THE MARK OF THE BEAST

THE MARK OF THE BEAST

EDITED BY

DEBRA HASSIG

ROUTLEDGE
A MEMBER OF THE TAYLOR & FRANCIS GROUP
NEW YORK AND LONDON

First paperback edition published in 2000 by
Routledge
29 West 35th Street
New York, NY 10001

Published in Great Britain
Routledge
11 New Fetter Lane
London EC4P 4EE

Routledge is an imprint of the Taylor & Francis Group

Library of Congress Cataloging-Publication-Data

The mark of the beast / edited by Debra Hassig.
       p. cm.
       Includes bibliographic rreferences and index.
       ISBN 0-8153-2952-0 (case : alk. paper)
       ISBN 0-415-92894-X (pbk.)
       1. Bestiaries–History and criticism. 2.Didactic
literature, Latin (Medieval and modern)–History and criticism.
3. Literature, Medieval–History and criticism. 4. Animals,
Mythical, in literature. 5. Animals, Mythical, in art. 6. Animals
in literature. 7. Animals in art.
PA8275.B4Z63 1999
809'.93362–dc21   98-36629
                                   CIP

Printed on acid-free, 250-year-life paper
Manufactured in the United States of America

10 9 8 7 6 5 4 3 2 1

for Jane Rosenthal
scholar, teacher, friend

Contents

Acknowledgments

A book of essays such as this is the result of much collective academic knowledge, commitment, and imagination. I must therefore thank first and foremost the authors, whose scholarly acumen, diligence, and creativity has manifested itself in this volume in a manner which I hope brings them great satisfaction. I would also like to thank Joyce Salisbury for the inestimable benefits of her time, knowledge, and good nature, and for providing encouragement, insightful comments and corrections on matters editorial, substantive, and conceptual.

I would like to thank Matt Strickland for generously providing me with a constant supply of references, scholarly analysis, and assistance of all kinds. Of the numerous other individuals who shared their time and expertise, I would like to thank especially Luuk Houwen, Matt Kavaler, Keith Busby, and Willene Clark. The acquisition of photographs and permission to reproduce them was greatly aided by the kind assistance of Martial Rose, Julia Hedgecoe, and Ken Harvey, as well as the efficient personnel of manuscripts and photographic departments in the British Library, Bodleian Library, Cambridge University Library, Pierpont Morgan Library, Bibliothèque Nationale, Paris; Eton College Library, St. John's Library, Cambridge; Christ Church Library, Oxford; University of Nottingham Library, Norwich Cathedral, J. Paul Getty Museum; Bern Burgerbibliothek, and the Westminster Abbey Library. Finally, I would like to thank the University of Oklahoma for a generous photographic subsidy.

This book is dedicated with affection and gratitude to Professor Jane Rosenthal, my mentor and continuing source of support and art historical inspiration. Her encouragement and instruction from the very beginning of my graduate training have helped me greatly over the years to better understand and to take immense pleasure in the study of medieval art.

Introduction

Animals were a ubiquitous presence in medieval life. The wild ones were hunted and feared, while the domestic ones lived side by side with their human owners, often performing various agricultural, transportation, and courtly tasks. Animals provided food, clothing, and companionship, and certain individuals won lasting fame for their loyalty and devotion to heroes and saints,[1] so is it really surprising that imaginative thinking about animals became a medieval preoccupation? With a gradually accumulated and rich store of symbolic associations, animals were excellent, figurative vehicles for religious allegory, political satire, and moral instruction. The medieval bestiary was the culmination and apogee of allegorical functions for animals, assembling stories and pictures of beasts and birds for purposes of moral instruction and courtly entertainment. It is indisputable that the bestiaries were an important medieval contribution to didactic religious literature. But far from comprising an isolated, specialist's genre available only to the religious and literate elite, bestiaries also addressed concerns central to virtually all walks of Christian life. That is, familiarity with the bestiary stories did not necessarily require direct access to the bestiary manuscripts, as the stories were available from a multitude of sources, some textual, some visual, some word of mouth.[2]

The present collection of essays rides the tide of accelerated academic interest in the medieval bestiary witnessed during the last couple of decades. The result of this interest has been a number of published studies that have greatly advanced our interpretations of this complex genre as well as deepened our understanding of the significance of animals during the Middle Ages. These include books and articles on the bestiaries per se,[3] translations into English of key

texts relevant to bestiary studies,[4] major investigations of the literary
and historical significance of animals in the Middle Ages,[5] and a
number of interdisciplinary anthologies that address medieval animals
and their social and symbolic significance.[6] Art historical treatment of
this material has been greatly aided by the publication, often in color, of
collections of bestiary imagery,[7] including complete facsimiles and
editions of bestiary manuscripts.[8]

One explanation for the increased attention to bestiaries during
recent years is the double recognition of the necessity for
interdisciplinary approaches to problems in medieval studies, and of the
inherently interdisciplinary content of the bestiaries themselves. In
addition, the influence of the bestiaries was not contained between their
covered boards but rather extended to many other genres either
dedicated to elucidating the wonders of nature or to exploiting the
symbolic potential of animals in such varied outlets as biblical
commentaries, nature treatises, encyclopedias, romances, epic,
exempla, and fables. Even a cursory survey of this literature reveals
certain commonalities and borrowings, which are almost always
grounded in or related to the Early Christian *Physiologus* and the later
medieval bestiaries. Hence, the bestiaries are the logical starting point
for understanding animal allegory and imagery found in many other
contexts.

The goal of the present collection of essays is not to hand down
truths on the ultimate significance of the bestiaries or to argue for one
consistent symbolic meaning for a given animal or to suggest but a
single function for these books. Rather, the individual studies all expose
accumulated layers of meaning developed in the bestiary stories and
attached to the animals themselves and seek therefore to make visible
their numerous ambiguities and contradictions as compelling testimony
to the flexibility and power of the genre. In addition, it is clear that the
bestiaries exerted a strong influence in other spheres, in that animal
imagery in other types of manuscripts (such as psalters and Books of
Hours) and in other artistic forms (such as monumental sculpture and
romance) carries with it associations drawn from the bestiaries that
informed and enriched its meaning in the new contexts. It is also
apparent that not only their texts and iconography but also the way the
bestiaries were read and perceived owed much to Classical tradition
and interpretations of animals, both real and imaginary.

Emphasis in all of these essays is on art historical and literary
analysis. Equal consideration is paid to texts and images with an eye

toward connecting specific artistic and literary features of the bestiaries with broader issues in medieval art, life, and literature. Still, given their varying topical concerns, I have grouped the essays into four distinct categories.

SOCIAL REALITIES

In the first section, I have included a pair of studies focused on single bestiary entries that address particularly important contemporary social and political issues. In Margaret Haist's study of the lion, that issue is no less than the legitimacy of the English monarchy. Taking as her point of departure a passage in Genesis quoted in the Bern Physiologus lion entry, she traces changing ideas about the importance of bloodline and qualities appropriate to a king as revealed in the later bestiary images and commentaries on the lion. These ideas helped legitimize the king's position in England by emphasizing rights to the throne through heredity and by suggesting that secular power was an earthly manifestation of heavenly authority. By the early thirteenth century, visual messages pertaining to kingship were incorporated into the seemingly conventional bestiary illustrations of the lion, and these changes paralleled ideas about kingship available in contemporary political tracts. Within this analytical framework, the bestiary leopard entry is also relevant as a vehicle for the condemnation of particular English kings.

The second essay that addresses a specific social concern is Mariko Miyazaki's study of the owl as a symbolic locus for medieval anti-semitism. Discussion centers on sculpted owl bosses and misericords in Norwich Cathedral and their relationship to the various owls pictured and described in the bestiaries, as a means of demonstrating how the bestiaries contributed to anti-Jewish sentiment in a city that experienced an especially intense division between Christians and Jews. The relationship between the owl and the ape as co-representatives of sin and evil is also examined in order to highlight the flexibility of the owl as a symbol, subject to multiple interpretations appropriate to both monastic and secular audiences.

MORAL LESSONS

In a very practical sense, moral lessons were the *raison d'être* of the bestiaries and hence at least the indirect subject of all of the essays in this collection. However, those comprising the second section are distinguishable from the others in that they examine directly particular moral or religious problems that blurred the lines between social mores and theological preoccupations. Carmen Brown has analyzed several different bestiary entries for their didactic potential in communicating the dangers of the two deadly sins of pride and lust. Bestiary entries related to these two sins are exceptionally numerous, so much so that certain animals were eventually invested with emblematic value as signs of specific sins, which they carried to a variety of artistic settings. Lion and goat imagery is especially revealing in this regard, transmitting a clear warning at once religious and social, in contexts both within and outside the bestiary proper.

The sin of lust is also the subject of my own essay on sex in the bestiaries. I am primarily interested in charting changing theological views of sex as revealed in a number of bestiary entries concerned with this theme, including the siren, beaver, and fire rocks. I try to show how bestiary characterizations of sex are consistently negative and generally condemn women as the impetus behind sexual misconduct. I trace a shift in emphasis over time by contrasting the ways in which the theme of sex functions as a theological guidepost in the Latin prose bestiaries with its later function in the *Bestiaire d'amour*. Written by Richard of Fournival, the latter is essentially a love-plea that skillfully reworks the meanings and imagery of the traditional bestiaries from the service of theological moralization to that of private seduction.

The most intensely theologically focused of the essays in this section is the study of the phoenix by Valerie Jones. The precise nature of the resurrection, whether physical or spiritual, was a matter of ongoing dispute throughout the Middle Ages. This essay links phoenix imagery in the bestiaries to contemporary beliefs concerning the resurrection at the end of time. In medieval literature and exegesis, the ancient myth of the phoenix's self-immolation and subsequent revival was adopted as a metaphor for Christ's self-sacrifice and resurrection, a metaphor transferred to and further developed in the bestiary phoenix entries. The essay explores how the phoenix images functioned as pictorial allusions to Christ and to Christian ideas of sacrifice and salvation, providing insight into views on the resurrection predominant at the time of their production as well as into more general beliefs regarding the ultimate fate of humankind.

CLASSICAL INHERITANCES

That the medieval bestiaries were dependent upon and informed by a rich accumulation of Classical lore and animal iconography is by now a commonplace, but the two essays included in this section explore this idea in especially detailed and insightful ways. Pamela Gravestock tackles the important, often-asked but little-answered question of whether or not medieval readers believed in the existence of imaginary bestiary creatures such as the unicorn, griffin, and bonnacon. Not surprisingly, the answer to the question is an involved one. The essay first examines the different approaches taken by modern scholars in the study of fantastic animals and then critiques those that seek one-to-one matchups between imaginary creatures and "real" animals as a continuation of the Classical tradition of rationalism. Among the issues examined are whether or not inclusion of certain animals in the bestiaries is tantamount to simple cases of "mistaken identity," to what extent their inclusion constitutes a continuation of Classical beliefs and ideas and whether or not imaginary animals may have served a didactic function in the bestiaries comparable to that of the "real" and recognizable beasts.

J. Holli Wheatcroft's essay on Classical influences in the bestiaries is an iconographical study but one that is fully integrated with ancient ideological influences that were incorporated into new Christian contexts, which distinguishes this study from previous ones that have provided important insights into the artistic origins of medieval animal imagery. The analyses of the bestiary snake and phoenix show how visual evidence of earlier religious practices were adopted and modified to serve the newer demands of emerging Christian doctrine. The analysis concentrates on correspondences between the significance of the snake and the phoenix in ancient Rome and on concomitant connections between the Roman cult of the dead and emerging Christian beliefs surrounding death and salvation. The essay deals directly with the bestiary's syncretic nature and the function of the *Physiologus* as a pathway from Roman religion to medieval Christian practice, an aspect of the genre that is often overlooked.

READING BEASTS

The last two essays in the collection provide lively and in-depth text and image analyses of two very important illuminated manuscripts. The first of these, by Alison Syme, is a study of Bodley 764, one of the most celebrated of the thirteenth-century English bestiaries. Using the tools and methods of psychoanalysis, references to specific taboos connected with death, sex, and decay are shown to play a large role in the formal structuring of the illuminations as well as to motivate the content of the text. Interestingly, however, these taboos are consistently "hidden"—cloaked in the guise of spiritual instruction—yet concern with avoiding them provides a bridge between biblical commandments, medieval exegesis, the bestiaries, and the work of modern theorists, including Freud and Derrida.

Finally, Michelle Bolduc calls attention to the compelling associations between the bestiary and late medieval romance despite their disparate pictorial and textual traditions. To this end, her essay examines the influence of bestiaries on an important thirteenth-century French romance, *Le Roman de Silence*. Included among the fourteen narrative images that illustrate the only extant manuscript copy of this work are three portraits of hybrid creatures. Providing a marked contrast with the dynamic, narrative imagery devoted to the romance's protagonists, the hybrid images make both direct references to—and indirect invocations of—the bestiary tradition, which reciprocally enriches and multiplies the levels of meaning in the romance.

I would only add that all of these essays aim to celebrate the medieval bestiary as an amazingly complex, well-loved, and versatile genre in its own right as well as to contribute to the process of removing it from intellectual and scholarly isolation as a charming but insignificant collection of animal stories. Together, the essays clearly demonstrate how bestiaries both address and further develop some of the most important concerns of the Middle Ages, bearing on such central institutions as the Church, the monarchy, and everyday social relations. In this sense, all of the authors assembled here have a common goal, which is to demonstrate that medieval bestiaries cannot be separated from their cultural milieu because they in fact played a significant role in its creation.

NOTES

1. Among the latter must be counted Alexander the Great's brave horse, Bucephalus; the loyal and avenging dog of King Garamantes; and the compassionate sea otters who dried the feet of St. Cuthbert.

2. See Willene B. Clark, "Twelfth and Thirteenth-Century Latin Sermons and the Latin Bestiary," *Compar(a)ison* 1 (1996), 5-19.

3. Xenia Muratova, *The Medieval Bestiary* (Moscow, 1984); *Beasts and Birds of the Middle Ages: The Bestiary and Its Legacy*, ed. Willene B. Clark and Meradith T. McMunn (Philadelphia, 1989); Wilma George and Brunsdon Yapp, *The Naming of the Beasts: Natural History in the Medieval Bestiary* (London, 1991); Debra Hassig, *Medieval Bestiaries: Text, Image, Ideology* (Cambridge, 1995). Comprehensive bibliography on bestiaries, including journal literature, may be found in Clark and McMunn (1989). For the earlier literature, see the bibliography in Florence McCulloch, *Mediaeval Latin and French Bestiaries*, rev. ed. (Chapel Hill, 1962).

4. These include Richard of Fournival, *Master Richard's Bestiary of Love and Response*, trans. Jeanette Beer (Berkeley, 1986); Albert the Great, *Man and the Beasts: De animalibus (Books 22-26)*, trans. James J. Scanlan (Binghamton, 1987); Hugh of Fouilloy, *The Medieval Book of Birds*, ed. and trans. Willene B. Clark (Binghamton, 1992); *A Medieval Book of Beasts: Pierre de Beauvais' Bestiary*, trans. Guy Mermier (Lewiston, 1992); *Bestiary: Being an English Version of the Bodleian Library, Oxford M.S. Bodley 764*, trans. Richard Barber (Woodbridge, 1993).

5. Jan M. Ziolkowski, *Talking Animals: Medieval Latin Beast Poetry, 750-1100* (Philadelphia, 1993); Joyce Salisbury, *The Beast Within: Animals in the Middle Ages* (New York, 1994). While not focused on the medieval period, interesting anthropological insights into animal-human relations are revealed in *What Is an Animal?*, ed. Tim Ingold (London, 1994).

6. Besides Clark and McMunn 1989, the most recent of these include *The Medieval World of Nature*, ed. Joyce Salisbury (New York, 1993); *Animals in the Middle Ages*, ed. Nona C. Flores (New York, 1996); and *Animals and the Symbolic in Mediaeval Art and Literature*, ed. L. A. J. R. Houwen (Groningen, 1997).

7. Ann Payne, *Medieval Beasts* (New York, 1990); Janetta Rebold Benton, *The Medieval Menagerie: Animals in the Art of the Middle Ages* (New York, 1992).

8. *Vollständige Faksimile-Ausgabe im Originalformat der Handschrift Ms. Ashmole 1511-Bestiarium* (Graz, 1982), with translation and commentary by Franz Unterkircher, *Bestiarium: Die Texte der Handschrift Ms. Ashmole 1511 der Bodleian Library Oxford in lateinischer und deutscher Sprache* (Graz, 1986); Muratova (color facsimile of the St. Petersburg Bestiary); *Deidis of Armorie: A Heraldic Treatise and Bestiary*, 2 vols., ed. L. A. J. R. Houwen (Edinburgh, 1994). Barber 1993, while not a facsimile publication, provides an English translation and all of the images (in color) of Bodley 764.

Abbreviations

Bible quotations given in the *Notes* sections of essays follow the Douay-Rheims translation of the Latin Vulgate. In excerpts transcribed from manuscripts, abbreviations have been expanded and capitalization and punctuation have been added, but spellings have not been normalized nor has grammar been corrected.

Barber 1993
Bestiary, trans. Richard Barber (Woodbridge, 1993).

Beer 1986
Richard of Fournival, *Master Richard's Bestiary of Love and Response*, ed. Jeanette Beer (Berkeley, 1986).

Camille 1992
Michael Camille, *Image on the Edge: The Margins of Medieval Art*, (London, 1992).

Clark 1992
Willene B. Clark, *The Medieval Book of Birds, Hugh of Fouilloy's Aviarium* (Binghamton, 1992).

Clark and McMunn 1989
Beasts and Birds of the Middle Ages: The Bestiary and Its Legacy, ed. Willene B. Clark and Meradith T. McMunn (Philadelphia, 1989).

Curley 1979
Physiologus, trans. Michael J. Curley (Austin, 1979).

Friedman 1981
John Block Friedman, *The Monstrous Races in Medieval Art and Thought* (Cambridge [MA], 1981).

Graz 1982
Vollständige Faksimile-Ausgabe im Originalformat der Handschrift Ms. Ashmole 1511—Bestiarium (Graz, 1982).

Hassig 1995
Debra Hassig, *Medieval Bestiaries: Text, Image, Ideology*, (Cambridge, 1995).

Klingender 1971
Frances Klingender, *Animals in Art and Thought to the End of the Middle Ages* (London, 1971).

McCulloch 1962
Florence McCulloch, *Mediaeval Latin and French Bestiaries*, rev. ed. (Chapel Hill, 1962).

Morgan 1982
Nigel Morgan, *Early Gothic Manuscripts (I), 1190-1250* (London, 1982).

Morgan 1988
Nigel Morgan, *Early Gothic Manuscripts (2), 1250-1285* (London, 1988).

Muratova 1984
Xenia Muratova, *The Medieval Bestiary* (Moscow, 1984).

PL
Patrologiae latina, ed. J. P. Migne, 221 vols. (Paris, 1841-64).

Payne 1990
Ann Payne, *Medieval Beasts* (London, 1990).

Rackham 1940
Pliny: Natural History, Books 8-11, trans. H. Rackham (Cambridge [MA], 1940).

Randall 1966
Lilian Randall, *Images in the Margins of Gothic Manuscripts*
(Berkeley, 1966).

Rowland 1973
Beryl Rowland, *Animals with Human Faces* (Knoxville, 1973).

Rowland 1978
Beryl Rowland, *Birds with Human Souls* (Knoxville, 1978).

Salisbury 1994
Joyce E. Salisbury, *The Beast Within: Animals in the Middle Ages*
(New York, 1994).

Scanlan 1987
Albert the Great, *Man and the Beasts: De animalibus (Books 22-26)*,
trans. James J. Scanlan (Binghamton, 1987).

Segre 1957
*Li Bestiaires d'amours di Maistre Richart de Fornival e li Response du
Bestiaire*, ed. Cesare Segre (Milan, 1957).

White 1954
T. H. White, *The Book of Beasts* (London, 1954).

Figure A. Pardus. Oxford, Bodleian Library, MS Bodley 764, f. 9v.
Photo: The Bodleian Library.

z via ingredunt ad cos
cu auro multo. Et au
tem z aliud animal.
qd formicaleon dicit.
eo qd z formicau leo.
ul certe formica z leo.
Et n animal partu
formicis fatis recilum.
ita ur se Tpuluere
centauro. et prius de siren

abscondat. z formicat
frumenta gestantes
inficiat. vnde aute
leo z formica uocat?
qa alijs animalibus
ur formica z: formi
cis aute ur leo.

De siren z homo.

Figure B. Siren and centaur. Los Angeles, J. Paul Getty Museum, MS Ludwig
XV/3, f. 78. Photo: The J. Paul Getty Museum, Los Angeles, California.

Figure C. Peacock. Oxford, Bodleian Library, MS Bodley 764, f. 84v.
Photo: The Bodleian Library.

cum amicas meis epularer.

Figure D. Goat. Oxford, Bodleian Library, MS Bodley 764, f. 36v.
Photo: The Bodleian Library.

Figure E. Unicorn and virgin. London, British Library, MS Royal 12.F.XIII,
f. 10v. Photo: by permission of the British Library.

Figure F. Beaver. Oxford, Bodleian Library, MS Bodley 764, f. 14.
Photo: The Bodleian Library.

dicentes. Non habem' regē nisi cesarem. Hunc
autem nescim' unde sit. & magis dilexert te
nebs q̄ luce. Tunc dūs comūtit se ad nos gen
tes. & illuminauit nos sedentes in umbra
mortis & tenebris. Vnde scriptū est. habitā
tib; in regione. um. m. lux. or. ē eis. De hoc po
pulo saluator p ppħam dic. popl's quē n̄ cogno
ui seruiunt m. rtm. filii alieni mentiti st m:
filii alieni inuetaiti se. & clau. a se. suis. Et alibj.
Vocauj n̄ plebem meā s; plebē meam. & n̄ di
lectam meā. Hic dicorax ipsa est & noctua. &
ē auis lucifuga. & solem uidere n̄ patitur.

Est aliud uolatile q̄d dr̄ fenix aricħie. ut ara
bie auis. eo q̄d colorē feniceū habeat uel

Figure G. Phoenix. New York, Pierpont Morgan Library, MS M. 81, f. 62v.
Photo: The Pierpont Morgan Library.

Figure H. Phoenix. Oxford, Bodleian Library, MS Bodley 764, f. 70v.
Photo: The Bodleian Library.

De naturis serpentium.

Raco maior cunctor serpentiu siue anī
mantium omniū sup terrā. hunc gre
ci draconta uocant. unde & deruatū
est in latinum. ut draco diceret. Qui sepe
ab speluncis abstractus fert in aerem. conci
tatur ppt eum aer. Est aute cristat. ore
paruo. & artis fistulis p quas trahit spm.
& linguam exerat. Vim aute non in dentib;

Figure I. Elephant and dragon. New York, Pierpont Morgan Library, MS M. 81,
f. 78. Photo: The Pierpont Morgan Library.

paulo fenioz: obliuiofuf.e. ce indoalif. Caladrius.

Caladruif ficut dicit phiſiologuſ totuſ e albȝ nullã
parte hñſ nigrã. Cuiuſ intioz fimuſ curat oculoȝ
caligine. Huic in atriſ regũ inuenit. Siqſ.e. in egritu
...

Figure J. Caladrius. London, British Library, MS Harley 4751, f. 40.
Photo: by permission of the British Library.

Figure K. Ibis. Oxford, Bodleian Library, MS Bodley 764, f. 66.
Photo: The Bodleian Library.

PART 1

Social Realities

The Lion, Bloodline, and Kingship

Margaret Haist

The lion is the most ubiquitous of the bestiary animals, and is also one of the relatively few to carry strong associations beyond the bestiary, especially in medieval heraldry. Often positioned first and described in the bestiaries as the "king of beasts," it is interesting to consider the relationship between the bestiary characterization of the lion and contemporary notions of kingship. This essay will explore this relationship, beginning with Old Testament interpretations of the lion emphasized in the *Physiologus* that later provided a useful model for contemporary notions of pure bloodline, kingly virtues, and just rule. Although evidence for royal patronage of bestiaries is inconclusive, it is suggested here that the bestiary lion entry addressed ideas of immediate concern to readers, who, if not themselves monarchs, were certainly living under monarchial rule. Most importantly, connections between the bestiary, heraldry, and contemporary views of kingship show how the lion as a symbol accrued new meanings over time through the skillful manipulation of both texts and images.

* * * * *

In the ninth-century Bern Physiologus, the opening miniature accompanying the earliest extant lion entry depicts Jacob blessing the lion of the tribe of Judah above a frieze of paired animals (figure 1).[1] The accompanying text first proclaims the lion the king of beasts and then summarizes Jacob's blessing according to Genesis 49.[2] Turning to Genesis directly, Jacob's blessing emphasizes the prophecy that Judah and his direct bloodline will lead the tribe until it produces the ruler whom the whole world awaits:

Juda is a lion's whelp:
To the prey, my son, thou art gone up:
Resting thou has couched as a lion,
And as a lioness, who shall rouse him?
The scepter shall not be taken away from Juda,
Nor a ruler from his thigh,
Til he come that is to be sent,
And he shall be the expectation of nations (Gen. 49:9-10).

This passage affirms the importance of bloodline and implies that keeping it uncontaminated will maintain the strength required to fulfill the ultimate prophecy, which, according to medieval interpretation of this passage, was the triumph of Christ.[3] As we shall see, this idea is reinforced in the Bern Physiologus image as well as the text through allegorical comparison of Judah to the lion by reference to the idea of generation.

In the Bern illumination, the lion is positioned on a hillock above all of the other animals, representing on one level the animal world ruled by the king of beasts and on another "all nations" awaiting their supreme king. The particular species illustrated stand for different categories of animals subsequently described in the *Physiologus,* including domestic animals (cattle), exotic beasts (bears), and other quadrupeds (deer). Each animal type is represented by a matched pair rather than a single animal—the deer are thus rendered as a stag and a doe—which suggests sexual pairing, reproduction, and species continuity, in harmony with the Genesis passage. That is, the use of distinct animal types and the representation of paired species allegorically suggests the preservation of bloodline condoned in Genesis 49. In this, the Judah image is also related to both the iconography and meaning of representations of the Flood, in which animals are depicted two-by-two as a means of preserving the species, following God's instructions to Noah (Gen. 9:15-19).[4]

Although the lion pictured here is clearly identified in the text as the lion of the tribe of Judah, he also represents Christ, the culmination of Judah's bloodline. This identification is reinforced in the three subsequent lion images in the Bern manuscript (ff. 7v, 8), which picture the lion erasing his tracks with his tail, sleeping with his eyes open, and reviving his dead whelps; as allegorical figures of Christ's incarnation, death, and resurrection, respectively.[5] Most important among these is the visual and verbal explication of how the lion's whelps are born dead and then revived after three days by their father, just as Christ was revived after three days by Our Father (f. 8).

In the Bern manuscript, the three miniatures depicting the specific lion habits seem to form a series apart from the Judah illumination, and in fact, the Judah image drops out entirely in the later bestiaries as emphasis shifts to the resurrection allegory. However, this image is important and worthy of careful scrutiny because it describes the point at which Old Testament prophecy and Christ's sojourn on earth intersect. It is also true that although the specific iconography is not repeated in the later bestiaries, ideas expressed therein are nevertheless incorporated in various ways, to be discussed below.

This first lion in the Bern Physiologus represents Judah himself, to whom Jacob speaks, but he is also a manifestation of Jacob's prophecy, which according to medieval Christian interpretation is Christ's appearance on earth and ultimate triumph over evil. This is suggested by the rubric directly under the illumination, which indicates that the lion is the king of all beasts (*Est leo regalis omnium animalium et bestiarum*), thus connecting the lion's position in the animal kingdom to that of Christ as King of Kings,[6] and in turn, to earthly kingship. It is also true that the presence of the halo suggests a Christ identification for the human figure, who is revealed as Jacob only if the viewer reads the text.[7] Like the lion, the human figure also carries a double identification as the fusion of the Old Testament (as Jacob) and the New Testament significance of Jacob's prophecy (Christ).

In addition to the rubric, the idea of kingship is signaled by the mountain on which the lion stands. That is, Isaiah, speaking of the ascendency of Judah to Jerusalem, refers to the "holy mountain of the Lord" (Is. 2:1-3). According to the *Physiologus* and later bestiaries, the lion loves to roam in the mountains, just as the mountain is God's seat on earth, forming another parallel between natural and sacred history.[8] This idea helps reinforce the lion's identification as Christ, linking the Old Testament to the New: the mountain is the site of God; therefore the lion (as Christ), assumes the mountain position. Thus, the link between the figure of the lion with bloodline and kingship was established at very early date in the *Physiologus*, and this connection continued to be strengthened with the development of the later bestiaries.

* * * * *

The early twelfth-century bestiaries continued the theme of bloodline in the lion entries, albeit with different pictorial emphases. Laud Misc. 247 is a particularly interesting example.[9] While the Bern Physiologus devotes separate miniatures to the lion sleeping with open eyes— compared to the ever-vigilance of Christ—and reviving the whelps, Laud Misc. 247 conflates these two subjects in a single miniature (figure 2). A pair of lions lie at the base of the folio with open eyes, while above them, the lion parents hold a dead whelp between them. The lion on the right is licking the cub's nose, while the left lion appears to blow life-giving breath, as indicated from the wavy lines issuing from the mouth. The reviving lions are positioned above the "sleeping" lions as a sign of their greater importance, and indeed the resurrection allegory became the focus of bestiary lion imagery from the late twelfth century onwards. Finally, it is interesting to note that above the image is a long list of all of the animals subsequently treated in the bestiary, beginning with the lion (*leo*). It is as though the frieze of animals pictured in the Bern Physiologus image has been replaced by the written word, still representing a gathering of all of Creation under the care of the lion/Christ (figures 1, 2).

The sleeping lions in Laud Misc. 247 are worth closer inspection in light of the *Physiologus'* emphasis on the Genesis passage, which still accompanies the image. First of all, there are two lions rather than just one. It is also notable that the "sleepers" are stretched out side by side. Perhaps this pair of lions sleeping together represent Judah and his lioness as described in Genesis 49, while simultaneously referring to the theme of resurrection. Thus, God rouses, or resurrects, not only his son (as allegorically depicted above the "sleepers") but also the tribe of Judah, including the faithful who inherit the tribe's legacy through Jesus Christ. Layered onto this is the idea of generation of family line, which in Judah's case culminates in the birth, death, and resurrection of Christ, as summarized in the lion revival scene and which in turn signifies the resurrection of all Christians at Christ's second coming.[10]

In Laud Misc. 247, then, the lion iconography has maintained the emphasis on typological associations inspired by the connections between the lion's nature and Old Testament prophecy concerning the coming of Christ as well as New Testament ideas about his resurrection. However, during the later twelfth century, an interesting text addition was made to the lion entries that suggests a shift in focus from strictly typological concerns to more contemporary ones. The additional text describes the lion's treatment of his enemies as represented by the relevant passage in the St. Petersburg Bestiary: "Around men, the lion is one with nature and is not unnecessarily angered. Rational men should heed this example, and not allow themselves to be angered and oppress the innocent, because the law of Christ directs that even the guilty should go free."[11] The text goes on to explain how the lion spares those who prostrate themselves before him.

The new text addition was accompanied by important pictorial changes that complemented the newly-introduced, merciful dimension of the lion's character. The most obvious of these was the direct illustration of the lion sparing prostrate men, as observable in the Ashmole Bestiary (f. 10), the Cambridge Bestiary (f. 1), and St. John's 61 (f. 3v), among other manuscripts.[12] Other iconographical innovations were more subtle, including a new emphasis on licking as opposed to breathing life onto the young as well as the involvement of both parents in the care-giving process (figure 3). Another new feature was the depiction of live young rather than stillborn whelps. Stillborn offspring are depicted in the earlier manuscripts stiff and immobile as if dead, with closed eyes (figure 2). Such representations contrast with the live young, shown as ambulatory with open eyes and alert expressions as depicted in the Morgan Bestiary (figure 3).

Caring for the young—family responsibility—in conjunction with the well-understood resurrection theme of the earlier lion compositions, delivers a new message, namely that Christian salvation depends on the assimilation of such values. Family and caring for the young may be seen as one aspect of the tolerance of the innocent condoned in the newly-added text passage cited above. It may be understood also in the more general context of good Christian behavior as outlined in the Bible, for example, as expressed in the final verse of Malachias: "And he shall turn the heart of the fathers to the children, and the heart of the children to their fathers: lest I come, and strike the earth with anathema" (Mal. 4:6). This is a theme articulated and pictured elsewhere in the bestiary, most notably in the entry on the hoopoe, which is focused both on caring for the young and on filial piety.[13]

This emphasis on the lion's merciful character runs counter to biblical characterizations of the lion and is a new addition to the discussion of the biblical lion's strength and courage found in the earlier bestiaries, including Laud Misc. 247 (f. 140v). In Old Testament times, lions were widespread in the Near East and posed a real threat to humans. It is likely that the lion's characterization as powerful and fearless in the Bible was founded on actual lion behavior, and Old

Testament use of the lion as a symbol holds generally to this reputation in biblical episodes that stress the lion's strength and ferocity as the ultimate formidable obstacles, as in the stories of Samson and the lion or Daniel in the lion's den.

Of particular interest in light of bestiary characterizations and notions of kingship is that the figure of the lion, as a powerful and aggressive animal, was used in the Old Testament to symbolize the power of the kings of Israel:

> And say: Why did thy mother the lioness lie down among the lions, and bring up her whelps in the midst of young lions? And she brought out one of her whelps, and he became a lion: and he learned to catch the prey, and to devour men. And the nations heard of him, and took him, but not without receiving wounds: and they brought him in chains into the land of Egypt. But she seeing herself weakened, and that her hope was lost, took one of her young lions, and set him up for a lion. And he went up and down among the lions, and became a lion: and he learned to catch the prey, and to devour men (Ezek.19:2-9).

The same emphasis on the strength and power of the lion found in the Bible is also found in the bestiaries, which proclaim the lion the king of all beasts, based on the animal's superior courage and strength.[14] According to the later bestiary texts, the lion's courage is located in his breast, and his strength is in his head.[15]

* * * * *

Given Old Testament emphasis on lion ferocity as a symbol of mighty kings, might the bestiary description of the merciful lion have been added in order to support more contemporary notions of kingship? In fact, during the later Middle Ages, the importance of a merciful ruler was expressed in other contexts, most notably in political treatises. For example, Book 4 of John of Salisbury's highly influential *Policraticus* (written 1154-59), which addresses the subject of the ideal prince, emphasizes the importance of tempering justice with mercy.[16] This idea expressed in the form of the lion allegory was also applied to specific rulers. For example, Orderic Vitalis in his *Ecclesiastical History* remarks of William Rufus, "The noble lion's wrath can spare the vanquished/ Do likewise all who govern on this earth."[17] The importance of the merciful ruler was an idea that was reiterated in later centuries, including by Machiavelli in *The Prince*.[18] Most interestingly, a fifteenth-century heraldic bestiary comprising part of the *Deidis of Armorie* addresses knightly concerns and so includes a "chivalric moral" in the text that accompanies the image of the lion charge. This moral explains that the man who bears the lion in arms is brave and valiant but also sweet and gracious towards his companions, citing the bestiary story of how the lion spares the prostrate.[19]

In fact, the development of coats-of-arms during the second quarter of the twelfth century may be viewed in relation to the bestiary lion and other bestiary animals which together functioned as allegorical figures of the English kings. Most relevant in this regard are the arms of England, the famous Plantagenet lions, created under Richard the Lionheart in 1195. It was at this point that Richard transformed the shield with one or possibly two facing lions rampant that he had borne until then—and that had possibly been borne by his father, Henry II— into a shield with three lions *passant guardant* that have functioned as the arms of England ever since (figure 4).[20]

Richard is an especially significant ruler vis-à-vis lions and the bestiary. His nickname, "Coeur de Lion" was first applied by Ambroise, a minstrel-historian of the Third Crusade, when Richard first sighted Acre and Saladin's camp on 8 June 1191.[21] The epithet was later rationalized by a rather gruesome thirteenth-century legend which details how Richard, during the time of his imprisonment by King Modard of Almayn, tore out the heart of a lion sent to devour him.[22] In an impressive act of terrorism, Richard proceeded to eat the lion's heart in front of the king and his court, creating a vivid image subsequently immortalized in the Chertsey tiles and in the Peterborough Psalter in Brussels (f. 33), among other later medieval works of art.[23]

According to the chronicler Richard of Devizes, however, Richard's reputation as a military "disciplinarian"—imposing equal and severe punishment on everyone who deserved it—earned him the name of "The Lion" from the inhabitants of Sicily.[24] This characterization of Richard would seem to be a return to the earlier Old Testament and *Physiologus* emphasis on the lion's ferocity rather than emphasis on merciful rule. Richard's reputation for cruelty is acknowledged in the twelfth century by Gerald of Wales in his *On the Instruction of Princes*, although Gerald, in keeping with contemporary Western opinion, interprets Richard's behavior as a justifiable war strategy. Interestingly, he also implies a shift to more merciful conduct:

This stain of cruelty he evidently had incurred without cause; for this reason, the causes for a while ceasing, he put on kindness and clemency, and without being over-hard, and certainly far from being careless and lax, that severity by degrees subsided and approached the golden mean. Moreover, He who gave nature gave also the passions of nature; for to restrain the fiercest impulses of his mind, this our lion is more than lion, is harassed like a lion by the torture of a quartan ague, by which although he is not afraid, yet he so almost constantly trembles, that with his trembling he uses the whole world to shake and fear.[25]

Later in this same treatise, Gerald again employs the symbolic relationship between rulers and the motifs borne on their arms in order to criticize the Plantagenets and to laud the Capetians, by reference to their heraldic lions and lilies, respectively:

And whereas, other princes cause figures of fierce and devouring beasts, such as bears, leopards, and lions, to be represented in outward appearance before men, and bear them before them painted on their arms and banners as an index of their ferocity; these alone, by a laudable gentleness of character, desire by every means in their power to observe a due moderation in their words and behavior, as well as in their actions, and wishing to avoid all arrogance and pride, mark and adorn their shields and banners, as well as their other armor, with only the simple small flowers of the lily.[26]

This passage also recalls the Scriptural passage that expresses a similar sentiment by way of the same animal metaphors: "As a roaring lion, and a hungry bear, so is a wicked prince over the poor people" (Prov. 28:15).

Somewhat confusing is the fact that the three Plantagenet lions adopted by Richard were subsequently referred to as "leopards" on the continent. This is likely a semantic attempt to distinguish between a heraldic lion, normally depicted with a heavy mane and in profile, and a heraldic leopard, shown with less hair and with its head turned full face (or *guardant*). Since leopards in heraldry were normally depicted as *passant*, the lions *passant guardant* of England were seen to fulfill all leopard requirements and therefore were so labeled. However, contemporary chroniclers, such as Matthew Paris, seemed unsure of how to identify these heraldic beasts, referring alternately to the arms of

England as "lions" and "leopards."[27] But because the leopard became a heraldic charge in its own right beginning in the thirteenth century, the beasts of the royal arms of England should be described as lions and not leopards.[28] That leopards were also used in coats-of-arms is of great interest in that, like the lion, the leopard carried with it certain bestiary associations and was used symbolically to denote the character of certain English rulers.

The bestiary leopard is given the Latin name *pardus*, confusingly described as the offspring of a lion and a pard, and consistently described as swift, vicious, and bloodthirsty.[29] The development of the leopard as a vehicle for condemnation of violence and bloodthirstiness may be related to clerical criticism of knightly behavior at the time when the leopard emerged as a new bestiary entry.[30] That is, the leopard does not appear in the *Physiologus* or the early twelfth-century manuscripts, but is commonly included among the thirteenth-century bestiary rosters. Its later invention might suggest that the bestiary leopard entry provided a means of isolating and channeling the aggressive characteristics traditionally attributed to the lion, and that this in turn might have functioned as an anti-model for kingship, as well as a symbolic means of highlighting contaminated bloodlines. References to pards and leopards in contemporary descriptions of certain monarchs suggest this was the case.

It is perhaps no coincidence that the three Plantagenet lions invented by Richard I are rendered identically to some of the bestiary leopard images, such as that depicted in Bodley 764 (figure A, p. xxii). It is likely, however, that this is more properly understood the other way around: the leopard may have taken on heraldic form in the bestiaries in response to perceived characteristics of the English kings. For example, in the *Song of Lewes*, written towards the end of 1264, an unknown author maintained the bestiary opposition between the lion and the pard in order to condemn the behavior of Edward I:

> He, lion-like in fierceness and pride
> Is also like the pard, so mutable
> This man, and pliable; his fickleness
> Leads him to break his word, and fail to keep
> His promises, so that with blandishments
> And soft words of appeasement he is forced
> To make excuses to acquit himself.[31]

Equally interesting is the characterization of Edward I in the *Siege of Caerlaverock* (c. 1300), in which the author adheres to the bestiary characterization of the leopard when he asserts of the royal arms, "In [Edward I's] banner were three leopards *courant* of fine gold set on red, fierce, haughty and cruel; thus placed to signify that, like them, the king is dreadful, fierce, and proud to his enemies, for his bite is slight to none who inflame his anger."[32] It is possible, then, given the heraldic nature of some of the bestiary leopards and their resemblance to the Plantagenet lions, that readers would have viewed the bloodthirstiness of this animal in relation to specific contemporary monarchs, perhaps Edward I in particular (figures 4, A, p. xxii).

As well as signifying viciousness and bloodthirstiness, the leopard also represented a contamination of bloodline, as the bestiaries stress that the leopard is the adulterous product of a lioness and a male pard, or of a male lion and a female pard.[33] This idea is reiterated quite clearly in the heraldic bestiary portion of the *Deidis of Armorie*, which declares in the entry accompanying the leopard charge that a leopard is a very cruel beast, generated of adultery. Merlin the prophet is then cited as the first man to bear the leopard in arms, because of the circumstances of his own contaminated bloodline, being "born of a faarie in adultery."[34] While it is unclear whether there are direct implications of contaminated bloodline in contemporary comparisons between particular English monarchs and leopards, more extensive investigation of this problem may produce such links. For example, it is perhaps suggestive that William Longespée, illegitimate son of Henry II, adopted the arms of his grandfather, Geoffrey le Bel, rather than the supposed arms of his father or of his legitimate brother, Richard the Lionheart. William's arms, observable on his tomb effigy in Salisbury Cathedral, consist of small gold lions—or possibly leopards—on a field of blue (*azure a semy of lioncels or*).[35]

* * * * *

Bestiary patronage may be of some relevance in considering the extent to which connections between the bestiary felines and contemporary notions of kingship would have been perceived. By the thirteenth century, bestiary owners almost certainly included aristocratic lay patrons for whom the idea of kingship was an immediate political concern; the same patronage patterns are also true of other types of thirteenth-century illuminated manuscripts such as apocalypses. Bestiary entries on the lion and leopard featuring images of beasts in heraldic poses, therefore, are perhaps functionally related to apocalypse illustrations showing members of Satan's army as contemporary knights and, in one instance, carrying the arms of known enemies of the English Crown.[36]

Certain of the connections between the lion in the bestiaries, heraldic treatises, and contemporary descriptions of English kings are also indirectly reinforced in lion imagery found in other types of manuscripts. For example, the Missal of Henry of Chicester includes a full-page illumination of the Virgin and Child, with three lions at the base of the throne, one *couchant*, one *rampant*, and the other *passant*.[37] In this context, the lions most certainly carry their bestiary associations with Christ and the resurrection, and given that three are depicted, perhaps a reference to the Trinity is also implied. In addition, the lions might also refer to Judah and his bloodline, which culminates in Christ, as depicted in the main image above. Most interesting also is an image of a resuscitating lion in a thirteenth-century Old Testament and Apocalypse, which forms part of a typological series of miniatures that addresses the concept of the resurrection but that is also connected to the Seventh Commandment to which the folio's caption refers: "Thou shalt not commit adultery" (figure 5).[38] Interestingly, the lion roundel on this folio shows an adult lion standing over another of equal size, which is visually more suggestive of male-female coupling than a lion-cub relationship. This particular combination of text and image simultaneously draws upon the bestiary lion's associations with pure bloodline as a figure of Judah and in opposition to the leopard, as well as with the resurrection, resulting in an economical combination of ideas that would otherwise have been very difficult to draw together.

The importance of lineage, the power it bestows, and the safe-keeping it requires are strong messages communicated by the bestiary lion illuminations, beginning with the ninth-century Bern Physiologus illustration's emphasis on these concepts according to the Old Testament and the typological mandates of the accompanying text. While the resurrection allegory remained the most important aspect of lion symbolism from the theological point of view, verbal and visual analogies drawn between the lion's conduct and that of specific English kings suggest that these more secular concerns would have been familiar to later bestiary readers and likely informed their perceptions of the lion entries. The transferral of the negative lion traits of ferocity and bloodthirstiness to the leopard, in combination with the heraldic depictions of this beast and its allegorical value as a symbol of contaminated bloodline and of adultery, is further witness to the bestiary's power as a genre and its ability to accommodate changing political and social concerns.

NOTES

1. See *Physiologus Bernensis*, ed. Christoph von Steiger and Otto Homburger (Basel, 1964) (facsimile) and Helen Woodruff, "The Physiologus of Bern: A Survival of Alexandrian Style in a Ninth Century Manuscript," *Art Bulletin* 12 (1930), 246.

2. "Ideo et Iacob benedicens Iuda dicebat, 'Catulus leonis Iuda filius meus,' et cetera" (Bern 318, f. 7).

3. See for example, Rabanus Maurus, *Allegorie in universam sacram scripturam* (*PL* 112:983A-C).

4. von Steiger and Homburger 1964, 32.

5. For the images and German translation, see von Steiger and Homburger 1964. See also Curley 1979, 3-4.

6. Apoc. 17:14, 19:16.

7. It has been suggested that the halo is meant to signal the visionary character of the Jacob figure (von Steiger and Homburger 1964, 32).

8. Bern 318, f. 7v; Curley 1979, 3; Barber 1993, 24.

9. The image is said to be similar to that in another surviving *Physiologus* manuscript from the tenth century (Brussels, Bibliothèque Royale, MS 10074), although its text is closer to that of Bern 233, unillustrated and dated from the eighth to ninth centuries (C. M. Kauffmann, *Romanesque Manuscripts 1066-1190* [London, 1975], 76).

10. On the relationship between Christ's resurrection and the resurrection of the faithful at the end of time, see Jones in this volume.

11. "Circa hominem leonum natura est ut nisi lesi nequeant irasci. Ad cuius exemplum rationabiles homines respicere debent, qui non lesi irascuntur et innocentes opprimunt, cum iubeat xpiana [christiana] lex noxios dimittere liberos" (St. Petersburg Bestiary, f. 10).

12. See Morgan 1986, pls. 63, 66, and 146.

13. See Hassig 1995, 93-103.

14. On the lion's strength and power, see Prov. 19:12, 20:2, 28:1, 30:30; and 2 Macc. 11:11, among other Scriptural passages.

15. "... uirtus eorum in pectore, firmitas autem in capite" (Bodley 764, f. 3).

16. John of Salisbury, *Policraticus*, ed. and trans. Cary J. Nederman (Cambridge, 1990), 49-53.

17. *The Ecclesiastical History of Orderic Vitalis*, ed. Marjorie Chibnall (Oxford, 1973), IV, 131.

18. Niccolò Machiavelli, *The Prince*, ed. Quentin Skinner (Cambridge, 1988), 67-68.

19. The *Deidis of Armorie* was translated from French into Scots c. 1494. See *Deidis of Armorie: A Heraldic Treatise and Bestiary*, 2 vols., ed. L.A.J.R. Houwen (Edinburgh, 1994), I, xvi, 20.

20. On Richard's arms, see Adrian Ailes, "Heraldry in Twelfth-Century England: The Evidence," *Proceedings of the 1988 Harlaxton Symposium*, ed. Daniel Williams (Woodbridge, 1990), 1-16.

21. Ambroise, *L'Estoire de la Guerre Sainte*, ed. G. Paris (Paris, 1897), line 2310. See J.O. Prestwich, "Richard Coeur de Lion: *Rex Bellicosus*," in *Richard Coeur de Lion in History and Myth*, ed. Janet T. Nelson (London, 1992), 1.

22. For the legend, see *Der Mittelenglische Versroman über Richard Löwenherz*, ed. K. Brunner (Vienna, 1913), lines 738-1118. See also John Gillingham, "Some Legends of Richard the Lionheart: Their Development and Their Influence," in Nelson 1992, 51-69.

23. See Roger Sherman Loomis, "Richard *Coeur de Lion* and the *Pas Saladin* in Medieval Art," *Publications of the Modern Language Association* 30 (1915), 509-28.

24. *Chronicle of Richard of Devizes of the Time of Richard I*, ed. and trans. J.T. Appleby (London, 1963), 16-17; Prestwich 1992, 13.

25. Gerald of Wales, *On the Instruction of Princes*, trans. Joseph Stevenson in *The Church Historians of England* (London, 1858), vol. V, pt. 1, 193. On the effectiveness of Richard's rule, see Prestwich 1992, in which it is argued that Richard's reputation as a tyrant is undeserved.

26. Stevenson 1858, 236.

27. Adrian Ailes, *The Origins of the Royal Arms of England: Their Development to 1199* (Reading, 1982), 16-17. On the debate surrounding Richard's development of the royal arms, see pp. 64-73.

28. Ailes 1982, 17.

29. White 1954, 13-14; Barber 1993, 34-35. Modern scholars have used both "pard" and "leopard" as translations for the bestiary name, *pardus*. "Pard" would appear the better choice, as the thirteenth-century bestiarists use the designation *leopardus* only very rarely. On the other hand, the term "leopard" more clearly expresses the hybrid nature of the beast. Therefore, in this essay, the term "pardus" is translated as "leopard" because whether or not the two terms are strictly equivalent (which is difficult to determine owing to inconsistent and interchangeable usage in the sources), they are used

interchangeably in the modern secondary literature. The bestiary leopard is normally depicted not as a naturalistic, spotted beast but rather as a large generic feline, usually of a single color, such as blue.

30. See Matthew Strickland, *War and Chivalry: The Conduct and Perception of War in England and Normandy, 1066-1217* (Cambridge, 1997), 55-58; 70-75. For the later period, see Maurice Keen, "Chaucer and Chivalry Revisited," in *Armies, Chivalry, and Warfare in Britain and France in the Middle Ages: Proceedings of the 1995 Harlaxton Symposium*, ed. Matthew Strickland (Stamford, in press).

31. *The Song of Lewes*, trans. Tufton Beamish, in *Battle Royal: A New Account of Simon de Montfort's Struggle Against Henry III* (London, 1965), 174.

32. *The Siege of Carlaverock in the XXVIII Edward I, A.D. MCCC*, trans. Nicholas Harris Nicolas (London, 1828), 22-23.

33. "Leopardus ex adulterio leene nascitur et pardi, et tertiam originem efficit sicut et Plinius in *Naturali Historia* dicit" (Ashmole Bestiary, f. 12v-13). This passage suggests that the "pard" and the "leopard" are two different types of animals. But see also n. 29, above.

34. Houwen 1994, I, 20; II, 122-23. On Merlin's birth, see J. S. P. Tatlock, *The Legendary History of Britain* (New York, 1974), 171-74.

35. Reproduced in Peter Coss, *The Knight in Medieval England 1000-1400* (Dover, 1993), 73.

36. Oxford, Bodleian Library, MS Douce 180 (Douce Apocalypse), p. 31; see A.G. Hassall and W.O. Hassall, *The Douce Apocalypse* (New York, 1961), 22. Identifications of coats-of-arms in English bestiaries have so far been limited to the Bodley 764 image of the elephant (Ronald Baxter, "A Baronial Bestiary: Heraldic Evidence for the Patronage of MS Bodley 764," *Journal of the Warburg and Courtauld Institutes* 50 [1987], 196-200). On bestiary and apocalypse patronage patterns, see Hassig 1995, 176-77.

37. Manchester, John Rylands Library, MS lat. 24. See Richard Marks and Nigel Morgan, *The Golden Age of English Manuscript Painting 1200-1500* (New York, 1981), 54, pl. 8.

38. "Non mecaberis" (f. 5v). The caption within the lion roundel reads, "Reddit per flatum catulum leo uiuificatum" (By its breath, the lion brings its cubs back to life). See Avril Henry, *The Eton Roundels: Eton College, MS 177* (Aldershot, 1990) (color facsimile of typological images), 125.

Figure 1. Jacob blessing the lion Judah. *Physiologus*. Burgerbibliothek Bern, cod. 318, f. 7. Photo: Burgerbibliothek Bern.

Figure 2. Lions. Oxford, Bodleian Library, MS Laud Misc. 247, f. 139v.
Photo: The Bodleian Library.

Incipit lib de naturis bestiarū ce eaꝛ significationibȝ.

estiarum uocabulum
pprie conuenit leonibȝ
pardis ce tigribȝ. lupis
ce uulpibȝ. canibȝ ce simi
is. vrsibȝ. ce ceteris queut
oꝛe uꝼunguibȝ seuuunt ex
ceptis serpentibȝ. Bestie
autem dicte a ui qua se
uiunt. fere appellate
eo quod naturali utan
tur libertate. ce desiderio suo ferant̄. Sunt
enim libere eaꝝ uoluntates ce huc atȝ il
luc uagantur. ꜩ quo animus duxerit
eo feruntur. De naturis leonum.

Figure 3. Lions with initial B. New York, Pierpont Morgan Library, MS M. 81,
f. 8. Photo: The Pierpont Morgan Library.

Figure 4. King Edward III and St. George. Walter de Milimete, *Liber de Officilis Regum*. Oxford, Christ Church Library, MS Ch.Ch. 92, f. 3. Photo: The Bodleian Library, by permission of The Governing Body of Christ Church, Oxford.

Figure 5. Lion resuscitating whelp and typological scenes. Typological
miniatures and Apocalypse. Eton College Library, MS 177, p. viii.
Photo: by permission of the Provost and Fellows of Eton College.

Misericord Owls and Medieval Anti-semitism

Mariko Miyazaki

Medieval bestiaries made available to their readers a wide range of verbal and visual information about birds, animals, and fabulous creatures. Moreover, bestiary images were easily adaptable to changing contemporary social and religious currents once separated from their texts and executed in a variety of different media. Once divorced from their traditional manuscripts contexts, it is likely that particular social conditions or public sentiments generated a need to invest certain bestiary themes with additional meanings. In this essay, I will focus primarily on the subject of the owl in order to illustrate how bestiary imagery was modified and developed in late medieval public church decoration, primarily in the form of the sculpted choir-seats known as misericords. The owl provides a good case study of this process as it was an especially popular misericord motif and its artistic and literary characterizations were largely informed by—but not limited to—the bestiaries. I shall try to analyze how this rather ubiquitous bestiary creature took on different meanings depending on where and under what circumstances a given image was executed. In this regard, the focus will be on owl imagery in Norwich Cathedral, where contemporary circumstances mandated a particular interpretation of the owl that helps explain its repeated depiction in the church's decorative program.

Compelling evidence of the transmission of bestiary imagery to other media may be found in misericords produced all over Europe but especially in England owing to the exceptional popularity of the bestiary tradition here. G.L. Remnant's extensive catalog of English misericords lists more than seventy identifiable animals; their close link with the bestiaries is apparent in the frequent representation of popular bestiary exotics, including the griffin and the siren, as well as depictions of more ordinary animals, such as the fox and the stag, whose allegorical significance was developed mainly in the bestiaries.[1] Good examples include the well-known bestiary story of the hunter throwing down a mirror to divert a tigress as depicted on a Chester Cathedral misericord and a ferocious hyena devouring a corpse on a misericord in Carlisle Cathedral.[2]

Surviving examples suggest that misericord carvers were more attracted to certain bestiary creatures, including the siren, unicorn, pelican, and elephant, while others, such as the panther, beaver, and phoenix, failed to hold their attention. It is unlikely that such choices were made simply on grounds of religious associations since the bestiaries assign to the latter-named and other "rejected" animals equally important theological significance.[3] One possible explanation for the selectivity shown by the sculptors may have been their indirect acquaintance with bestiary stories by way of sermons and fables, and these, in turn, privileged certain creatures.[4] It is likely that these creatures were so privileged because they were allegorically associated with characteristics especially relevant in public church settings.

ENGLISH MISERICORDS: FORM AND FUNCTION

In England as elsewhere, stern discipline at first required all monks to stand during the daily recitation of the Divine Office. But by the beginning of the twelfth century, a concession had been granted which was accompanied by the construction of the first misericords, ingeniously constructed ledges on which the clergy could rest during services without seeming to do so. The reasons for the presence of often elaborate carvings on misericords, visible only when the ledges are tilted upwards, is not clearly understood; they may have been intended to celebrate the indulgent purpose of the misericords or may simply constitute one manifestation of the medieval love of ornamentation. In some cases, they may also have carried significant theological messages. It has been theorized recently that certain narrative or emblematic images—especially those involving sin or damnation— may have been deliberately located "beneath" the monks, who could then figuratively and literally suppress them.[5] This might help explain why many of the misericord motifs and vignettes are negative or have some connection to the idea of sin, which, as we shall see, the case of the owl so emphatically demonstrates.

English misericords, which form the focus of this analysis, are distinct from their continental counterparts in three main respects.[6] First, English carvers showed more pronounced interest in animal themes than French artists, who preferred the depiction of daily human activities. Second, on both sides of the central subject, English misericords often have subsidiary carvings called supporters, a feature not common in France, which allows for "adjunct" figures and motifs related in some way to the central image. Most significantly for the present analysis, misericord production reached its peak in England in the fourteenth and fifteenth centuries, a century earlier than in continental Europe, and thus many English examples were executed closer to the thirteenth-century heyday of the medieval bestiaries.

Because of the relative rarity of iconographical unity across a given misericord ensemble, it is probable that the artists enjoyed greater freedom in the selection and treatment of subjects. This situation likely contrasts with the usual case for architectural sculpture or stained glass, for which it is generally assumed the artist was required to follow a theological program formulated by the clergy.[7] However, monastic patrons were ultimately responsible for the final design of misericords and could withhold payment indefinitely if commissioned work was unsatisfactory.[8] Moreover, a wide variety of subjects in misericords parallel those known from medieval sermons, in which metaphors drawn from nature and daily life presented in the form of *exempla* often provided spiritual instruction.[9] Such animal parables were incorporated into daily preaching and may well have been better known than the bestiary accounts. That sermon versions of animal lore probably exerted a more immediate influence on carving design than the illustrations of precious manuscripts should not be surprising, given that sermons were delivered by religious who commissioned misericords, and their audiences included craftsmen who, in turn, furnished the church decoration. These factors, viewed in light of misericord functions, suggest that the carved subjects met with monastic approval and held potential religious significance, which is why the misericord owls will be approached from a primarily theological point of view.

ICONOGRAPHICAL SOURCES

Some misericord carvings of animal subjects continue a tradition of animal representation carried over from Romanesque sculpture, in which animals sometimes involved in human activities were used as vehicles of humor and satire.[10] Towards the end of the thirteenth century, such animal motifs increasingly found their place in wood carvings, and fascination with the upside-down world continued.[11] In addition to architectural sculpture, animal imagery in the margins of illuminated manuscripts may have provided especially attractive models for misericord artists, owing at least in part to their common aesthetic functions: marginalia enlivened serious, devotional texts, just as misericords enlivened a solemn and holy location in the church.[12]

Another important influence on the development of misericord animal iconography was popular literature. A good example of such correspondence may be observed on a misericord in Beverley Minster, which includes a lively portrait of an owl on the left supporter. The central subject, a fox friar and his ape assistant preaching before a congregation of geese, was influenced by the *Roman de Renard*, a twelfth-century animal epic which achieved enormous popularity throughout Europe in the later Middle Ages and often served as a source of inspiration for marginal decoration, sculpture, and stained glass.[13] I will return to the possible significance of the owl in this context, but suffice it to say at this point that it likely refers to the idea of sin, especially given the mock-religious content of the main scene.

There are other more didactic animal tales which helped promote the popularity of animal imagery in England, such as the collections of fables by Odo of Cheriton and Marie de France.[14] The influence of a specific popular literary work is observable in a misericord in Ely Cathedral, which juxtaposes an energetically rendered owl holding a mouse with a beguiling small bird sheltered by ivy leaves.[15] This image was likely inspired by *The Owl and the Nightingale*, a well-known bird story written in the mid-thirteenth century and a source for later *exempla*.[16] *The Owl and the Nightingale* describes a dispute between the two birds in order to underscore the dichotomy between the monastic and the secular life.[17] With its monastic theme and metaphysical symbolism, this poem also reveals an amusing rivalry between the two avian characters that is especially appropriate on church furniture used by the monks themselves.

THE OWL IN THE BESTIARIES

Important visual and literary iconographical sources as outlined above doubtless informed some misericord owl images, but the overwhelming influence on this imagery was the medieval bestiaries. Since antiquity, the owl carried mostly negative connotations, ranging from death and evil to stupidity and sloth.[18] The idea of the owl as a primarily negative bird was perpetuated by the bestiarists, whose primary contribution to owl symbolism was to identify the owl with sinners in general and with the Jews in particular.

Several different types of owls are discussed in different bestiary entries, resulting in a somewhat confusing array of terminology. The *nycticorax, noctua, bubo,* and *ulula* can be traced back to Pliny and, ultimately, to Aristotle.[19] All four of these bestiary owls together reveal a decidedly negative view of this class of bird and also provide strong symbolic associations that are especially appropriate in ecclesiastical decoration.

The bestiaries incorporated the *Physiologus* chapter on the *nycticorax,* usually translated as "night crow" or "night raven," always classified and understood as a type of owl. The *Physiologus* first connects the *nycticorax* to Christ by quoting the Psalms: "I have become like an owl in the house" (Ps. 102:6).[20] But subsequently, the bird is identified with the Jews who, like the *nycticorax* who prefers the night and shuns the daylight, prefer the darkness of ignorance to the light brought by Christ, saying, "We have no king but Caesar, we know not who this man is" (John 19:15).[21] This anti-Jewish characterization was also applied to the *noctua,* which is not described in the *Physiologus* but which appears frequently in the thirteenth-century bestiaries.[22]

A more detailed discussion of the *nycticorax* and the *bubo* may be found in Hugh of Fouilloy's *De avibus,* the most important contemporary treatise on birds that was often excerpted or incorporated in its entirety into the bestiaries.[23] Interestingly, Hugh presents a radically different interpretation of the *nycticorax,* in which he compares the bird's habit of shunning the light to Christ, who desires to convert sinners.[24] Both types of owls appear in illustrated copies of Hugh's aviary as recognizably owl-like, with hooked beaks, ears, and large round eyes.[25]

The aviaries and bestiaries also have a separate entry for the *bubo,* another type of owl which, owing to its abominable foulness and idleness, signifies all sinners and is assailed by other birds just as a sinner arouses outrage and repulsion among righteous people.[26] Some of the thirteenth-century bestiaries, such as Bodley 764, offer another chapter on the *ulula* or screech-owl, whose shrieks foretell disaster and symbolize the wailing of the sinner in hell. Like the *nycticorax* and *noctua*, the text connects the *ulula* to the Jews, albeit indirectly, citing Isaiah 13:21, a passage concerning the destruction of Babylon.[27]

Most of the bestiary owl illustrations show little attempt to visually complement the moral lessons provided by the texts in that they are often simple portraits. However, some bestiary owl imagery carries specifically anti-Jewish meanings. For example, in both Bodley 764 and Harley 4751, the large *bubo* is shown harassed by small birds, thus underscoring its identification with loathsome sinners (figure 1). In addition, given the anti-Jewish nature of the owl texts, the image is a reference to the Jews, hated by Christians just as owls are hated by more virtuous birds. Anti-Jewish meaning may also be assigned to the Bodley 602 *nycticorax*, shown closing its eyes and pecking a corpse in front of a collapsing temple, which likely alludes to the ruin of Babylon and to the Synagogue, and thus to the destruction of the Old Law (figure 2).[28]

Owls depicted in other medieval contexts also represent the Jews in various ways. For example, an image of St. Francis preaching the birds from a thirteenth-century psalter shows a prominent owl sitting on a branch as a representation of the Jews and therefore central target of the sermon.[29] The opening miniature in the famous thirteenth-century notebook of Villard de Honnecourt depicts an owl and a pelican flanking a central image of a seated bishop, symbolizing the light-shunning Jews and Christ's resurrection, respectively.[30]

Furthermore, the close examination of certain bestiary renderings of the *bubo*—although technically exempt from anti-Jewish "taint" in many of the bestiary texts—reveals a focused attempt to anthropomorphize the bird in a way that bears an unmistakable resemblance to contemporary portraits of Jews. For example, the Harley 4751 *bubo* has a beak skillfully turned into a hooked nose, a physiognomical feature common to most pejorative representations of Jews (figure 1).[31] Even more obvious is the *bubo* in the Westminster Abbey Bestiary, with its recognizably human face with prominent horns (figure 3).[32] These examples suggest that in the bestiaries the identification with the Jews had already been extended to all of the owls.

The owl's horns, such as those observable in the Westminster image, are of particular interest in the analysis of the bird's anti-Jewish significance. That Jews themselves had horns was an idea exploited by medieval Christians in order to characterize the Jews as wholly diabolical.[33] The Church reinforced the association between horned devils and Jews by issuing a decree which prescribed the Jews' obligatory wearing of the *pileum cornutum,* a pointed or "horned" hat.[34] Bestiary and misericord artists further promoted the demonic implications of horns by including them in owl representations, thus creating a simultaneously naturalistic and pejorative visual sign.

That there are both horned and unhorned owls in nature was obviously known to medieval artists, given their indiscriminate use of horns for various of the bestiary owls.[35] Therefore, a horned owl in the bestiaries or in misericord carving may be read as either ornithologically descriptive or as an aspect of the bird's anti-Jewish characterization, or possibly both, depending on context. For example, an owl depicted on a misericord in Gloucester Cathedral, beleaguered by aggressive small birds, has clearly noticeable horns.[36] Perhaps the Gloucester image depicts an actual horned owl, nothing more. However, this cannot totally eliminate its negative implications, because the horn-like tufts could have been readily understood as nature's "evidence" for a demonic-Jews theory, in keeping with the medieval view that every natural phenomenon is a manifestation of God's will.[37] In addition, a ritual murder accusation was brought against the Jews of Gloucester in 1168 which may have provided historical justification for anti-Jewish imagery in the cathedral.[38]

A natural history connection can also be found for images of the owl's harassment. In nature, an owl is often attacked by other birds when it ventures out into daylight, because it is virtually blind and therefore tactically disadvantaged. Medieval hunters were well aware of this behavior and often snared small birds by using a real or stuffed owl as bait.[39] However, it is clear that this natural process also acquired mystical significance, as the owl's blindness caused by glaring light was moralized in the bestiary owl descriptions. For example, Guillaume le Clerc's *Bestiaire* entry for the *nycticorax* refers to the spiritual blindness of the Jews who "are in the darkness and see not the truth."[40] This general insult is given a christological interpretation in fr. 14969 (f. 13), in which Guillaume's text is accompanied by an image of an angel covering the eyes of a Jew who is being pushed away from the baptism of Christ by a demon.[41] The stigmatization of the Jews as blind is expressed most prominently in representations of Synagoga, the ubiquitous female personification of the Jews, who often carries a broken spear and wears a veil over her eyes as expressive of Jewish spiritual "blindness."[42] Finally, another of the medieval claims concerning the alleged physical abnormalities of the Jews was that Jewish children were born blind and needed Christian blood to recover their sight.[43]

For those misericords that present a simple portrait of the owl with no visual reference to its nature and moralization, it is more difficult to establish the direct relationship with the bestiaries. While the bestiaries themselves often depict the owl in the form of a portrait, it should be noted in some manuscripts the owl is depicted as a crow-like or heron-like bird, whereas misericord versions always have recognizably owlish appearances with large eyes and a sharply curved beak on a characteristically round face (figure 4).[44] In part, the more naturalistic representations of the misericord owls are explained as part of a general tendency toward the more accurate rendering of birds in later medieval English art, especially during the fourteenth and fifteenth centuries.[45]

In most cases, the owls in misericords are either depicted alone or else are shown with small birds which at times meekly hide in bushes and at others bravely attack their common enemy. In the absence of accompanying texts, the visual elements of the misericord owls do not seem to clearly express anti-Jewish sentiment as directly as the images in Harley 4751 or Bodley 602. However, analysis of the contexts and locations of individual owl misericords may provide clues as to how they participated in this social reality.

OWLS AT NORWICH CATHEDRAL

Norwich Cathedral provides an excellent case study, as it incorporates into its decorative program an unusually high number of owl images, including three misericords and three roof bosses, which emphasize themes of hostility.[46] Two of the misericords employ a mobbing theme for the main carving: one depicts the owl unaware of an imminent raid under branches full of small birds, while the other portrays a moment of frightening assault in an elaborate symmetrical composition (figure 4). The third misericord, which lacks a negative connotation, shows a single owl with a mouse in its beak as a subsidiary carving to a central image of Samson rending the lion's jaws.[47] In the cloister, one of the roof bosses depicts small birds pecking a larger owl's head (figure 5), and two others represent the owl perching in a tree.[48] Given bestiary interpretations of the owl as a sign of the Jews, the possible reason for its recurrent depiction at Norwich Cathedral may be sought in the social history of the city, in particular, in the markedly tense Christian-Jewish relations of the twelfth and thirteenth centuries.

Medieval Norwich was one of the designated cities in which Jewish settlements were built under the protection of the secular authorities after the Norman Conquest of 1066.[49] Not all English towns had such Jewish quarters, and only about fifteen to twenty such large communities were maintained prior to the expulsion of the Jews from England in 1290.[50] In spite of—or perhaps owing to—a significant Jewish presence, Norwich was one of the cities in medieval England where anti-Jewish sentiments were particularly intense.

The fear, mistrust, and hatred of the Christian public reached a fevered pitch when Norwich Jews were wrongfully charged with the ritual murder of the little boy William, who was to become a martyr saint, in 1144.[51] This was a notorious example of other similar accusations for which hundreds of Jews were imprisoned and executed all over Europe, as a manifestation of Christian fears that Jews would abduct and slaughter Christian children during the Passover. Despite papal denunciation of such charges, local Church authorities were usually in the forefront of anti-Jewish campaigns as was the case in Norwich.[52]

In the following century, as more Jews fled to England after their expulsion from many parts of continental Europe, anti-Jewish activities rapidly escalated, resulting in numerous riots, boycotts, and persecutions against the newcomers.[53] Although such conflicts were by no means confined to Norwich and took place in many English towns near Jewish settlements, tensions were especially acute in the eastern regions which necessitated royal intervention as well as special protective legislation. For example, when Norwich Jews were exposed to savage attacks in 1190 and 1235, they were allowed to take refuge in a Norman castle and thus escape massacre.[54] When the provincial council of the Church held at Oxford in 1222 promulgated a series of anti-Jewish canons including prohibitions against new synagogues, the employment of Christian servants in Jewish households, and the entry of Jews into churches, Norwich was one of only three dioceses in which these laws were strictly enforced, the other two being Oxford and Lincoln.[55] On a more individual level, the famous thirteenth-century Jewish Receipt Roll, which derides Isaac of Norwich and other contemporary Norwich Jews by picturing them in league with demons and the Antichrist, graphically testifies to the profound suspicion and hostility towards Jews at this time and place.[56]

Strictly speaking, in the bestiaries it is the *bubo,* a symbol of sinners, towards which the rage of other birds is directed, while specific references to the Jews are reserved for the *nycticorax* and the *noctua.* However, considering the strong anti-Jewish current here, it is not surprising if in Norwich the iconography of the mobbed owl depicted in two misericords and again as a roof boss in the cloister was interpreted as an allegory of justifiable attack on the Jews by righteous Christians. This interpretation also has implications for bestiary images of the *bubo* mobbed by birds, especially if such an image may be seen as part of a larger group of anti-Jewish texts and images that might be included in a given bestiary.[57] An extension of anti-Jewish meaning to virtually all of the owls is also explained by the possibility that the misericord carvers—whether or not they had direct access to bestiary manuscripts—did not differentiate between the various bestiary owls.[58]

Indeed, bestiary texts themselves anticipate the confusion of the owl identities. The Cambridge Bestiary distinguishes the *noctua* from the *bubo* simply on grounds that the latter is larger and, after stating that the *nycticorax* is itself an owl, discusses the owls together as collective figures of the Jews.[59] Bodley 764 contains an especially ambiguous description: "The night-owl is not the owl (*bubo*), for the owl (*bubo*) is bigger. The night-raven is the same as the night-owl, which loves the night."[60]

In considering their anti-Jewish significance, it is important to note that the roof bosses and misericords in Norwich Cathedral were executed during the fourteenth and fifteenth centuries,[61] long after the period of greatest Christian-Jewish conflict that culminated in the expulsion of the Jews from England in 1290. However, there is ample evidence of persistent anti-semitism in Norwich and other English cities even in the absence of the Jews themselves. Most notably, the negative portrayal of the Jews as sinister, treacherous, and foolish continued to be commonplace in popular sermons, often in the form of *exempla* as compiled in the fourteenth-century *Gesta Romanorum,* and notoriously anti-Jewish religious dramas such as the N-Town plays, known to have been performed in Norwich.[62] Interestingly, both the *Gesta Romanorum* and the mystery plays have been identified as sources for the cathedral roof boss iconography.[63]

Reference to the Jews' involvement in ritual murder also continued well after the English expulsion. For example, *The Jew's Daughter,* a widely-circulated popular ballad, tells of a Jewish girl who lures and brutally kills a Christian boy called Hew, obviously referring to Hugh of Lincoln who, like William of Norwich, was believed to have been slaughtered by the Jews.[64] Anti-Jewish motifs are found in more famous literary works as well. In *The Prioress's Tale,* Chaucer portrays a nun who expresses an intense hatred towards the Jews. After narrating a story of a little boy's murder by Jews, the Prioress recaps the notorious Lincoln incident: "O yonge Hugh of Lincoln, slayn also / With cursed Jewes, as it is notable / For it is but a litel whyle ago."[65] The degradation of the Jews in English art was also perpetuated in post-expulsion visual messages, such as the continued production of images of the blindfolded Synagoga, as observable for example on the west fronts of Lincoln and Rochester cathedrals.[66]

Anti-Jewish sentiment in Norwich died particularly hard, continuing well beyond the medieval period. The relics of William of Norwich were venerated until the arrival of Protestantism, and although the peak of his cult occurred in the second half of the twelfth century, offerings were still made and canons carried out repairs on his shrine in the cathedral in the fifteenth century.[67] As late as 1753, when Jewish residents were finally given official permission to become naturalized without taking the Sacrament, the outrage of the public swept through England and in Norwich the bishop who confirmed the government's decision was insulted by angry citizens in more than one part of his diocese.[68]

The identification of the owl with the Jews was probably stronger in places with a long history of Christian-Jewish hostility, like Norwich, where the imagery of the owl mobbed by small birds had become a symbol of the righteous indignation of Christians against the wickedness of the Jews. This iconographical motif, together with the representations of horned owls, may point to the artist's possible practice of natural observation but not without moral considerations. When the misericord owls carry anti-Jewish symbolism, they demonstrate social aversion to the Jews as well as anti-Jewish propaganda promoted by the Church. The latter aspect seems to be of particular significance in Norwich because one of the local saints was said to have been murdered by the Jews. Anti-Jewish representations therefore were important reminders of Jewish evil, not only to the cathedral chapter but also to the citizenry, and probably also aided in the effort to attract as many pilgrims as possible to the shrine of the martyr-saint. In fact, it has been suggested that the blame for William's murder was placed on the Jews ultimately for economic reasons, in that a shrine to a local saint who died for the faith was needed to attract pilgrims and donations and, in this context, the Jews functioned as the most convenient non-Christian murderers.[69]

In addition, it may be significant that the Norwich misericords were funded by bequests and donations from numerous prominent local benefactors, such as Thomas Erpingham, apparent from the numerous carved coats-of-arms that function as supporters on many of the misericords.[70] Lay involvement in the commissioning of choir stalls for a monastic cathedral suggests that these images may have served or communicated the particular interests of the non-clergy as well as the monks. If viewed as an ensemble, the subjects represented in the Norwich misericords include a number of non-controversial themes, such as combat and domestic life, which do not seem to carry anti-Jewish meaning or to bear social significance particular to Norwich. However, by this time, anti-Jewish sentiment grounded in social unrest regularly infiltrates other religious contexts. Examples include the sermons and mystery plays already mentioned as well as illuminated apocalypses, bestiaries, and the fifteenth-century *Biblia pauperum*.[71] As for Norwich Cathedral, the inclusion of numerous owls in the cathedral's decorative program may well constitute a case of anti-Jewish visual commentary in an otherwise conventional misericord program that communicates both religious and social concerns.[72]

SINFUL PARTNERS: THE OWL AND THE APE

While the anti-Jewish significance of medieval owls was quite emphatic in certain contexts, it would be misrepresentative to suggest that every owl necessarily expresses anti-Jewish sentiment. The owl was a popular motif in medieval art because it also functioned as a more general sign of sinners. The notion of the sinner owl was discussed at length by Hugh of Fouilloy who, as noted above, equated the *nycticorax* with Christ and reserved his negative comments for the *bubo*. For Hugh, the filthiness of the *bubo* signifies the sinner's wayward behavior which dishonors others, and its idleness his reluctance to engage in good deeds. He also draws an analogy between the heavily-feathered body of the *bubo* and excessive carnal desire, as well as between its habit of living in a cave and the avoidance of confession. The hostility of other birds towards the *bubo* therefore symbolizes the stern rebuke of virtuous people directed to those who openly indulge in sinful acts.[73]

Neither bestiary painters nor misericord carvers attempted to illustrate the various individual vices ascribed to the owl; rather, they chose to represent the fatal consequences awaiting sinners, mainly though depictions of the menaced owl. Medieval artists further developed the theme of sin by coupling the owl with other animals of well-established negative character. One of the most notorious of such negative animals is the ape, used to suggest lust and irreverence in many medieval artistic contexts.[74] A combined image of the owl, ape, and fox on a Beverley Minster misericord has been already noted. In this context, the owl and ape likely represent the wickedness of the deceitful Reynard, who poses as a religious. Also, given that the main scene depicts the delivery of a sermon and that the misericord itself is located in the church choir, the owl, in particular, might function as a sign of the unrepentant sinner. Two other misericords, one in Winchester Cathedral and the other in Wells Cathedral, show the owl held by the ape, images that satirize the aristocratic activity of hawking.[75] The wry humor conveyed by the ape imitating a knight becomes even more pointed by the substitution of the owl for the falcon because of the uselessness of the dim-sighted owl in daytime hunting. Although such imagery was no doubt meant to amuse, it was nonetheless based on contemporary moral notions. One clue to a possible interpretation of this scene may be found in the Luttrell Psalter (f. 38). An image of the ape hunting with the owl appears on the Beatus page, whose text begins: "Blessed is the man that walketh not in the counsel of the ungodly, nor standeth in the way of sinners, nor sitteth in the seat of the scornful" (Ps. 1:1), creating an antithetical relationship between text and image. Indeed, the owl and ape enjoyed a popular partnership precisely because they were both such ubiquitous symbols of vice and evil.

There are several important parallels between the medieval characterizations of the owl and ape, which may further explain the pairing of these two creatures in manuscript marginalia and on misericords. Firstly, the owl was regarded as the worst bird *(turpissima avis)* while the ape was believed the worst beast *(turpissima bestia)*. Therefore, both were characterized as outcasts and ostracized by their own communities.[76] The owl, like the ape, bears a certain resemblance to humans: it is the only bird with its eyes in the front of its face. The owl has demonic associations owing to its horns and penchant for darkness, and the ape symbolizes the devil himself: the ape has a head but no tail because the devil had his beginning in heaven but lost his tail because of hypocrisy.[77] Another common aspect shared by the owl and ape is their physical and spiritual uncleanness. The owl is accused of dirtying its own nest with dung and is said to linger among tombs all day in the stench of decaying flesh.[78] The ape's uncleanness manifests itself primarily through its sexuality. Remarks on the sexual perversity of the ape can be found in a fourteenth-century commentary on Dante and in a Franciscan *exemplum* circulated during the same period; both comment on the male ape's lust for human females.[79] In the Peterborough Cathedral ceiling and in the Luttrell Psalter, the uncleanness of the owl and ape is reinforced by its proximity to the goat, another unclean beast consistently associated with lechery in the bestiaries.[80] In the Peterborough image, the ape rides backward on the goat, reminiscent of the forced ride by medieval criminals on their way to execution and used in pictorial art as an expression of shame and evil.[81]

In an extremely interesting prefatory miniature to a thirteenth-century English psalter, the owl and ape are witnesses to Abel's murder by Cain (figure 6).[82] At first glance, the somewhat whimsical depiction of the owl, together with the playfulness of the ape archer, may appear incongruous in regard to the seriousness of the main subject. However, given their negative associations, the inclusion of these two animals in this context is appropriate in all respects. On one level, their presence emphasizes the bestial nature of fratricide. On another level, the sinful pair may be a reminder of the collective guilt of the Jews who, like Cain, inhumanly abused their own flesh and blood when they rejected Christ.[83] The view of Cain as the prototype of the Jews, which originated in the writings of the early Church Fathers such as Ambrose and Augustine, became a widely accepted notion,[84] and the use of the owl motif provided a visually economic means of further underscoring the anti-Jewish interpretation of this event.

CONCLUSION

Different layers of meaning embodied in the image of the owl were undoubtedly perceived by medieval viewers. The owl could be a witty character in popular tales, an ominous bird foretelling doom, a symbol of religious and social prejudice, and a conveyer of moral lessons.

Medieval views of the owl were for the most part unfavorable, and the prevalent opinion expressed by bestiary and misericord artists in conjunction with literary characterizations related this bird to the Jews on the one hand and to all kinds of sinners on the other. It should be emphasized that these two concepts were not mutually exclusive. Indeed, these meanings were probably interchangeable, depending on particular social contexts in which the image was presented and on individual viewer interests, unless contemporary circumstances mandated a stronger identification of the owl with the Jews as in the case of Norwich Cathedral. Towards a more thorough understanding of the latter, a full-scale study of the cathedral imagery and its patrons would allow the assessment of the owl and its function as an anti-Jewish symbol in a broader context. The presence of the owl in cooperative images of evil, particularly in partnership with the ape, also strengthened its identification with sin by association. The power and richness of the owl as a pictorial motif therefore lies in its versatility and long tradition of negative traits, such as blindness and uncleanness, that were readily adaptable for anti-Jewish commentary as well as for the expression of more general ideological beliefs.

NOTES

1. G.L. Remnant, *A Catalogue of Misericords in Great Britain* (Oxford, 1969); M.D. Anderson, "The Iconography of British Misericords," in Remnant 1969, xxxv-xxxvi.

2. George C. Druce, "The Mediaeval Bestiaries and Their Influence on Ecclesiastical Decorative Art," *Journal of the British Archaeological Association,* n.s. 25 (1919), 51-56, fig. 2 of pl. IV, fig. 2 of pl. VII. The latest study of English misericords is Christa Grossinger, *The World Upside Down: English Misericords* (London, 1997).

3. The panther and phoenix signify Christ and the resurrection, respectively, while the beaver is a figure of chastity. See Hassig 1995, 72-92, 156-66; and Jones in this volume.

4. On the relationship between bestiary stories and contemporary sermons, see G.R. Owst, *Literature and Pulpit in Medieval England* (Oxford, 1966), 196-204. An opposing view—arguing for a minimum contribution of bestiaries to sermons—has been recently put forward by Willene Clark, "Twelfth and Thirteenth-Century Latin Sermons and the Latin Bestiary," *Compar(a)ison* 1 (1996), 5-19.

5. Camille 1992, 93-95.

6. Anderson 1969, xxvii. On the differences between English and French misericords, see also Henry Kraus, *The Hidden World of Misericords* (New York, 1975), 171-72.

7. Kraus 1975, x; Anderson 1969, xxiv; Arthur Gardner, *English Medieval Sculpture* (Cambridge, 1951), 277.

8. Anderson 1969, xxvii; M.D. Anderson, *History and Imagery in British Churches* (London, 1971), 142-55.

9. On *exempla*, see Frederich Tubach, *Index exemplorum: A Handbook of Medieval Religious Tales* (Helsinki, 1969).

10. Klingender 1971, 310-16. For example, see the archivolts of the twelfth-century churches at Berfreston, Kent and Aulnay, Poitou, on which the owl joins a larger procession of monstrous creatures, such as a centaur and a harp-playing ass (*Ibid.*, fig. 191). Other well-known and early examples of sculpted animal drôleries include the twelfth-century crypt capitals in Canterbury Cathedral (Deborah Kahn, *Canterbury Cathedral and Its Romanesque Sculpture* [Austin, 1991], 35-94) and twelfth-century sculpture in Yorkshire (Xenia Muratova,"Les cycles des Bestiaires dans le décor sculpté des églises du XIIe siècle dans le Yorkshire, et leur relation avec les manuscrits des Bestiaires enluminés," *Atti del V Colloquio della International Beast Epic, Fable and Fabliau Society* [Alessandria, 1987], 337-54).

11. Klingender 1971, 433.

12. On the functions of manuscript marginalia, see Randall 1966, 3-20; and Camille 1992, 11-55.

13. Randall 1967, 366-67, 416-18 and figs. 249-51. See also Kenneth Varty, *Reynard the Fox* (Leicester, 1967), especially Chapter 4, "The Fox Religious" and Chapter 5, "The Fox and Ape," 51-67.

14. Odo of Cheriton, *The Fables of Odo of Cheriton*, trans. and ed. John C. Jacobs (Syracuse, 1985); Marie de France, *Fables*, ed. and trans. Harriet Spiegel (Toronto, 1994).

15. Edward G. Tasker, *Encyclopedia of Medieval Church Art* (London, 1993), fig. 7.102.

16. *The Owl and the Nightingale*, trans. Brian Stone (Harmondsworth, 1971). See also Klingender 1971, 365-66, 435.

17. The allegorical use of birds is also found in Part I of Hugh of Fouilloy's *De avibus*, which contrasts the dove and the hawk as symbols of the contemplative and active lives, respectively. See Clark 1992, 13-19; 116-47.

18. Paul Vandenbroeck, "Bubo significans: Die Eule als Sinnbild von Schlechtigkeit und Torheit, vor allem in der niederländischen und deutschen Bilddarstellung und bei Jheronimus Bosch I," *Jaarboek van het Koninklijk Museum voor Schone Kunsten-Antwerpen* (1985), 40. See also Heinrich

Schwarz and Volker Plagemann, "Eule," in *Reallexikon zur deutschen Kunstgeschichte* 6 (1973), cols. 267-322; and Edward A. Armstrong, *The Folklore of Birds,* 2d rev. ed. (New York, 1958), 114-15.

19. By *nycticorax,* Aristotle probably meant the eared-owl (Curley 1979, 72). On owl classifications, see Pliny, *Natural History* 10.16 (Rackham 1940, 314-15).

20. Curley 1979, 10.

21. The *nycticorax's* association with the Jews is not mentioned in the Y version of the *Physiologus,* which is regarded as closer to the Greek original. The anti-Jewish characterization appears in the B version on which the English medieval bestiaries were dependent. See Curley 1979, 10-12; McCulloch 1962, 22-25. See also Muratova 1984, 164.

22. White 1954, 134.

23. Clark 1992, 173-75 (nycticorax); 216-19 (bubo).

24. *Ibid.,* 172-75.

25. *Ibid.,* figs. 11, 12. It has been hypothesized that Hugh himself was responsible for the *De avibus* images. See Charles De Clercq, "Hugues de Fouilloy, imagier de ses propres oeuvres?" *Revue du nord* 45 (1963), 31-42.

26. Clark 1992, 217-19; Barber 1993, 148-49.

27. Bodley 764, f. 84v; Barber 1993, 170-71.

28. George C. Druce, "Notes on Birds in Mediaeval Church Architecture," *Antiquary* 50 (1914), 384; Hassig 1995, 97-98.

29. New York, Pierpont Morgan Library, MS M. 72, f. 139v (Schwarz and Plagemann 1973, cols. 301-302 and fig. 5).

30. Paris, Bibliothèque Nationale, MS fr. 19093, f. 1 (Hans R. Hahnloser, *Villard de Honnecourt,* 2d rev. ed. [Graz, 1972], 269 and pl. 1).

31. On physical distortions used in pejorative representation of Jews, see Ruth Mellinkoff, *Outcasts: Signs of Otherness in Northern European Art of the Late Middle Ages,* 2 vols. (Berkeley, 1993), I, 127-29.

32. Hassig 1995, 97.

33. Exodus 34:29 describes Moses descending from Mount Sinai with the second set of Law tablets. In the passage, reading, "And behold the skin of his face sent forth beams," Jerome translated the Hebrew word *karan,* meaning "shine," incorrectly as "horns" (Joshua Trachtenberg, *The Devil and the Jews,* [Philadelphia, 1943], 44-46). See also Ruth Mellinkoff, *The Horned Moses in Medieval Art and Thought* (Berkeley, 1970), 1-5.

34. Trachtenberg 1943, 44-46.

35. Brunsdon Yapp, *Birds in Medieval Manuscripts* (New York, 1981), 39-42 and figs. 24-31.

36. Tasker 1993, fig. 7.101.

37. According to St. Paul, "Ever since the creation of the world, his invisible nature, namely, his eternal power and deity, has been clearly perceived in the things that have been made" (Rom. 1:20).

38. Cecil Roth, A *History of the Jews in England,* 3d ed. (Oxford, 1964), 13.

39. Bird hunting with an owl placed on a limed branch had been a common practice since ancient times, as depicted in a late Roman mosaic in Oderzo (Ranuccio Bianchi, *Rome: The Late Empire,* trans. Peter Green [New York, 1971], 115 and pl. 95). See also Clark 1992, 219; Yapp 1981, 37.

40. Guillaume le Clerc, *Bestiaire*, trans. George Druce (Ashford, 1936), 25-26.

41. See Mellinkoff 1993, I, 102-3; II, pl. IV.10.

42. *Ibid.,* I, 48-51, 64-65, 217-20.

43. Trachtenberg 1943, 50-51.

44. Various physical characteristics attributed to the bestiary owls may be related to the problematic translation of the term *nycticorax,* applied to certain owls, which literally means a "night raven" or a "night crow" but has been translated by some as "night heron." See also Yapp 1981, figs. 24-31.

45. Brundsdon Yapp, "Birds in Bestiaries: Medieval Knowledge of Nature," *The Cambridge Review* 105 (Nov. 1984), 183-90.

46. The owl images are located as follows. Misericords: (1) owl surrounded by birds (choir, north side, third [from east]); (2) owl supporter (choir, north side, sixth [from east]; see also below, note 47); (3) owl mobbed by birds (transept crossing, south side, ninth [from east]) (figure 4). Cloister bosses: (1) owl mobbed by birds (south alley, twelfth bay [from W], second [from N]) (figure 5); (2) owl with mouse in its beak perched in a pear tree (north alley, third bay [from east], eighth); (3) owl with mouse in its beak with two small birds (north alley, sixth bay [from east], eighth). See M. Rose, *The Misericords of Norwich Cathedral* (Dereham, 1994), 28, 53, 57; Tasker 1993, figs. 7.99 and 7.100; A.B. Whittingham, *Norwich Cathedral Bosses and Misericords* (Norwich, 1981); and M.R. James, *The Sculptured Bosses in the Cloisters of Norwich Cathedral* (Norwich, 1911). See also Martial Rose, "The Vault Bosses," in *Norwich Cathedral: Church, City and Diocese 1096-1996,* ed. Ian Atherton et al. (London, 1996), 363-78. The recently published monograph by Martial Rose and Julia Hedgecoe *(Stories in Stone: The Medieval Roof Carvings of Norwich Cathedral* [London, 1997]), with spectacular color photography, neither describes nor reproduces the owl bosses.

47. The owl with the mouse constitutes the right supporter, while the left supporter is an image of a crane, neither of which carry negative meaning in this context.

48. E.W. Tristram, "The Cloister Bosses," in *Norwich Cathedral Cloister* (Norwich, 1938), 8-9, 30; James 1911, pl. III.

49. Roth 1964, 5-14.

50. *Ibid.*, 91-93.

51. V.D. Lipman, *The Jews of Medieval Norwich* (London, 1967), 49-57.

52. Norwich Bishop William Turbe, St. Pancras Prior Dom Aimar, and a Benedictine monk Thomas of Monmouth, who wrote *The Life and Miracles of St. William of Norwich* about 1173, were the most ardent supporters for William's popular canonization. See Lipman 1967, 53-54; Ronald C. Finucane, *Miracles and Pilgrims: Popular Beliefs in Medieval England* (London, 1977), 119-20; and most recently, John M. McCulloh, "Jewish Ritual Murder: William of Norwich, Thomas of Monmouth, and the Early Dissemination of the Myth," *Speculum* 72/3 (1997), 698-740.

53. Roth 1964, 53-59.

54. Lipman 1967, 57-58, 62-63.

55. *Ibid.*, 58-59.

56. Cecil Roth, *Essays and Portraits in Anglo-Jewish History* (Philadelphia, 1962), 22-25. One of the caricatured Jews, Moses Mokke (shown on the left wearing the prominent funnel-hat), was executed as responsible for the alleged circumcision of a Christian boy and his property was confiscated by the Crown about 1140 (Lipman, 59-62). See also Mellinkoff 1993, I, 93; II, pl. III.125. The triple-faced Antichrist may be compared with the representation of the two-faced figure on a misericord in Norwich Cathedral, identified as a personification of Deceit (Tasker 1993, 204 and fig. 6.74).

57. Other especially anti-Jewish bestiary entries include the caladrius and hyena. On the caladrius, see George C. Druce, "The Caladrius and Its Legend, Sculptured upon the Twelfth-Century Doorway of Alne Church, Yorkshire," *Archaeological Journal* 69 (1912), 381-416. For a reproduction of the extremely anti-semitic caladrius image found in fr. 14969 (f. 9), see Mellinkoff 1993, II, pl. III.121. On the hyena, see Hassig 1995, 145-55.

58. M.D. Anderson, *Animal Carvings in British Churches* (Cambridge, 1938), 9-11.

59. White 1954, 133-34.

60. "Noctua autem non est bubo, nam bubo maior est. Nicticorax ipsa est noctua, que noctem amat" (Bodley 764, f. 73). Barber (1993, 147) translates the first sentence of this passage rather differently, and also renders *bubo* as "screech-owl."

61. The choir stalls and misericords were executed in two campaigns, from 1415-25 and 1472-99 (Veronica Sekules, "The Gothic Sculpture," in

Atherton et al. 1996, 208). The cloister bosses were carved from the second decade of the fourteenth century (Rose 1996, 364).

62. The N-Town plays were performed publicly in Norwich as recently as 1952 (*The Passion Play from the N. Town Manuscript*, ed. Peter Meredith [London, 1990], vii, 9). See also "The Council of the Jews," in *English Mystery Plays*, ed. Peter Happé (Harmondsworth, 1975), 409-31; and Trachtenberg 1943, 185-86. Anti-Jewish *exempla* are included in Jacques de Vitry, *The Exempla or Illustrative Stories from the Sermones Vulgares of Jacques de Vitry*, ed. Thomas Frederick Crane (New York, 1890), 124-25; and the *Gesta Romanorum*, trans. Charles Swan (New York, 1970), 161-62, 184-85.

63. Rose 1996, 372.

64. Bernard Glassman, *Anti-Semitic Stereotypes without Jews* (Detroit, 1975), 43. Hugh of Lincoln was murdered in 1254.

65. Geoffrey Chaucer, "The Prioress's Tale," lines 684-686 (*The Canterbury Tales: Nine Tales and the General Prologue*, ed. V. A. Kolve and Glending Olson [New York, 1989], 214). Chaucer probably wished to satirize the simplicity and sentimentalism of his character. However, this kind of story may have helped perpetuate the old stereotypes of the Jews (Glassman 1975, 37-40). See also Glassman's analysis of *The Jew of Malta* by Christopher Marlowe and *The Merchant of Venice* by Shakespeare (pp. 65-60).

66. The Rochester Synagoga is reproduced and described in Tasker 1993, 201 and fig. 6.68.

67. Roth 1964, 9; Finucane 1977, 120.

68. Roth 1964, 216-18.

69. Lipman 1967, 56. One of the peculiar facts concerning the cult of William of Norwich is the high proportion of the lower clergy among the pilgrims who benefited from the saint's miracles (Finucane 1977, 121).

70. Sekules 1996, 208; all of the coats-of-arms are reproduced in Rose 1994. See also Charles Tracy, *English Gothic Choir Stalls, 1400-1500* (Woodbridge, 1990), 32.

71. On anti-Jewish aspects of English illuminated apocalypse manuscripts, see Suzanne Lewis, "*Tractatus adversus Judaeos* in the Gulbenkian Apocalypse," *Art Bulletin* 68 (1986), 543-66. Various anti-Jewish aspects of English medieval bestiaries are discussed throughout Hassig 1995. The *Biblia pauperum* characterizes Christ's tribulations and murder as a Jewish plot, especially in the scenes of his arrest and mockery. See Avril Henry's facsimile and translation of the Schreiber Edition, dated c. 1460 (*Biblia Pauperum* [Aldershot, 1987], a, b, c [second alphabet]).

72. On anti-Jewish misericords outside England, see Elaine C. Block, "Judaic Imagery on Medieval Choir Stalls," *Reinardus* 8 (1995), 33-37.

73. Clark 1992, 219. Hugh's identification of the *nycticorax* with Christ may have been derived from Rabanus Maurus's *De natura rerum*, in which this bird symbolizes Christ or a holy man who scorns the unbeliever (Clark 1992, 173). See Rabanus Maurus, *De natura rerum* 8.6 (*PL* 111:251).

74. The most comprehensive study of medieval ape symbolism is H. W. Janson, *Apes and Ape Lore in the Middle Ages and the Renaissance* (London, 1952).

75. Remnant 1969, 57, 136; Anderson 1969, 58. Related scenes are observable on the ceiling of Peterborough Cathedral as well as in the margin of the Luttrell Psalter (Janson 1952, 166) (see below). See also Beryl Rowland, "'Owls and Apes' in Chaucer's *Nun's Priest's Tale*," *Mediaeval Studies* 27 (1965), 323; and Yapp 1981, 36-37.

76. Janson 1952, 181-82.

77. White 1954, 34-35; Barber 1993, 48-49.

78. Bodley 764, f. 74; Barber 1993, 149.

79. Janson 1952, 115-16, 268-69.

80. White 1954, 74-76. Of the various bestiary goats, *hircus* is normally associated with lasciviousness. On this characteristic of goats, see also Hassig and Brown in this volume.

81. Rowland 1965, 324-25. See Ruth Mellinkoff, "Riding Backwards: Theme of Humiliation and Symbol of Evil," *Viator* 4 (1973), 154-66.

82. See Morgan 1988, 182-83.

83. Janson 1952, 182. See also Ruth Mellinkoff, *The Mark of Cain* (Berkeley, 1981), 74-75 and figs. 19, 20.

84. Mellinkoff 1981, 92-98.

Figure 1. Owl mobbed by birds. London, British Library, MS Harley 4751, f. 47. Photo: by permission of the British Library.

enuncozace in eodem plalmo dicir. factus sum fi
cur nuncozax in domicilio. fucticozax imund est

Figure 2. Nycticorax. Oxford, Bodleian Library, MS Bodley 602, f. 6.
Photo: The Bodleian Library.

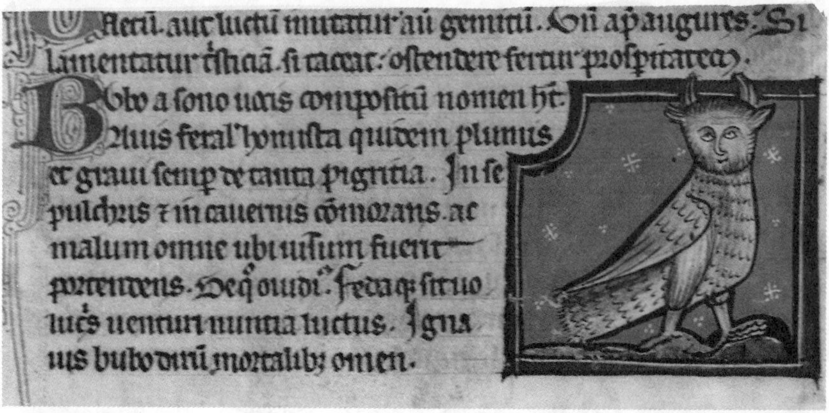

...ferri. aut luctu mutatur au gemitu. Cū ap augures: Si lamentatur ishaā si taceat: ostendere fertur prospitatea. Bubo a sono uocis compositū nomen ht. Auis feral' homista quidem plumis et graui semp de tanta pigritia. In sepulchris ꞇ in cauernis cōmorans. ac malum omne ubi uisum fuerit portendens. Deꝗ ouidi'. feda ꝗ sit uo lucꝭ uenturi nuntia luctus. Ignauus bubo dirū mortalibꝰ omen.

Figure 3. Owl. London, Westminster Abbey Library, MS 22, f. 40.
Photo: by courtesy of the Dean and Chapter of Westminster.

Figure 4. Owl mobbed by birds. Misericord. Norwich Cathedral.
Photo: Ken Harvey.

Figure 5. Owl mobbed by birds. Roof boss, cloister. Norwich Cathedral.
Photo: Julia Hedgecoe.

De cajm quimferat Abel fraurm suū. ſc. uıŋ.

Figure 6. Cain murdering Abel. Prefatory miniature to a psalter. Cambridge, St. John's College, MS K.26, f. 6. Photo: by permission of the Master and Fellows of St. John's College.

PART 2

Moral Lessons

Bestiary Lessons on Pride and Lust
Carmen Brown

"To instruct and delight," wrote Horace, is the poet's chief aim, and clearly it was advice that medieval artists, poets and painters alike, followed closely.[1] The coexistence of didacticism and entertainment was not necessarily detrimental for either purpose, and often the mark of artistic genius was made manifest in their skillful combination. It is true that often one intention was more important to its author and therefore received greater emphasis. If we take as an example the medieval bestiaries, their primary function was to instruct—not only a monastic audience but a secular one as well.[2] The highly allegorized meanings and characteristics attributed to various animals, birds, and Monstrous Races; the text heavily laced with passages from Scriptures; and the inclusions of the Creation cycle and account of the Fall of humankind all contribute to the bestiary's value as an instructional text. Yet for those who were illiterate and for all who wished to remember firmly the lessons imparted by the text, the images of birds and animals, both familiar and exotic, were powerful mnemonic devices.[3] As it was, the bestiary ably fulfilled Horace's dictum and did so for several centuries, enjoying a great popularity, especially during the twelfth, thirteenth, and fourteenth centuries. The lavishly illustrated psalters and Books of Hours which later supplanted the bestiary in popularity owed it a great debt. As we shall see, some of their imagery was derived from bestiary iconography, and their margins were often filled with tiny animals and birds familiar from the traditional bestiary rosters.[4]

It seems fairly clear that the bestiaries succeeded in delighting their readers. If, however, their main aim was to instruct, were they equally successful in this endeavor? There is no way to tell for certain. We can only learn what they intended to teach: lessons on proper Christian behavior and the ways of good moral life. These subjects were the topic of many medieval books. Yet the bestiaries were able to present a special view of human moral successes and failures by constructing the behaviors of animals and birds in order to reinforce the values important in medieval society.[5] The use of animals instead of humans focused the moralized message more clearly. For if an irrational animal—unendowed with human reason and without knowledge of the Divine Word—was able to embrace a Christian way of life, should not a rational human be able to do so that much more easily?[6] Conversely, moral failure in animals was excusable, for the same reason given above, while for humans it was not. Consequently, the fact that animals were employed to teach about the power of God's love and about the dangers of sin suggests a deep concern to turn the audience from its "beastly" ways and back to the behavior which would be best for the soul.[7]

The purpose of this essay is to examine some specific aspects of bestiary instruction, particularly those pertaining to the most deadly sin of pride. I will investigate the animals associated with this and related vices and their place in the bestiaries as well as the implications this symbolism held for readers. Finally, the bestiary texts and images will be compared to related imagery in other types of manuscripts, which I will suggest were tantamount to new "translations" of the bestiary illuminations.

In spite of the well-known medieval love of allegorical interpretations, it would be incorrect to ascribe absolute values to the bestiary animals. Some animals could represent more than one deadly sin and depending on the context, one animal could and often did have both positive and negative attributes as will be examined in more detail below.[8] However, we should not infer that the allegorical meanings of the bestiary animals are themselves arbitrary but rather that they are dependent upon the text which the images accompany. The periodic discrepancy between bestiary texts and images is a complicated matter, which might alternately signal the artist's ignorance or misunderstanding of the text, the independent transmission of texts and images, or the artist's deliberate attempt to contradict meanings suggested by the text.

Many of the bestiary entries treat the concept of sin. John Cassian (c. 360-435) was one of the first of the Church Fathers to categorize the various sins and prescribe remedies for them. A century and a half later,

Gregory the Great discussed the seven deadly sins in his *Moralia in Job*. St. Augustine developed the idea of sin and its necessary relationship to free will in many of his most influential writings.[9] Of the sins discussed by the various Fathers, pride emerged as the deadliest sin, as indicated in the Scriptures: ". . . for pride is the beginning of all sin" (Eccl. 10:15). Although it has been argued that avarice slowly became equal with pride or even replaced it as the deadliest sin with the gradual emergence of a monetary economy,[10] one still might reasonably expect to find ample pictorial representations of pride in a bestiary. The bestiaries did not follow the common arrangement of addressing pride first, perhaps because their main intention was to emphasize the good, Christian ways of living or more likely because the *Physiologus* tradition had provided an organizational schema that remained influential in the later bestiaries. For whatever reason, the animals that symbolized pride were scattered throughout the bestiaries, and only by reading the texts and studying the various images would one receive the complete lesson concerning this sin.

A first lesson concerning the dangers of pride may be found in the story of the tiger. The tigress, renowned for her speed, suffers the theft of her cub and immediately chases after the hunter in a frantic attempt to recover it. The hunter, knowing that he cannot hope to outrun the swift mother, effects his escape by a ruse. He throws down a mirror and the tigress is so deceived by the reflected image that she mistakes the mirror for her cub and stays with it while the hunter escapes with her offspring.[11] In many bestiary texts there is no allegory present in the tiger story, but given the generally negative portrayal of humans in the bestiaries, we may assume that the hunter has some association with evil—if he does not actually represent the devil himself—and that the tiger represents a sinner who does not realize the truth about her lost spiritual goodness until it is too late. But what does the story teach about pride?

The first element which captures our attention is the mirror. Some artists depicted much more detailed mirrors than others; some painted an accurate reflection of the tigress while others rendered undistinguishable circles. A few of the more luxurious bestiaries include reflective silver leaf, in imitation of a functioning mirror.[12] The top panel of the tiger illumination in Bodley 764 shows the mirror with the mother's reflection in some detail (figure 1). The mirror is obviously important to the narrative, as it is the instrument of deceit used by the hunter and the cause of the tigress' misfortune. Beyond its narrative function, though, it also has considerable allegorical merit. Mirrors often represented human vanity, especially female pride in their appearance. While the Latin prose bestiaries lack this statement, the French bestiary of Pierre de Beauvais (long version) indicates that the tigress delays her chase because she is so enraptured by the fair image she sees in the glass.[13] The Cambrai Bestiary characterizes the tiger as "a prisoner" because whenever she sees a mirror, she is "never so busy" that she fails to stop and look at her reflection.[14]

Richard of Fournival's *Bestiaire d'amour* entry on the tiger expresses a similar idea: "For however great its rage if its cubs have been stolen, if it comes upon a mirror it has to fasten its eyes upon it. And it so delights in gazing at the great beauty of its good form that it forgets to pursue the men who stole its cubs. It stands there as if captured."[15] It would seem, then, that the bestiary tiger story was eventually altered to emphasize the tigress' pride rather than her mere confusion upon seeing her reflection in the mirror.

Concern over women's excessive pride was articulated far earlier, however. From the eleventh century on, much ecclesiastical criticism was aimed at noblewomen and their passion for opulent accessories and "vanities."[16] Saint Paul wrote in his letters to Timothy (Tim. 2:9-10) and Peter (1 Pet. 3:2-4) that women's adornment ought to be purity of heart and good works rather than elaborately ornamented hair or clothing. Tertullian's *De cultu feminarum* contains one of the most famous diatribes against women's excessive concern with personal adornment, which provides a point of departure for the explication of their inherently evil natures.[17]

Later ecclesiastics adopted a similarly critical position on women's interest in fashion. In the mid-thirteenth century, Vincent de Beauvais composed a tract concerning the education of royal children in which he cautions that young women and girls should not wear tightly-fitting dresses with trains, silk, hair ribbons, precious belts, or anything else that might incite lust.[18] Pride in relation to appearance was a sin ordinarily imputed to women; thus it seems to be no accident that it is the tigress rather than the male tiger who is guilty of excessive pride in the bestiaries.

If the mirror is the instrument of deceit, what then might be made of the larcenous hunter? In fact, a second, more subtle, representation of pride occurs in the figure of the fleeing thief. In most of the bestiaries, the thief is mounted in accordance with the text description, and he is depicted holding the stolen cub cradled under one arm and either a second mirror, a sword, or the reins in his other hand (figure 1).[19] Furthermore, he is dressed as a nobleman, sometimes as a knight, usually in the flowing mantle and robes of the wealthy. In the Ashmole Bestiary, the face of the knight is mostly obscured by his chain mail and helmet, but in Bodley 764 (figure 1) and Royal 12.C.XIX, the hunter is a bearded youth, carefully coifed and wearing a rich mantle. The Bodley 764 image shows the hunter's robes flying back from the speed of his escape, a realistic touch which reveals the hunter's shapely leg. The tiger image in the St. Petersburg manuscript shows the hunter in long robes which do not cover his lower legs, revealing bright blue stockings.

These specific aspects of the hunter's appearance were the very things on which various ecclesiastics focused in their criticism of how noblemen chose to dress. Bumke writes that "masculine beauty manifested itself most conspicuously in the legs and what covered them" and that this shameful display was "especially offensive" to ecclesiastical writers.[20] Courtly fashion for noblemen included tight hose, short undergarments or robes which had been strategically slit, and tightly-fitted overgarments, and French fashion after the eleventh century dictated that the modern man wore his hair long and curly. Young men were clean-shaven while middle-aged men wore a carefully trimmed beard, sometimes with a moustache.[21] Thus, the costly chain mail, noble attire, and the possession of a horse exhibited by the tiger hunters all attest to a high social position.

With these elements in place, we can suggest that the hunter himself is a symbol of pride. Of particular support to this hypothesis are the ubiquitous medieval representations of pride as a mounted horseman who is in the process of falling from his horse.[22] Horses played a fundamental role in both the feudal system and the definition of a chivalric knight. Huizinga argues that pride was "the sin of the feudal and hierarchic period" while later scholars claim that pride was a sin of power which manifested itself in abuses against the powerless.[23] If power mainly sprang from the possession of land, then it would be the nobility who were most likely to commit such abuses. It then follows that the nobility would be more often portrayed in contemporary representations of the sin of pride. In some medieval texts, pride was connected directly with the nobility. For example, in his late thirteenth-century *De monstruosis hominibus*, the Clerk of Enghien declared of the prideful giants:[24] "For the nature of [giants], I wish to lead you now to the present; these are some great earthly lords."[25] Therefore, the bestiary's youthful noble, with clean-shaven face, carefully pressed curls, and elaborate clothes, provides a suitable representation of pride in a hierarchical, social context. Other visual support for this interpretation includes the hunter's placement relative to that of the tigress. That is, the structure of most of the tiger compositions invites the viewer to survey the image from the center to the periphery, directing attention first to the hunter and only secondarily to the tigress. For example, in the Ashmole Bestiary, the centrally-positioned knight is leaning backward to throw the mirror, creating a sense of motion in the direction of the tigress, positioned at the far left of the picture plane and regarding herself in the mirror after it has been thrown. This composition creates the illusion of a time sequence in that we first see the mirror about to be thrown and then we see it depicted a second time, lying before the tigress after it has landed. In Bodley 764, a sense of time is suggested through the division of the action into upper and lower registers, although it is not clear whether this is merely a spatial division, as the hunter is shown holding the cub but not tossing the mirror (figure 1). Once again, however, the hunter catches the viewer's attention first, given his large size and the fact that his head trespasses across the frame, nearly invading the tigress' pictorial space. In other words, it is the hunter rather than the tiger who appears to be the central focus of the bestiary images in spite of the text emphasis on the fate of the hapless tigress. This may have been done in order to highlight a well-known image of pride, the young nobleman mounted on a horse, in order to visually connect the idea of this sin with the tigress herself.

The hunter's head in the Bodley 764 image raises another important aspect of relative positioning. The same violation of the frame may be observed in other images, such as the St. Petersburg Bestiary, in which the mounted hunter is so tall that his entire head escapes the frame. On the one hand, these compositions may be explained as the result of space requirements needed to accommodate a well-proportioned human figure, but another explanation is also possible. In medieval thought, each deadly sin corresponded to a certain part of the body. For example, anger was related to the tongue, envy to the heart, and gluttony to the mouth. The sin of pride was associated with the head.[26] In Ulrich of Lilienfield's *Concordantiae caritatis,* in which the vices were coordinated with their respective body parts, pride is paired with *caput,* depicted as a small figure pointing to his head.[27] The fact that the hunter's head in the bestiary tiger images exceeds the boundary of the frame is suggestive: pride cannot be contained. Hence, relative placement of the hunter and tigress with respect to the frame emphasizes visually that the allegorical message of the bestiary entry concerns the dangers of pride.

Pride as a mounted nobleman continued as a popular iconographical motif in later medieval manuscripts. For example, in a French Book of Hours made for Jean Dunois in the mid-fifteenth century, Pride is depicted with Envy.[28] A young, clean-shaven man is seated on a lion, wearing a crown, rich robes, and the gold medallion of a high office.[29] He arranges his long robes with his left hand in such a way that a large portion of his bare leg and foot show through the folds, and in his right hand he carries a sword. Another image of pride occurs in Morgan 1001, another fifteenth-century French Book of Hours (figure 2). Again, a clean-shaven, richly-clad youth is mounted on a lion. His long, wavy hair is held in place by a circlet. In his right hand he holds a scepter. Interestingly, the details of this portrait lend a decidedly feminine touch: the young man holds a mirror in his left hand in which his reflection is clearly visible. The intensity of his gaze and his self-absorbed expression are similar to that often observable in bestiary depictions of the siren (figure B, p. xxiii). While taking pride in one's appearance was not limited to women, it was normally associated with women, and it is therefore telling to see the same activity transferred to a man. In fact, the soft features of the man's face and hair might be described as feminine as well. This androgynous quality of the face may have been deliberately rendered by the artist to suggest that the sin of pride was not limited to women or perhaps to imply that pride caused a loss of virility in men. In either case, the correspondence of pictorial details with the earlier bestiary images indicates a continuation of pride's strong iconographical tradition.

As mentioned, the young man gazing into a mirror is a detail well known from the bestiary depictions of the siren and was likely transferred from that context. This is an appropriate borrowing, in that the siren, like the tiger, embodied the theme of pride in the bestiaries. Part woman, part bird (or alternatively, part woman, part fish), the siren was well known to the Ancients through Homeric epic and Greek myth. In brief, sirens lured sailors to their doom by singing beautiful songs and lulling them to sleep. Once the sailors were asleep, the sirens tore them apart. The same story may be found in the bestiaries, after having undergone extensive Christian moralization.[30] Generally speaking, the sirens represent sin and spiritual danger. However, the iconographical treatment of the siren suggests that the bestiary artists may have had more specific sins in mind. The Ashmole Bestiary (f. 65v) includes a siren with a long fish tail, holding in her right hand a slightly convex object, not immediately identifiable and which partially extends into the surrounding frame. Its shape and detail suggest a toothed object such as a comb, but the manner in which the siren holds it suggests that is a mirror. Both the comb and the mirror were symbols of female vanity and pride, and the bestiary siren illuminations often showed the siren holding one or the other or both. An especially revealing image in Ludwig XV/3 shows a contented siren absorbed with a mirror, which she holds in her right hand while primping her hair with her left (figure B, p. xxiii). This illustration calls to mind a passage from Ovid quoted by Andreas Capellanus in his *De arte honeste amandi*: "Every woman, not only a young one but even the old and decrepit, strives with all her might to exalt her own beauty; this can come only from pride . . . and pride follows beauty."[31] To the siren's right is a centaur, who appears to be galloping away from the siren. However, the centaur's attention seems to have been caught by the sight of the lovely creature. In spite of his leg movements, his torso is twisted in her direction and his face is turned towards her. Both figures bear some resemblance to courtly persons. The siren's face, hair, and overall posture suggest a life of relative ease and luxury, and the centaur, like the earlier tiger hunters, is clean shaven with medium length, wavy hair, over which he wears a gold circlet. As we shall see, these two figures not only imply pride but also the closely related sin of lust.

It is interesting to note that the siren and the centaur are human from the waist up and animal from the waist down. These hybrid renderings are on the one hand the continuation of Classical tradition, but we may speculate that they are also significant from the contemporary theological point of view. Though the figures have human heads and therefore presumably have the capacity for advanced reasoning, their half-animal natures suggest that their behavior is governed by their baser physical instincts. Pride and lust alike exist in physical things, pride being the misplaced value of worldly, physical (including corporeal) objects over spiritual matters and lust being the desire to experience physical, corporeal pleasure. Hence, the siren and centaur are both particularly good choices as carriers of meaning related to these two sins. In addition, the text that accompanies the bestiary siren identifies her as an "aquatic harlot," which also serves to connect her to the sin of lust by way of prostitution.[32]

As the examples of both the tigress and siren demonstrate, pride was a sin associated in the bestiaries specifically with women. However, the bestiaries also allow that men were susceptible to this sin as well, certainly as implied by the presence of the hunter in the tiger images. A common thread between both genders is the manifestation of pride in areas related to personal appearance. This leads to a third bestiary entry focused on pride: the peacock, the magnificently ostentatious—and male—bird. As with many of the other bestiary creatures, the text on the nature of the peacock is not uniformly positive or negative. The peacock's brightly-colored feathers are said to signify the Gentiles who have been adorned by Christ with "the grace and splendor of many virtues."[33] The careful and detailed rendering of the "eyes" of the peacock's tail in many of the bestiaries may be an artistic attempt to create a pictorial equivalent of the text.[34] The peacock in Bodley 764 is shown in its pride (figure C, p. xxiv). However, even peacocks painted with their tails lowered often retained detailed or enlarged feathers. The St. Petersburg Bestiary artist created his peacock with slightly less detailed "eyes" but with bright colors not actually observable on a real peacock's tail (f. 56).[35] The peacock in the Ashmole Bestiary has its tail lowered, but the angle at which the tail is turned allows the viewer to see the enlarged details of the "eyes" in a manner that would not be possible if viewed from the side. The effect is that we see the peacock's tail in its pride, while the rest of the bird remains in profile.[36]

Despite the peacock's connection with "grace and the splendor of many virtues," the bird also signifies the sin of pride. This is clearly indicated in Hugh of Fouilloy's *De avibus* entry for the peacock, which was incorporated into many of the medieval bestiaries. Hugh includes an extensive moral analysis in which the peacock represents "the sensualist," and then remarks:

> The peacock, while it is praised, raises its tail, because some prelate or other lifts his mind in vainglory to the praises of flatters. . . . When the [peacock's] tail is raised, its rear end is exposed, and thus that which is praised in the [teacher's] action is scorned in [his] pride.[37]

Not only does the peacock not raise its tail unless praised, but because of its ugly feet, it does not wish to fly. Pliny described the peacock as being "not only ostentatious but also spiteful."[38] While some of the bestiaries do not mention the peacock's pride, the images imply that the artists were aware of this association. Bodley 764 (figure C, p. xxiv), the Ashmole Bestiary, and the St. Petersburg Bestiary all share a similar iconographical element: the peacock's tail, whether raised or lowered, extends beyond the frame of the image. Like the hunter's head in the tiger image that extends beyond the frame, the trespassing peacock tails suggest that pride cannot be contained. The association of pride with the peacock remains even to this day, when we describe someone as being "proud as a peacock," and when various birds (such as peacocks and turkeys) present their tail feathers, they are described as being "in their pride."

In moral treatises, the peacock remained a symbol of pride throughout the Middle Ages. In the Austrian moral treatise, *Lumen animae* (c. 1330), attributed to the Carmelite Matthias Farinator, the vices and virtues are described as each riding an animal, wearing a helmet and a mantle, and carrying a shield. The helmets, mantles, and shields all bear symbolic decoration. Pride comes first in the procession, riding a dromedary and carrying a sword. On her helmet is a peacock, on her mantle is an eagle, and on her shield, a lion.[39] A Venetian Office of the Virgin of the late 1500s depicts the seven-headed dragon of the Apocalypse (Apoc. 13:1-3).[40] The seven heads are identified with the seven deadly sins, which are pictured with a human figure and at least one accompanying animal. Pride, who rests on the central head, is depicted as a richly dressed, seated woman, who looks into a mirror, flanked by a horse and a peacock.

From these images, we may conclude that pictorially, pride was often connected with excessive concern with one's appearance. While the nobility, particularly noblewomen, seem to have been the target audience for this lesson, it is unlikely that the message was restricted only to one social class or gender. After all, sumptuary laws were in effect which restricted the style and material of clothes worn by the lower classes who sought to emulate the nobles in their dress.[41] The magnificent dress worn years before the growth of a merchant class has been described as the "prerogative of the nobles."[42] With the emergence of a money-based middle class, however, more people had the financial ability to dress richly, even if they were not members of the court. This situation is suggested by examples of immoderate dress cited in preachers' handbooks of the period and in the numerous sumptuary laws that were enforced, ostensibly to restrict extravagance but also to prevent commoners from climbing above their proper social position.[43] Viewed in this light, the emphasis placed on discouraging people's pride in their appearance was in part a reaction against the changing social structure.

As noted in the foregoing discussion of the siren, the sins of pride and lust were closely related in the bestiaries. Another creature intimately associated with the sin of lust in particular is the goat, especially the *hircus*, who in the bestiaries is said to be so full of lust that he is "always burning for coition" (figure D, p. xxv).[44] The tradition of the goat as a lustful animal may also be observed in other manuscript contexts. In the Dunois Book of Hours, *Luxuria* is pictured as a well-dressed noblewoman seated on a large goat.[45] Interestingly, though, in light of the iconography of pride, her face is turned towards her mirror, which she holds in her left hand, while in her right hand she clutches two arrows. Furthermore, in the background, David at the window watching Bathsheba in her bath connects this image of Luxuria with a biblical story concerning both pride and lust (II Kings 11).

Luxuria's use of the mirror ties together the concept of lust with pride in appearance, which is in keeping with the bestiary tradition of the siren, also associated with both lust and pride, and often holding a mirror. The pairing of these two sins is also in keeping with the religious view of their interrelationship. Ecclesiastical writers repeatedly criticized noblewomen's manner of dressing because they felt that it encouraged lust in men. One critic exclaimed, "Their clothes are so tight that it strikes me as an abomination; for in the clothes the body entices with a shameful readiness."[46] Luxuria's arrows visually recall another bestiary creature, the centaur, also known for his lechery and for toting arrows, and closely associated with the siren (figure B, p. xxiii).[47]

The goat is also featured in the image of Lust found in Morgan 1001 (figure 3). In this image, the personification of Lust is a young nobleman riding a goat, clutching one of the goat's horns in his left hand, and holding a small bird—possibly a nightingale—in his right hand. Like the youthful figure of Pride in the same manuscript (figure 2), the man has long, wavy hair and is clean shaven, in opposition to the goat's long beard. He also wears riding boots with long spurs. In contrast to many of the bestiary images (figure D, p. xxv), the goat here has horns of moderate length but very prominent genitals, which serve to remind the viewer of his moral significance that by now was very familiar from the bestiary descriptions of *hircus*. Together, the goat and human figure in the Morgan 1001 image combine iconographical features of both lust and pride, underscoring the interrelationship between these two sins known from contemporary theological tracts as well as the medieval bestiaries.

The vivid images and stories of the bestiaries largely account for their popularity, and the bestiary artists created numerous images as captivating as they were instructive. And while myth and fantasy—which often seem intrusive at worst and irrelevant at best to our scientific, modern sensibilities—played a large part in the bestiary entries, to characterize the bestiary as a work of "flawed science" or fantasy is to miss the point.[48] These were books intended to instruct, and their creators were shrewd enough to realize that instruction is received and retained much better when paired with detailed and enjoyable visuals. Furthermore, the influence of fantasy and moral allegory did not hinder the depiction of very realistic details such as combs, mirrors, and aspects of contemporary dress, all of which had come to symbolize certain sins of paramount importance, both socially and theologically. In many respects, the bestiary images were just as instructional as the texts. In a society where literacy was usually a mark of wealth or station, it should not be surprising to find pictures that teach so well.

NOTES

1. Horace, "The Art of Poetry," in *Latin Poetry in Verse Translation*, ed. L.R. Lind (Boston, 1957), 138.

2. Willene Clark, "The Illustrated Medieval Aviary and the Lay-Brotherhood," *Gesta* 21 (1982), 63-74; Hassig 1995, 176-78.

3. Beryl Rowland, "The Art of Memory and the Bestiary," in Clark and McMunn 1989, 12-25; Mary J. Carruthers, *The Book of Memory: A Study of Memory in Medieval Culture* (Cambridge, 1990), 126-27. See also McCulloch 1962, 7.

4. See Debra Hassig, "Marginal Bestiaries," in Houwen 1997, 171-88.

5. For example, Christian moral values such as loyalty and chastity are prominent in the bestiaries. The dog, horse, and hoopoe are faithful to their masters or elders (in some cases, until death); the turtledove and beaver demonstrate the ideals of chastity. See White 1954, 61-67 (dog), 84-88 (horse), 131-32 (hoopoe), 145-46 (turtledove), 28-29 (beaver); and Hassig 1995, 84-92 (beaver), 93-103 (hoopoe).

6. In some bestiary entries, this question was posed directly. In the case of the faithful hoopoe: "Now observe, if these birds, being without the faculty of reason, do these mutual kindnesses to each other, how much the more ought

rational men to return the care of their parents?" (White 1954, 131-32). Similarly, the *Physiologus* entry on the turtledove concludes, "Take note, therefore, all you souls of the faithful, how much chastity is found in a small bird. All you who bear the person of the turtledove in the visage of the soul, imitate her chastity" (Curley 1979, 57).

7. On animals as human exemplars, see Salisbury 1994, 103-36.

8. For example, the siren could represent pride and lust (as discussed at length below), the dog envy and gluttony, and the mouse greed, gluttony, and in some cases, sloth. See Hassig 1995, 104-15 (siren); White 1954, 67 (dog); and Rowland 1973, 127-29.

9. Morton Bloomfield, *The Seven Deadly Sins*, (Michigan, 1952), 69.

10. J. Huizinga, *The Autumn of the Middle Ages*, trans. R. J. Payton and U. Mammitzsch (Chicago, 1996), 25-27; Lester K. Little, "Pride Goes Before Avarice: Social Change and the Vices in Latin Christendom," *American Historical Review* 76 (1971), 15-17; Stanford M. Lyman, *The Seven Deadly Sins: Society and Evil* (New York, 1978), 232-36.

11. White 1954, 12-13. Sometimes the mirror is described as a "glass ball."

12. See, for example, the Ashmole Bestiary, f. 12.

13. For the French prose text, see Charles Cahier and Arthur Martin, "Bestiaires," in *Mélanges d'archéologie, d'histoire et de littérature* (Paris, 1851), II, 140.

14. Trans. Guy Mermier, *A Medieval Book of Beasts: Pierre de Beauvais' Bestiary* (Lewiston, 1992), 312. See also Edward B. Ham, "The Cambrai Bestiary," *Modern Philology* 36/3 (1939), 234.

15. Trans. Beer 1986, 14. " . . . s'on li emble, ke s'ele encontre un mireoir qu'il ne li covingne ses iels aerdre. Et se delite tant a regarder la grant beauté de sa bone taille, k'ele oblie a cachier chiax ki li ont emblé ses faons, et s'areste illuec comme prise" (Segre 1957, 40-41).

16. Joachim Bumke, *Courtly Culture: Literature and Society in the High Middle Ages*, trans. Thomas Dunlap (Berkeley, 1991), 152-55.

17. *PL* 1:1417-1448. See also Hassig in this volume.

18. Vincent of Beauvais, *De eruditione filiorum nobilium*, ed. A. Steiner (Cambridge [MA]), 1938, 192; Bumke 1991, 338-39.

19. See also: Add. 11283, f. 2 (reproduced in Payne 1990, 20); Ashmole Bestiary, f. 12 (reproduced in Graz 1982); Royal 12.C.XIX, f. 28 (reproduced in Payne 1990, 20); St. Petersburg Bestiary, f. 36 (reproduced in Muratova 1984).

20. Bumke 1991, 146-47.

21. *Ibid.*, 148-49. See also Mary G. Houston, *Medieval Costume in England and France* (New York), 1996; and Françoise Pipponier and Perrine Mane, *Dress in the Middle Ages* (New Haven, 1997).

22. Pride depicted as a falling rider had become so common in the Middle Ages that it has been characterized as the "accepted model from which no one could depart." Examples are not limited to painting but are found also in sculpture, misericords, and stained glass (Emile Mâle, *The Gothic Image*, trans. Dora Nussey [New York, 1958], 110, 121).

23. Huizinga 1996, 25.

24. Giants are interpreted as symbols of pride in numerous medieval literary contexts, including bestiaries, such as Douce 88: "Gigantes sunt ultra humanum modum grandes quorum figuram superbi tenent qui super uolunt uideri quam sunt, qui dum laudes affectant uires excedunt" (f. 69v). See also Walter Stephens, *Giants in Those Days: Folklore, Ancient History, and Nationalism* (Lincoln [NE], 1989), 48, 69; and Andy Orchard, *Pride and Prodigies: Studies in the Monsters of the Beowulf Manuscript* (Woodbridge, 1995), 80-81.

25. Trans. Friedman 1981, 128. For the Latin text, see Alfons Hilka, "Eine altfranzösische moralisierende Bearbeitung des Liber de Monstruosis Hominibus Orientis aus Thomas von Cantimpré, De Naturis Rerum," in *Abhandlungen der Gesellschaft der Wissenschaften zu Göttingen: Philololgisch-Historische Klasse* 7 (Berlin, 1933), lines 265-67.

26. Bloomfield 1952, 221; 433, n. 121.

27. William M. Voelkle, "Morgan Manuscript M. 1001: The Seven Deadly Sins and the Seven Evil Ones," in *Monsters and Demons in the Ancient and Medieval Worlds: Papers Presented in Honor of Edith Porada*, ed. Ann E. Farkas (Mainz am Rhein, 1987), 105-106 and pl. XLI.

28. London, British Library, Yates Thompson III, f. 159 (Voelkle 1987, pl. XLV.14; Henry Yates-Thompson, *A Descriptive Catalogue of Fifty Manuscripts from the Collection of Henry Yates-Thompson* [Cambridge, 1898], 55). The figure of Envy depicted alongside Pride is a woman riding on a wolf.

29. Pride is a characteristic of the lion not found in the *Physiologus* text but emphasized in the later bestiaries; see Haist in this volume. It is also true that a given group of lions has been referred to as a "pride" since the Middle Ages (Rex Collings, *A Crash of Rhinoceroses: A Dictionary of Collective Nouns* [London, 1993], 126).

30. See Curley 1979, 23; Barber 1993, 150; McCulloch 1962, 167; and Hassig 1995, 106.

31. Andreas Capellanus, *The Art of Courtly Love*, trans. John J. Parry (New York, 1969), 206. Andreas' source is Ovid, *Fasti* I.149.

32. This passage derives from Isidore of Seville's *Etymologies* 12.3.30-31 (*PL* 82:423A). For a discussion of the relationship between the bestiary siren and prostitution, see Hassig in this volume.

33. Trans. Barber 1993, 170. "Et diuersos colores in pennis habet significat populum gentilem de longinquis partibus terre ad Christum uenientem, qui etiam eius gracia multarum uirtutum ornatu resplendet" (Bodley 764, f. 84v). This interpretation differs from that of Hugh of Fouilloy (see below).

34. However, not all of the bestiaries feature elaborate peacock renderings. For example, the peacock depicted in Fitzwilliam 379 (f. 25) is a generic, short-tailed, light brown bird. On the bestiary peacock, see also Syme in this volume.

35. Reproduced in Muratova 1984.

36. This image is reproduced in Graz 1982 and is discussed in Debra Hassig, "Beauty in the Beasts: A Study of Medieval Aesthetics," *Res* 19/20 (1990/91), 159-60.

37. "Nota etiam quod pavo, dum laudatur, caudam erigit, quia praelatus quilibet adulantiam laudibus per vanam gloriam mentem levat . . . Cum autem cauda erigitur, posteriora nudantur, et sic quod laudatur in opere, deridetur in elatione" (Clark 1992, 248-49).

38. Pliny, *Naturalis historia* 10.22.44 (Rackham 1940, 320-21).

39. Bloomfield 1991, 138.

40. New York, Pierpont Morgan Library, Acc. no. 15102, f. 146v; Voelkle 1987, 111 and pl. LI.

41. Bumke 1991, 128-30.

42. Barbara Tuchman, *A Distant Mirror: The Calamitous Fourteenth Century* (New York, 1978), 19.

43. *Ibid.*, 19-20. For example, see the *Fasciculus morum,* a collection of moralized tales organized around the theme of the seven deadly sins, beginning with pride (*Fasciculus Morum: A Fourteenth-Century Preacher's Handbook,* ed. and trans. Siegfried Wenzel [University Park, 1989]).

44. White 1954, 74.

45. Yates Thompson III, f. 172 (reproduced in Voelkle 1987, pl. XLVI.16).

46. *Reinfried von Braunschweig,* ed. K. Bartsch (Tübingen, 1871), lines 15211-17.

47. See Ludo Jongen, "Do Centaurs Have Souls?: Centaurs as Seen by the Middle Dutch Poet Jacob van Maerlant," in Houwen 1997, 139-54.

48. On this problem, see Gravestock in this volume.

Figure 1. Tiger. Oxford, Bodleian Library, MS Bodley 764, f. 6v.
Photo: The Bodleian Library.

Figure 2. Pride. Book of Hours. New York, Pierpont Morgan Library,
MS M. 1001, f. 84. Photo: The Pierpont Morgan Library.

Figure 3. Lust. Book of Hours. New York, Pierpont Morgan Library, MS M. 1001, f. 98. Photo: The Pierpont Morgan Library.

Sex in the Bestiaries

Debra Hassig

Medieval interest in animal behavior was part of a larger attempt to uncover evidence of God's plans for humanity.[1] Accordingly, animal habits and lore were constructed and interpreted in ways that contributed to prevailing theological beliefs and social attitudes. Using the technique of animal allegory, the medieval bestiarists presented verbal and visual expressions of many important social and religious concepts. For example, the tale of young hoopoes caring for their aging parents taught the importance of filial piety, and the story of the fox deceiving birds bespoke the dangerous wiles of the devil and of heretics.[2]

Animals also had various sexual associations, many of which were detailed and assessed in the bestiaries along spiritual lines in order to encourage proper Christian piety. This aspect of "animal sexuality" will form the focus of this essay. Most importantly, it is suggested here that the bestiary was able to accommodate shifting attitudes toward sex through changes in the genre itself, made manifest in both texts and images. That is, while the traditional Latin prose bestiaries concerned themselves primarily with the characterization of sex as formidable and dangerous—and principally promoted by women—the later development of the *Bestiaire d'amour* shifted this focus from strictly theological to more erotic and worldly concerns.

It should also be remembered that throughout the Middle Ages, animals were exploited for sexual purposes in contexts that had little to do with moral enlightenment, and these ways of thinking about animals undoubtedly helped establish a precedent for the sexual descriptions found in the bestiaries. The Church Fathers, exegetes, and authors of penitentials repeatedly addressed the sin of bestiality, first categorizing it with masturbation and eventually with adultery and homosexuality.[3] By the later Middle Ages, punishment for bestiality—often capital— was extended to animal as well as human offenders.[4] Sex with animals was also linked to the idea of demonic intercourse, as the devil was believed to transform himself for sexual purposes into an animal, commonly a serpent, dog, or goat.[5]

A metaphorical way of viewing animals in a sexual context— which was simultaneously a way of viewing women in a bestial context—may be observed in numerous literary descriptions that compare women to a whole menagerie of beasts, from lions to hares.[6] Similarly, small, furry animals, such as cats, rabbits, and squirrels, were used in both literary and visual arenas as emblems of female sexuality.[7] Various other sexual themes were expressed in illuminated manuscripts in animal marginalia, which sometimes featured animals performing lewd acts in seeming defiance of their accompanying religious texts.[8] Broadly speaking, these types of comparisons are part of the same tradition developed in the bestiaries, which consistently view animal behavior in terms of human moral conduct, with a special emphasis on the dangers of female sexuality.

Certain beasts had sexual connotations traceable to the Classical sources on which the bestiaries were largely based. For example, the bestiarists state that wild goats are stubborn, lascivious animals, always eager to mate, with eyes so full of lust that they look sideways (figure D, p. xxv). Thus, goats are compared to those who follow the depravities of the devil and clothe themselves in the shaggy hide of vice.[9] These early descriptions of the goat doubtless informed later convictions that the devil sometimes took on a goat's form for the purpose of copulating with women.[10] Another well-known bestiary creature with a sexual association is the unicorn, a fierce beast that could only be caught if baited by a virgin, whereupon hunters could seize and kill him. The entrapped unicorn thus became a popular figure of Christ's crucifixion. According to the bestiarists, the unicorn's horn signifies Christ's unity with his Father,[11] but the horn also had certain sexual connotations—as horns often did—especially when pictured in the lap of a nude virgin, as in the famous image from the thirteenth-century Rochester Bestiary (figure E, p. xxvi).[12] The virgin's nudity in this image emphasizes her receptive role in the hunting maneuver as well as the more general idea of female sexuality as a dangerous trap.

In medieval art, apes also enjoyed a long tradition of sexual associations and were often shown engaging in obscene activities in the margins of other types of illuminated manuscripts, such as psalters.[13] One especially unsavory example features an ape suckling a nun in an image that synthesizes ape lore and social satire, of which female religious are clearly the target.[14] However, the bestiarists do not generally discuss the ape's lustful nature but rather characterize apes as physically disgusting and akin to the devil.[15] Nevertheless, the image in the Bodley 602 bestiary very definitely suggests a sexual connotation for apes by juxtaposing them with a satyr, the mythological lecher par excellence, shown in the guise of a wildman, wearing an animal skin and carrying a club and a snake (f. 18v). During the Middle Ages, both the satyr and the wildman were infamous for their sexual excesses, rendering the apes in the Bodley 602 image guilty by association.[16]

Interestingly, the bestiary roster of creatures includes representatives of all four genders of male, female, hermaphrodite, and neuter, all of which are carefully illustrated and described. Male creatures, such as bulls, rams, and horses, are regularly included in the more expanded bestiaries and are sometimes rendered with male genitalia that looks more human than animal. Many of the bestiaries also describe female animals, such as the sow, ewe, and cow, which are sometimes depicted suckling their young. And certain female creatures, most notably the sirens, are often rendered nude from the waist up (figure B, p. xxiii).

But verbal and visual sexual identifications were made not simply for the sake of variety, balance, or voyeurism. Nor was the goal strictly to provide a representative sample of what kinds of creatures are found in nature, or to systematically explore different sexual orientations in the animal kingdom. Rather, gender and the degree of concupiscence attributed to a given beast was more often than not the primary gauge for determining that beast's value as an allegorical parallel for Christ or Satan, and concomitantly, as a model or antimodel for human moral behavior. What becomes obvious is that sex and evil go hand in hand: the more sexually involved the creature, the greater its perceived evil. As a corollary to this, freedom from sex is equated with moral virtue. Ultimate virtue is achieved only through complete denial of sex, and in this, the tenor of the bestiary harmonizes with contemporary ideas about the spiritual merits of celibacy and, to a lesser extent, marriage.

Some of the bestiary creatures lack sex entirely, and for this they receive the highest moral accolades. Examples include the phoenix, reproduced from its own ashes as a sign of the resurrection, and the bee, whose complete uninvolvement with sex allows it to live a virtuous communal lifestyle and in other contexts, inspired comparisons to the Virgin.[17] At the other extreme, some beasts betray the interests and anatomy of both males and females. The best example of the hermaphroditic type is the hyena, who is alternately male and female, and in the bestiaries, is appropriately equipped with both male and female genitalia, as in the extremely graphic image found in Harley 4751 (figure 1). The bestiary texts inform us that in addition to dual sex, the hyena has the unpleasant habit of breaking into graves and feeding on human corpses, an activity that generally provides the narrative focus of the bestiary images. However, it is the creature's sexual characteristics that carry a decidedly negative meaning. Specifically, the bestiarists characterize the hyena's double sex as unclean, and on this basis compare the animal to the "duplicitous Jews," who first worshiped the true God but were later given over to idolatry.[18]

The Harley 4751 hyena image corroborates the anti-Jewish focus of the text by presenting the hyena/Jew as a ravaging, fearsome beast with long fangs and monstrous aspect. Other bestiary hyena images communicate this ideology in different ways. For example, in the Bodley 764 hyena image, the elaborate church provides a striking backdrop for the graveyard the hyena is raiding in the foreground (f. 15). Given that the accompanying text directly compares the corpse-eating beast to the Jews and the Synagogue to an unclean animal, this image may also signify the ultimate dominance of the terrestrial Church over the "bestial" Jews, who feed on the corruption of pagan doctrine.[19]

It is interesting how dual sex and godlessness work together to present the over-sexed hyena as a sign of the worst enemy of Christianity second only to the devil himself—the Jew. Looking again at the Harley 4751 hyena (figure 1), the fact that the corpse is female rather than the usual male suggests that the image may be informed by a particular social concern which underscores the bestial nature of the Jews. According to medieval law, sex between a Christian and a Jew was tantamount to bestiality and punishable by death. Cases are recorded of such illicit intercourse, usually between a Christian man and a Jewish woman; a common punishment was to burn or bury the offenders alive.[20] This type of case points up a certain irony vis-à-vis medieval bestiality laws and the Jews. That is, the prohibition on sex between humans and animals was originally based on Jewish law

(Ex. 22:19, Lev. 20:13-16), yet the law-givers ultimately extended its application to the Jews themselves.[21] In the Harley 4751 image, then, the hyena may be identified as a Jew, in accordance with the accompanying text, and the fact that the corpse is female likely alludes to the Christian-Jewish sexual taboo. It should also be remembered that the primary reason for the sumptuary laws forced upon medieval Jews—the wearing of the "Jew badge" and the *pileum cornutum* (pointed hat)—was to prevent sexual relations between Christians and Jews, indicating that bestiality (at worst) and miscegenation (at best) were central issues in the history of Christian-Jewish relations.[22]

So from the point of view of sex, the hyena entry must be said to signify deviant and spiritually disastrous practice. By contrast, the bestiary elephant is a virtuous beast, valiantly upholding the well-known medieval paradox of the chaste marriage. Throughout the Middle Ages, the theologically mandated function of sex was reproduction and nothing more; any pleasure that might be derived from the act was considered sinful in varying degrees depending on particular circumstances. For example, in the thirteenth century, Alexander of Hales identified only three legitimate reasons for having sex. These were (1) to conceive a child, (2) to pay the conjugal debt, and (3) to avoid the danger of fornication.[23] In other words, these were the only circumstances under which one could have sex without sinning. In addition, medieval penitentials specified a considerable number of times during the year when married people were required to refrain from sex, based on the dual criteria of the wife's physiological cycle and the liturgical calendar.[24] According to one modern calculation, if all regulations were obeyed, medieval married couples (taking advantage of all available opportunities) could have had sex only about forty-four times annually.[25] Canon law, as codified in Gratian's mid-twelfth-century *Decretum* and its later commentators, reinforced the view that marital sex must be guided by principles of moderation and control, that procreation was its only acceptable function, and that pleasure should be avoided at all costs.[26]

The bestiary elephant's conjugal habits accord with the medieval marriage ideal. According to the bestiarists, elephants do indeed have sex but only once. After the female brings the mandrake root to the male, the two elephants travel eastward to Paradise to eat of the mandrake and to copulate, after which the female immediately conceives and later gives birth.[27] But otherwise, the elephant couple remains chaste, thus providing a model for all contemporary married couples who were encouraged by the Church to do likewise.[28] The Laud Misc. 247 bestiary elephant image conveys the idea of conjugal chastity particularly well (f. 163v).[29] Firstly, by juxtaposing the elephant pair with humanoid mandrake roots, the artist has implied a comparison between elephants and humans. The mandrake figures suggest a human counterpart to the elephants that may be read as the ideal, chaste couple, given their frontality and physical separation from each other as well as the accompanying text. A related parallel between elephant and human behavior is also suggested by a thirteenth-century misericord in Exeter Cathedral, which features an elephant flanked by the heads of woman and a monk, which may be read in light of bestiary elephant lore as figures of chastity.[30]

The case of bestiary fish is an interesting one in light of medieval understanding of aquatic sex. Fish were believed to reproduce in various ways, in some cases, without copulation, and those that were understood to copulate were never observed to do so in an "unnatural manner."[31] In all cases, fish were believed produced without semen and therefore, when eaten, not to excite human passions. This belief is perhaps one reason why fish became the food of fasting in monasteries.[32] Fish surface with some regularity in various Gospels episodes, such as the miracle of the loaves and fishes and the calling of St. Peter; they are not mentioned in the Old Testament story of Noah because they were not on the ark (nor, presumably, did they drown).[33] Given the importance of fish in various Christian contexts, it is curious that the bestiaries do not include many moralizations in the fish sections and that the two lengthiest ones are decidedly negative. These pertain to the boat-racing *serra,* interpreted as one who starts out on the path of righteousness but gives up when the going gets tough, and the whale, a symbol of the deceitful devil.[34] It would seem in these two instances that the general (and positive) fish associations were given over to a more negative narrative tradition in order to warn the reader of the dangers of letting down one's spiritual guard. Big fish eat little fish just as the strong attack the weak, thus leaving themselves open to attack from someone even stronger.[35]

On the whole, however, and not unlike the elephants, their moderate sex lives won for fish promotion to a higher spiritual position within the bestiary. Fish are praised for their manner of propagation, for their avoidance of adulterous contact with strange fish and their refusal to mate except with members of their own kind.[36] These sexual habits are contrasted with those of donkeys and horses, which are crossbred in a manner contrary to nature resulting in sin greater than mere fornication. Next, human beings are criticized not only for cross-breeding horses but also for other sexual crimes against nature, such as the mutilation of men to produce eunuchs. By contrast, fish are characterized as pure and unsullied, laying their eggs in an ocean personified as a surrogate parent that incubates the egg until it gently falls apart and a fish comes forth. It would seem, then, that an antiseptic birthing process provides additional grounds for a positive moral view of fish, probably because it contrasts with the bloody, painful method suffered by Eve and all of her female descendants as punishment befitting the Transgression.[37]

Of the numerous other examples of bestiary creatures whose moral significance is defined by sex in some way, three stand out as especially important from contemporary theological and social perspectives. These are the beaver, the siren, and the fire rocks, all of which were regularly included in English and French bestiaries of the twelfth and thirteenth centuries. The three creatures also provide the means to contemplate three different aspects of sex—celibacy, prostitution, and heterosexual lust, respectively. In what follows, it will also be noted to what extent texts and images complement or contradict each other vis-à-vis the intended moral lessons and also how interpretations or reactions to these words and pictures might have varied, depending upon the medieval reader's gender and social station. Like everything else in medieval society, sex had its aspects that varied depending on one's position in the social hierarchy, and the bestiaries provided a flexible format for multiple interpretations depending on the perspective of the individual reader. From inscriptions and other types of evidence, we know that the bestiary readership encompassed a certain variety, including religious, the baronial class, queens, and noblewomen, who doubtless brought different perspectives to their understanding of the bestiary stories.[38]

The story of the beaver provided an especially visceral, even painful, focus on sex. An image found in Bodley 764 is a particularly fine example of the popular iconography of the beaver attempting to escape destruction by the hunter, who pursues the beaver for his medicinally valuable testicles (figure F, p. xxvii). According to the bestiarists, the beaver saves his own life by castrating himself, by tearing off his testicles with his teeth and flinging them into the hunter's path. If the unfortunate beaver should confront another hunter, he need only expose himself and his mutilation, whereupon his pursuer will retreat, after finding the beaver worthless. The beaver, the bestiarists proclaim, is like the man of God, who casts off all vices and flings them in the face of the devil, who, seeing that he no longer has anything of value, departs in confusion.[39] The particular vehicle used to illustrate this figurative concept strongly suggests that sexual desire is one of those vices to be cast off. Once again, virtue is defined as absence of sexual desire, in this instance, owing to a quite literal detachment.

The beaver story must have seemed particularly poignant to religious, for whom chastity was a primary means of ascending from an earthly to a more spiritual existence.[40] Physically, of course, chastity took the form of celibacy. A pair of images from fr. 14969, a copy of the metrical *Bestiaire* of Guillaume le Clerc which emphasizes the role of mendicants in a series of allegorical images paired with narrative animal illustrations, clearly communicates a specifically monastic interpretation of the beaver story (ff. 28, 28v).[41]

Positioned just before a small image of the hunter pursuing a self-castrating beaver, the allegorical image emphasizes both the spiritual and physical aspects of the chastity metaphor. Persons accompanied by demons on the left are juxtaposed with ecclesiastics and a Franciscan punishing one of his brethren on the right. When read in conjunction with the image of the castrating beaver pictured on the following folio, the image suggests that religious seeking spiritual perfection, like the beaver, must renounce evil, both mentally and physically. In this sense, the beaver story was equally relevant to cloistered women, although given the specifics, it obviously spoke more directly to men. To the lay person, the idea of chastity may have had relevance in the context of marriage, albeit conveyed somewhat more indirectly than in the elephant story.

Nonmimetic devices in certain bestiary images underscore both the spiritual and physical meaning of this story. In some images, the beaver's testicles are already detached and disembodied, forming a focus for the narrative scene, as in the St. John's 178 beaver entry (f. 162v), where the testicles are prominently positioned in midair and highlighted by their rose coloring.[42] In other bestiary images, the testicles are rendered in bright orange or blue. Images that showcase disembodied, brightly colored, and/or centrally positioned testicles would seem to emphasize the significance of the cast-off vices, rather than the act of castration, making them somewhat less terrestrially focused than those images that graphically depict the beaver tearing his testicles off with his teeth (figure F, p. xxvii). Focus on the visceral act of castration was perhaps a means of conveying the difficulty of observing this aspect of the *Rule*, as well as notions of suffering in the attempt. Certainly the castration images suggest a sense of anxiety and loss, feelings likely experienced by the cloistered chaste.

Perhaps the bestiary creature most imminently suitable for a moral involving the evils of sex is the siren, a female hybrid well-known from antiquity.[43] Sirens were depicted in the bestiaries either as half-woman, half-fish (which became the standard during the Middle Ages) and less often, as half-woman, half-bird (which perpetuated Classical iconography).[44] In the Morgan Bestiary siren image (f. 17), the two types are combined in a siren trio, who have bird feet and wings but also fishtails.[45] According to the bestiarists, the water-dwelling sirens wait for ships to pass by in order to lull sailors to sleep with their lovely singing. The sirens then drag the sleepy sailors off to islands in order to have sex with them. If the men fail to perform, the sirens rip them to bits and devour their flesh.[46] This unpleasant maneuver is predictably interpreted in spiritual rather than earthly terms, as the bestiary moral warns that those who, like the sailors, become distracted by the pleasures of the terrestrial world do so to the detriment and ultimate peril of their immortal souls.[47]

Most significantly, the bestiary texts identify the siren as an aquatic harlot, or *meretrix* (meaning "she who earns"), the term for prostitutes used in canon law.[48] During the Middle Ages, prostitutes were a ubiquitous social presence, plying their trade in cities, towns, and rural areas; they were present at court; they were patronized by religious and they accompanied men on crusades. In other words, prostitutes formed part of the life of the entire community: they were not a subculture nor were they limited to one particular location.[49] In an extremely interesting image from the University Library Bestiary, the sirens are wearing contemporary female garb, including *chapels* tied under their chins and long-sleeved blouson tunics (figure 2). In fact, visually, their identity as sirens—obvious from their wings and tails—is momentarily camouflaged by their elaborate costumes. Given the accompanying text, the sirens' costumes suggest their identification with contemporary prostitutes, even courtesans. Emphasis on costume is in keeping with the major focus of contemporary regulations concerning prostitutes, which was sumptuary. What a prostitute was forbidden to wear—or alternatively, was required to wear—varied widely from place to place, but, much like the sumptuary laws applied to the Jews, the purpose of these regulations was to provide visual signals in order to prevent undesirable sexual alliances (that is, to differentiate the prostitutes from the "respectable" women). According to surviving records, the identifying garb worn by some prostitutes includes striped hoods or arm bands of various colors; regulations often specified that they were forbidden jewels, silks, or furs. However, it is assumed that these laws were routinely flouted, given their constant repetition.[50]

I am not suggesting that the sirens in the University College Bestiary document the precise type of clothing worn by medieval English prostitutes in a particular location.[51] The main significance of the garb in this image is that it serves to identify the mythical sirens with their human female counterparts, the *meretrices*. It is perhaps not entirely coincidental that the sirens' wearing of the *chapels* in this image corresponds with other representations of evil and/or lustful women in various manuscript contexts. For example, in the famous Morgan Old Testament, David's concubines are all shown wearing *chapels*.[52] Another interesting comparison may be made to a miniature devoted to the subject of marriage annulment in a late thirteenth-century French or Flemish copy of Gratian's *Decretum*. In this image, a husband accused of impotence is anatomically assessed by two expert witnesses, presumably "wise women" sent by the courts to conduct a hands-on investigation of the problem, both of whom wear *chapels* tied under their chins.[53] While conspicuous costume on women in other medieval artistic contexts has been said to imply sexual sin,[54] in the University Library image, given the accompanying text, such sin is denoted rather than merely implied.

The popular image of the siren combing her hair before a mirror was associated with the medieval sin of *luxuria*, or lust.[55] The hair-combing sirens were generally shown nude save for their fishtails, in the manner reserved for other representations of female figures intended to signify sin, sexual lust and dangerous evil.[56] Certainly all of these characteristics are applicable to the sirens and their modus operandi. In addition, during the Middle Ages, nakedness was often associated specifically with the insane, the dead, and most notably for our purposes, prostitutes.[57] An image from the Ludwig XV/3 bestiary pairs a hair-combing siren with the centaur, known in the bestiaries for his lasciviousness, which, when viewed in conjunction with the accompanying text, strengthens the siren's association with her human equivalent, the female prostitute (figure B, p. xxiii). Extending the analogy further, the centaur might be read as a client or perhaps even a *bawd* (the English medieval term for *pronuba*, meaning procurer).[58] Far-fetched as this might sound at first, it is worth remembering that throughout the Middle Ages, as in modern times, pimps procured customers for prostitutes and lived off their earnings.[59] Symbolically speaking, the centaur is a good choice for this role, given his close association with the siren in the history of the bestiary text transmissions as well as his hybrid form and his reputation as a lecherous, duplicitous rogue.[60]

The place of prostitutes in medieval Christian life was a paradoxical one. On the one hand, prostitutes enjoyed the sympathy of the Church because while their activity was uniformly frowned upon, it was still considered a necessary social evil. That is, in lieu of available women, the imagined alternatives—sodomy and sexual perversions— were believed to have far worse social and spiritual consequences.[61] Furthermore, prostitutes were considered prime conversion material, in the tradition of Saint Mary Magdalene and other prostitute-saints, such as Saint Mary the Egyptian.[62] The Church took an active role in the conversion effort: by the end of the twelfth century, Pope Innocent III offered extra spiritual rewards to men who married and reformed prostitutes.[63]

However, the Church's message of redemption for fallen women did not outweigh its more negative view of femininity, which equated virtually any female sexual activity with prostitution and rejection of God.[64] For example, according to monastic interpretations of the Bible found in patristic literature, prostitution is a metaphor for faithlessness.[65] Prostitutes, as signified by the sirens, are therefore not entirely out of place in a type of book primarily dedicated to spiritual matters. At the same time, however, the prostitute's inherently sexual nature insured the continuation of her association with strictly carnal affairs as allegorized in the story of the corrupt sirens of Classical lore.

Lay readers would have undoubtedly made the connection between the bestiary siren and the town prostitutes, who were often recognizable by their distinctive dress and who plied their trade in brothels and other designated areas.[66] Religious, ostensibly more concerned with the spiritual well-being of prostitutes, would have also known where to find them for other purposes, given that clergy made up a major portion of the prostitutes' intended clientele. In fact, some prostitutes were known to cater specifically to priests, who were preferred customers because they usually paid better.[67] Even bishops profited from the business of prostitution by collecting fines from brothels.[68] In short, prostitutes could be found wherever men gathered together, whether in lay or religious contexts.[69]

Given the varied readership of the bestiaries, it is possible that the siren entry may have been familiar to the prostitutes themselves. Interestingly, the siren story presents a general warning not only to men but also to women. Bestiaries became increasingly popular with female patrons from the thirteenth century on as part of a broader trend of expanding thirteenth-century manuscript patronage. That is, "unisex" spiritual moralization notwithstanding, the siren entry may be seen as part of the broader medieval expression of misogyny that was very well developed in the bestiaries. This misogynist sentiment points up one of the more compelling aspects of the medieval bestiaries, being their contradictory nature. On the surface, bestiaries are charming picture books about animals, interpreting beast behavior in allegorical ways that concern the betterment of the human soul. But at the same time, as well demonstrated by the hyena and siren entries, these same texts and images are de facto expressions of hostility toward women and Jews, albeit marketed as moral guidance.

Even more than the siren entry, the fire rocks entry is blatantly misogynist. Like the siren story, the fire rocks texts characterize women as temptresses, ostensibly to reinforce the value of chastity for both men and women. Whereas the beaver entry clearly focuses on men, the fire rocks story and moralization target women as the primary vehicles for sexual lust and the inevitable spiritual downfall experienced by those who give in to feminine wiles. Often, the fire rocks entry is the very last one in the bestiaries, a position of some importance, because it presents the subject on which the entire book draws to a close. Not surprisingly, the subject is sex as an evil enterprise instigated by women and the concomitant spiritual havoc wrought by indulgence in physical pleasure.

It is especially interesting that although the fire rocks are a type of stone, they are fully anthropomorphized. According to the bestiarists, fire rocks live in pairs on a mountain, and, most significantly, they are gendered: one is male and the other is female. As long as the male and female remain on opposite sides of the mountain, all is well, but if they come together, they burst into flames and destroy everything in the vicinity. The moral of the story is addressed to "men of God," who are instructed to separate themselves from women or risk moral peril.

Men are reminded that all women carry the burden of Eve, by whom
sin first arose which rages wildly in her "disobedient children" right up
to the present day.[70] Images of the fire rocks remove any remaining ambiguity
surrounding the meaning of this story by consistently picturing the
stones as a human man and woman, usually surrounded by flames
(figure 3). The idea of lust is most strongly emphasized in those images
that feature nude figures, which normally include half-naked women
somewhat reminiscent of the human portion of the siren (figure B,
p. xxiii). Surrounding the figures with flames reinforces the narrative
but at the same time also recalls the fire of lust and perhaps also the fire
of ultimate damnation. In addition, in some images, a "buck-passing"
series of gestures recalls representations of Adam and Eve shifting
blame before God in the Garden of Eden, also found in other medieval
contexts such as the twelfth-century mural at St. Botolph's in
Hardham.[71] The use of these gestures allows a simultaneous pictorial
reference to the Fall which underscores the theological focus of the
accompanying text.

So in many respects, the fire rocks texts and images harmonize and
mutually reinforce meaning, but they also contradict each other in at
least one important way. Although the texts are unequivocally
antifeminist in assigning guilt to Eve and all of her female descendants,
the images are essentially "egalitarian" in character. That is, there is
nothing inherently antifeminist about the images, nothing that visually
suggests the special female guilt imputed by the texts. On the other
hand, strong visual references to Adam and Eve, not only in the form of
the "buck-passing" gesture but also as a compositional parallel are
charged with misogynist meaning, given that the medieval
interpretation of the biblical account (recounted in the bestiary entry)
assigns blame to Eve as well as to females in general.[72] For example,
the Ashmole Bestiary image depicts the fire rocks as a nude man and
woman, flanking a tree in a setting that recalls the Garden of Eden.[73] As
in the fire rocks story, sex plays a pivotal role in the Genesis episode:
an important and primary outcome of the Fall was the unleashing of
libido.[74] It is therefore in keeping with the general equation made
throughout the bestiaries—as well as in medieval commentary and
exegesis—between sex and evil.

In theory, the fire rocks story provides a lesson applicable to
virtually all bestiary readers, male and female, religious and lay,
although its appeal for lay female readers is questionable, given its

strongly misogynist character. This may explain why the fire rocks entry was apparently excluded from certain bestiaries produced during the late thirteenth and early fourteenth centuries, a time when female patronage was on the rise.[75] While specific patronage for the bestiaries produced during this period is largely unknown, there is evidence in the form of dedications and inscriptions that some of the earlier bestiaries were composed for women, leading to the supposition that one function of the bestiaries was to provide entertainment for noblewomen.[76] It is also notable that two of the more elaborate late thirteenth-century bestiaries, Bodley 764 and Harley 4751, which exclude the fire rocks entries, instead include an unusually large number of images of both female animals and human females, which together suggests female patronage.

This was the same period that the popularity of the Latin prose bestiaries was on the wane, its position being usurped by a new type of bestiary traceable to Richard of Fournival, a canon and poet.[77] Richard wrote the *Bestiaire d'amour* during the late thirteenth century, thereby lifting the bestiary out of the spiritual realm and lowering it into the arena of courtly love. That is, in the *Bestiare d'amour*, Richard altered traditional descriptions of the various bestiary beasts and birds in order to produce new figures of sexual longing and fulfillment. The *Bestiaire d'amour*, then, is still a guide to human behavior but now with carnal rather than spiritual goals—in fact, it has been characterized as an instrument of seduction[78]—that simultaneously strengthens the metaphorical associations between humans and animals.[79] That he has as his ultimate goal the conquest of the woman to whom the *Bestiaire* is addressed is made clear near the beginning of the work, where Richard identifies himself as a cock crowing desperately for his lady's attention.[80] Ultimately, the lady is allowed a reply in the *Response du bestiaire*, which is sometimes appended and which to some extent rebuts Richard's love arguments point-for-point.[81]

Sometimes Richard's animal/love analogies tend toward the unpleasantly visceral, as when he compares his unsuccessful love-pleas to dog vomit cheerfully reswallowed:

> Alas! I have so often since repented that I entreated you and thus lost your sweet company. For if I could have acted like the dog, which is of such a nature that, after vomiting, it can return to its vomit and re-eat it, I would happily have swallowed down my pleading a hundred times, after it flew out through my teeth.[82]

The dog, then, in the *Bestiaire d'amour* is a sign of love's futility, nearly opposite in tone from the description of the dog found in the earlier Latin bestiaries, in which the wise and faithful watchdog is compared to the priest. On the other hand, the Latin bestiaries also compare the dog returning to his own vomit to those who repeatedly sin,[83] which implies, albeit indirectly, the futility of penance.

The *Bestiaire d'amour* was illustrated with miniatures largely dependent on the roster of creatures established in the Latin bestiaries, but these images also contain significant original variations and additions related to new meanings suggested by the text. In one manuscript, the *Response* is also fully illustrated where elsewhere it is limited to a single opening miniature.[84] In Douce 308, an early fourteenth-century copy of the *Bestiaire d'amour* produced at Metz, special emphasis is placed on the idea of the love-plea itself through repeated images of Richard and his lady interspersed among as well as integrated into the animal pictures. These figures function as commentators on the activity of the animals or more specifically, on their significance in the seduction process.

For example, in the first of the animal miniatures, Richard and his wimpled lady converse before a cock crowing on a perch (f. 87v), and in the next miniature on the same folio, the same two figures are shown recoiling from the braying ass. The presence of the human figures in these miniatures serves to remind viewers that the animals depicted are not only to be read as literal displays of animal behavior or according to their traditional bestiary moralizations but also as allegorical figures of Richard's pursuit of love. While, as noted above, the cock's crowing is compared to Richard's love-plea, the ass provides something of an object lesson. Because the wild ass eventually bursts from overly loud braying, Richard's efforts are better spent on penetrating speech than loud song.[85] At the same time, the crowing cock and braying ass contribute to the recurring theme of speech and the power of words as the only means by which Richard may hope to win over his lady. This is arguably the poem's most important theme, as it provides its *raison d'être*.

Death and revival is another theme developed throughout the *Bestiaire d'amour* in both the text and images. Richard speaks repeatedly of dying of love and appeals to his lady for resuscitation by means of her favors. The earlier Latin bestiaries contain a number of animal entries with death and revival themes, some of which Richard groups together. While retaining the traditional iconography, Richard imbues the imagery with new meanings. On a single folio in Douce 308, the weasel, lion, and pelican are all pictured and described in sequence (figure 4). According to Richard, the weasel's medicinal revival of her dead offspring, the lion's resuscitation of his stillborn cubs by roaring over them, and the pelican's restoration of life to his murdered chicks by sprinkling them with his own blood are all signs of the same thing: love-death and its remedy.[86] In all three cases, the traditional interpretation of animal resuscitation imagery as signs of Christ's sacrifice and resurrection has been replaced by a new reading that focuses on profane rather than divine love, a process that defines the essential nature of the *Bestiaire d'amour*.

Another way of reworking the traditional bestiary animals into a secular love framework is through the introduction of behavior that requires new iconographical presentations. For example, the traditional bestiaries consistently interpret the eagle's habit of physical rejuvenation—accomplished by flying toward the sun and then plunging three times into water below—as a sign of spiritual renewal through baptism.[87] Latin bestiary images of the eagle, therefore, almost always depict the eagle flying toward the sun and/or plunging downward into a pool of water in accordance with this important Christian theme. Richard, however, interprets the eagle as emblematic of the pride that stands in the way of love. The text relates how the eagle's beak eventually becomes overgrown and prevents him from eating, at which point he must shatter and resharpen it on a hard stone. The eagle shattering his beak is then compared to the humility that must be embraced before sexual favors may be dispensed.[88] Concomitantly, the eagle in Douce 308 is shown sharpening his beak rather than flying upward toward the sun (f. 104).

Goats, apes, hyenas, beavers, sirens, fire rocks—the medieval bestiaries are filled with visual and verbal references to sex, whether couched in the reputed behavior of the beasts themselves or compared to human sexual conduct. While sex functions quite consistently as a metaphor for sin and preoccupation with worldly concerns, a concept applicable to both men and women, a good deal of the discussion in the bestiaries centers on the dangers of female sexuality in particular, and therefore must be viewed in light of medieval antifeminist interests. That later the bestiary genre branched off in a new direction entirely devoted to the expression of erotic love is a strong indicator that popular medieval views of sex expanded to accommodate not only its theological significance but also its strictly terrestrial aspects. These more earthly preoccupations would find a wider reception among the lay patronage of Richard of Fournival's *Bestiaire d'amour*, a work that recasts the focus of the bestiary from communal concern with divine love to a private act of seduction.[89]

NOTES

1. See Hugh of St. Victor, *Eruditionist didascalicae* 7.3 (*PL* 176:814B); and Nicholas of Cusa, *Idiotae de sapientia* 1 (*Nikolaus Von Kues: Werke*, 2 vols., ed. Paul Wilpert [Berlin, 1967], I, 217).

2. White 1954, 131-32 (hoopoe), 53-54 (fox); Barber 1993, 171-72 (hoopoe), 65-66 (fox); Hassig 1995, 93-103 (hoopoe) and 62-71 (fox).

3. On punishments for bestiality, see *Medieval Handbooks of Penance*, trans. John T. McNeill and Helena M. Gamer (New York, 1990), 173, 176 (6th c.); 253-54 (7th c.); 303, 313 (9th c.); 355 (12th c.). For an excellent survey of changing attitudes toward bestiality as articulated in the penitentials and other contemporary sources, see Salisbury 1994, 84-100.

4. E.P. Evans, *The Criminal Prosecution and Capital Punishment of Animals: The Lost History of Europe's Animal Trials* (London, 1906), 146-52; Joyce E. Salisbury, "Bestiality in the Middle Ages," in *Sex in the Middle Ages* (New York, 1991), 178-79.

5. Jeffrey Burton Russell, *Lucifer: The Devil in the Middle Ages* (Ithaca, 1984), 67; Salisbury 1991, 182; 1994, 97-99.

6. Bruno Roy, "La belle e(s)t le bête: Aspects du bestiaire féminin au moyen âge," *Etudes françaises* 10/3 (1974), 319-27; Salisbury 1994, 155-59.

7. Roy 1974, 327-29; Madeline Caviness, "Patron or Matron? A Capetian Bride and a *Vade Mecum* for Her Marriage Bed," *Speculum* 68/2 (1993), 338-44.

8. On marginalia themes and functions, see Camille 1992, 9-55. On marginal animal antics, see Randall 1966, 192-94.

9. Isidore of Seville, *Etymologiae* 1.1.14 (*PL* 82:426B); *De bestiis et aliis rebus* 3.16 (*PL* 177:89B-C); White 1954, 74; Barber 1993, 83. Earlier, the goat's enthusiasm for mating was described by Pliny (*Naturalis historia* 8.202-203; Rackham 1940, 140-41).

10. Rowland 1973, 80-86.

11. White 1954, 20-21; Barber 1993, 36-37. On other religious aspects of the unicorn's horn, see J. W. Einhorn, *Spiritalis Unicornis* (Munich, 1976), 241-44.

12. On the phallic associations of the unicorn's horn, see Rowland 1973, 154.

13. See W.H. Janson, *Apes and Ape Lore in the Middle Ages and Renaissance* (London, 1952). On the ape, see also Miyazaki in this volume.

14. Manchester, John Rylands Library, MS fr. 2, f. 212 (reproduced in Camille 1992, 30, fig. 12). On ape marginalia, including *obscaena*, see Randall 1966, 56-65; and Camille 1992.

15. White 1954, 34-35; Barber 1993, 49.

16. Rowland 1973, 137-38; Richard Bernheimer, *Wild Men in the Middle Ages: A Study in Art, Sentiment, and Demonology* (Cambridge [MA]), 1952, 121-73). In the bestiaries, satyrs are sometimes shown nude and with enlarged phalli emphasizing their sexual nature. See for example Add. 11283, f. 6; and St. John's 178, f. 164v (reproduced in Hassig 1995, fig. 44).

17. See Hassig 1995, 72-83 (phoenix) and 52-61 (bee). On the phoenix, see Jones in this volume.

18. White 1954, 30-32; Barber 1993, 45-47.

19. Hassig 1995, 150 and fig. 155.

20. Guido Kisch, "The Jews in Medieval Law," *Essays on Antisemitism,* 2d ed., ed. Koppel S. Pinson (New York, 1946), 108; C. Davies, "Sexual Taboos and Social Boundaries," *American Journal of Sociology* 87 (1982), 1046.

21. Evans 1906, 152.

22. Prevention of sexual relations between Jews and Christians is the stated reason for the sumptuary laws articulated by Pope Innocent III in his decree following the Fourth Lateran Council of 1215. For the text, see Solomon Grayzel, *The Church and the Jews in the XIIIth Century* (Philadelphia, 1933, 308); and Jacob R. Marcus, *The Jews in the Medieval World* (New York, 1969), 138-39.

23. James Brundage, *Law, Sex, and Christian Society in Medieval Europe* (Chicago, 1987), 448.

24. *Ibid.*, 155-63. See also McNeill and Gamer 1990, 96 (6th c.); 208 (7th c.).

25. Jean-Louis Flandrin, *Un temps pour embrasser: Aux origines de la morale sexuelle occidentale (VIe-XIe siècle)* (Paris, 1983), 48.

26. James Brundage, "The Married Lover's Dilemma: Sexual Morals, Canon Law and Marital Restraint," paper presented at the Mid-America Medieval Association meetings, 26 February 1994. See also the very instructive (and witty) flowchart showing the sexual decision-making process in Brundage 1987, 162.

27. White 1954, 25-26; Barber 1993, 40.

28. Jean Leclercq, *Monks on Marriage: A Twelfth-Century View* (New York, 1982), 12-23; Jo Ann McNamara, "Chaste Marriage and Clerical

Sex in the Bestiaries   89

Celibacy," in *Sexual Practices and the Medieval Church*, ed. Vern L.
Bullough and James Brundage (Buffalo, 1982), 22-33; Dyan Elliott, *Spiritual Marriage:
Sexual Abstinence in Medieval Wedlock* (Princeton, 1993), especially pp. 132-
94; Pierre J. Payer, *The Bridling of Desire: Views of Sex in the Later Middle
Ages* (Toronto, 1993), 84-110.

29. Hassig 1995, 133 and fig. 131.

30. Reproduced in M.D. Anderson, *Misericords: Medieval Life in English
Woodcarving* (Harmondsworth, 1954), plate 2. A reference to conjugal fidelity
may be the elephant that functions as a foot base on the fifteenth-century brass
effigy of Lady Vernon, wife of Sir William Vernon, located in the nave of the
parish church in Tong, Shropshire. See Henry H. Trivick, *The Craft and Design
of Monumental Brasses* (New York, 1969), fig. 59.

31. Albertus Magnus, *De animalibus* 24.1.2-5 (Scanlan 1987, 326-28).
The Jewis Midrash (*Midrash Rabbah: Genesis*, trans. H. Freedman [London,
1951], I, 160) states that fish copulate face to face, like humans and serpents,
because at some point God spoke to them directly, suggesting that fish
intercourse mirrors a conversation with God (Salisbury 1994, 81).

32. Hannelore Zug-Tucci, "Il mondo medievale dei pesci tra realtà e
immaginazione," in *L'Uomo di fronte al mondo animale nell'alto medioevo*
(Spoleto, 1985), I, 300-301.

33. *Ibid.*, 326-27. That the fishes did not drown during the Flood is a point
highlighted by St. Anthony in his sermon to their aquatic descendants. See
Ugolino di Monte Santa Maria, *Fioretti* 40 (*The Little Flowers of St. Francis*,
trans. Raphael Brown [New York, 1958], 131-33).

34. White 1954, 199-200 (serra), 197-98 (whale); Barber 1993, 205
(serra), 203-205 (whale).

35. White 1954, 206-207. The source of the bestiary fish section text is the
anonymous *De bestiis et aliis rebus* 3.55 (*PL* 177:106C-107B), which is based
largely on Isidore's *Etymologiae* 12.6 (*PL* 82:450B-459A).

36. White 1954, 204-206. Hildegard of Bingen suggests that, owing to
their positive properties, fishes are spiritually beneficial when ingested by
humans (*Physica* 5.1; *PL* 197:1272).

37. On women's suffering in childbirth as punishment for the Fall, see
Elaine Pagels, *Adam, Eve and the Serpent* (New York, 1988), 133-37.

38. On bestiary readership, see Hassig 1995, 170-78.

39. *Etym.* 12.2.21 (*PL* 82:437B); *Physiologus latinus: éditions
preliminaires, version B*, ed. Francis Carmody (Paris, 1939), 32; *De bestiis* 2.9
(*PL* 177:61B-D); White 1954, 29-29; Barber 1993, 43-44.

40. Benedict of Nursia, *Rule* 4.59, 4.63 (trans. Leonard J. Doyle, *St.
Benedict's Rule for Monasteries* [Collegeville, 1948], 17).

90 *Debra Hassig*

41. Hassig 1995, 88-89, figs. 86, 87.

42. Reproduced in Hassig 1995, fig. 80.

43. The sirens are described by Homer (*Odyssey* 12). On the Christian interpretation of this tale, see Hugo Rahner, "Odysseus at the Mast," in *Greek Myths and Christian Mystery* (New York, 1963), 328-86.

44. On the iconographical development of the siren, see Edmond Faral, "La queue de poisson des sirènes," *Romania* 74 (1953), 433-506.

45. Color reproduction in Janetta Rebold Benton, *The Medieval Menagerie: Animals in the Art of the Middle Ages* (New York, 1992), 19.

46. Carmody 1939, 25-26; *De bestiis* 2.32 (*PL* 177:78A-C); White 1954, 134-35; Barber 1993, 150-51.

47. White 1954, 134-35; Barber 1993, 150-51.

48. The source of the *meretrix* identification is Isidore's *Etymologiae* (12.3.31): "Secundum veritatem autem meretrices fuerunt, quae transeuntes quoniam deducebant ad egestatem, his fictae sunt inferre naufragia" (*PL* 82:423A). On the medieval use of this term, see Vern L. Bullough, "The Prostitute in the Early Middle Ages," in Bullough and Brundage 1982, 35; and Ruth Mazo Karras, *Common Women: Prostitution and Sexuality in Medieval England* (Oxford, 1996), 11.

49. Karras 1996, 77-79, 95.

50. Margaret Wade Labarge, *A Small Sound of the Trumpet: Women in Medieval Life* (Boston, 1986), 200.

51. That works of art cannot always be interpreted as eyewitness contemporary records is discussed in Stella Mary Newton, *Fashion in the Age of the Black Prince* (Woodbridge, 1980), 102-109.

52. Los Angeles, J. Paul Getty Museum, Ludwig I/6 (f. 45, detached leaf). See Anton von Euw and Joachim M. Plotzek, *Die Handschriften der Sammlung Ludwig* (Cologne, 1979), I, 72-79; and John Plummer, *Old Testament Miniatures* (New York, 1969), facing p. 202.

53. Baltimore, Walters Art Gallery, MS W. 133, f. 277. See Jacqueline Murray, "On the Origins of 'Wise Women' in Causes for Annulment on the Grounds of Male Impotence," *Journal of Medieval History* 16 (1990), 235-49 and fig. 1. A better reproduction of the miniature may be found in Karras 1996, fig. 1.

54. Ruth Mazo Karras, "Holy Harlots: Prostitute Saints in Medieval Legend," *Journal of the History of Sexuality* 1 (1990), 26.

55. John Block Friedman, "L'iconographie de Vénus et de son miroir à la fin du moyen âge," in *L'erotisme au moyen âge*, ed. Bruno Roy (Montreal, 1977), 51-82.

56. On *luxuria* images, see Anthony Weir and James Jerman, *Images of Lust: Sexual Carvings on Medieval Churches* (London, 1986).

57. Margaret Miles, *Carnal Knowing: Female Nakedness and Religious Meaning in the Christian West* (New York, 1989), 81.

58. Karras 1996, 11.

59. *Ibid.*, 62, 74.

60. The centaur and siren descriptions are combined in the same text entry in the early Christian *Physiologus*, on which the medieval bestiaries were based. See Carmody 1939, 25-26; and Ludwig XV/3 (ff. 78v-79).

61. James Brundage, "Prostitution in Medieval Canon Law," in Bullough and Brundage 1982, 151; Charles Chauvin, *Les chrétiens et la prostitution* (Paris, 1983), 60-62; Karras 1996, 142.

62. See Karras 1990; and Jean LeClercq, *Monks on Marriage: A Twelfth Century View* (New York, 1982), 88-105.

63. Bullough 1982, 41-42; Jacques Rossiaud, *Medieval Prostitution* (Oxford, 1988), 47. For the text of Innocent III's decree, see *Corpus Juris Canonici*, ed. Emil Friedberg (Graz, 1959), II, 667.

64. Karras 1990, 31.

65. Leclercq 1982, 87.

66. G.T. Salusbury, *Street Life in Medieval England* (Oxford, 1948), 153-54; Chauvin 1983, 19-22; Labarge 1986, 198; Rossiaud 1988, 57-58.

67. Rossiaud 1988, 41; Karras 1996, 77.

68. Ruth Mazo Karras, "The Regulation of Brothels in Later Medieval England," *Sisters and Workers in the Middle Ages*, ed. Judith M. Bennett, et al. (Chicago, 1989), 124-26.

69. On crusaders and prostitutes, see James A. Brundage, "Prostitution, Miscegenation and Sexual Purity in the First Crusade," in *Crusade and Settlement*, ed. Peter W. Edbury (Cardiff, 1985), 57-65.

70. Carmody 1939, 13-14; *De bestiis* 2.19 (*PL* 177:67A-B); White 1954, 226-27.

71. See Otto Demus, *Romanesque Mural Painting* (New York, 1970), fig. 228. The origins of the motif appear to be Carolingian. See for example the image of Adam and Eve before God in the Moutier-Grandval Bible (London, British Library, Add. MS 10546, f. 5v); and the image of Adam and Eve confronted by God on the bronze doors (dated 1015) of the cathedral at Hildesheim. In the bestiaries, examples of gesturing in the fire rocks entries may be found in Laud Misc. 247 (f. 141v), Add. 11283 (f. 41), and Bodley 602 (fig. 124). For descriptions and reproductions of these images, see Hassig 1995, 119-20.

72. The most articulate if not the most venomous statement to this effect is found in Tertullian's *De cultu feminarum* 1.1.1-2 (*PL* 1:1417A-1419A; trans. F. Forrester Church, "Sex and Salvation in Tertullian," *Harvard Theological Review* 68 (1975), 84), in which women are "the devil's gateway" (*janua diaboli*).

73. For a fuller discussion of this image, see Hassig 1995, 123-24.

74. John Bugge, *Virginitas: An Essay in the History of a Medieval Ideal* (The Hague, 1975), 134-37.

75. On female patronage of later medieval illuminated manuscripts, see S. G. Bell, "Medieval Women Book Owners: Arbiters of Lay Piety and Ambassadors of Culture," in Bennett et al. 1989, 135-61; and Suzanne Lewis, "The Apocalypse of Isabella of France: Paris, Bibl. Nat. MS Fr. 13096," *Art Bulletin* 72/2 (1990), 224-60. On female patronage of bestiaries, see Francis Avril and Patricia Danz Stirnemann, *Manuscrits enluminés d'origine insulaire VIIe-XXe siècle* (Paris, 1987), 98-99. For a fuller discussion of the exclusion of the fire rocks entries in particular bestiaries, see Hassig 1995, 126-27.

76. Xenia Muratova, "Bestiaries: An Aspect of Medieval Patronage," in *Art and Patronage in the English Romanesque*, ed. Sarah Macready and F. H. Thompson (London, 1986), 121.

77. On what little is known of Richard's life and work, see Yvan G. Lepage, *L'Oeuvre lyrique de Richard de Fournival* (Ottawa, 1981), 9-11.

78. Sylvia Huot, *From Song to Book: The Poetics of Writing in Old French Lyric and Lyrical Narrative Poetry* (Ithaca, 1987), 142-45. On the text/image technique of seduction, see also Helen Solterer, "Letter Writing and Picture Reading: Medieval Textuality and the *Bestiaire d'Amour*," *Word & Image* 5/1 (1989), 133, 141.

79. Salisbury 1994, 158-59.

80. Beer 1986, 3.

81. The *Response* is today attributed to a different (anonymous) author (Lepage 1981, 15). The tone of the *Response* is decidedly negative and has been interpreted as an early expression of feminist principles (Beer 1986, xxii-xxvi).

82. Trans. Beer 1986, 5. "Elas! et si me sui puis tantes fois repentis de c[h]ou ke je vous avoie proié, por vostre douce compaignie perdre. Car se jou puisse faire ausi comme li chiens, ki est de tel nature ke quant il a vomi, k'i repaire a son vomite et le remangüe, jou eüse volentiers me proiere regloutie cent fois, puis k'ele me fu volee des dens" (Segre 1957, 14-15).

83. White 1954, 61-67; Barber 1993, 71-77.

84. Paris, Bibliothèque Nationale, MS fr. 412 (13th c.). A full-scale art historical study of the *Bestiaire d'amour* and *Response* miniatures has yet to be undertaken.

85. Beer 1986, 3-4. "Et la raison de ce que li desessperés a plus fort vois si est prise, je quit, en la beste del monde ki plus s'esforce de braire et ke plus a laide vois et orrible, c'est li asnes salvages. Car sa nature si est qu'il ne recane onques, fors quant il a tres erragie faim et il ne puet trover en nule maniere de quoi il se puist soeler. Mais adont met il si grant paine a racaner qu'il se desront tous. Et por chu me covient il, quant je ne puis en vous trover merci, metre grengnor paine c'onques mais, ne mie a forment canter, mais a forment et atangnamment dire" (Segre 1957, 10).

86. Beer 1986, 19-20; Segre 1957, 53-57.

87. White 1954, 105-107; Barber 1993, 118-19.

88. Beer 1986, 31-32. "Li bes de l'aigle senefie l'orgueil ki est encontre amors. Car adont brise li bes, quant on se humelie tant ke on deferme le forteresce ki est devant la langue, a chu k'ele puist reconoistre et otroier" (Segre 1957, 91-92).

89. Huot 1987, 138.

Figure 1. Hyena. London, British Library, MS Harley 4751, f. 10.
Photo: by permission of the British Library.

Figure 2. Sirens. Cambridge, University Library, MS Kk.4.25, f. 77.
Photo: by permission of the Syndics of Cambridge University Library.

Figure 3. Fire Rocks. Oxford, Bodleian Library, MS Ashmole 1511, f. 103v.
Photo: The Bodleian Library.

Figure 4. Weasel, lion, pelican. Richard of Fournival, *Bestiaire d'amour*. Oxford, Bodleian Library, MS Douce 308, f. 96v. Photo: The Bodleian Library.

The Phoenix and the Resurrection
Valerie Jones

The issue of the resurrection at the end of time is one of the most controversial in Christian history and thus has been a matter of debate in theological writings for centuries. In early Christian thought, the exact nature of Christ's resurrection, and thus the Christian conception of humanity's resurrection at the end of time, took the form of two opposing views: the corporeal resurrection as maintained in Judeo-Christian faith and the strictly spiritual understanding that grew out of Hellenistic philosophy.[1] The problem of the resurrection is not directly addressed in Scriptures, thus leaving theologians both modern and ancient to decide what is implied in ambiguous biblical passages. The crux of the problem remained whether the resurrection would involve a revival of the flesh or solely of the spirit. The development and resolutions of this debate are allegorized in medieval interpretations of the phoenix myth, in that conflicting views of the resurrection expressed in Christian literature are also observable in images of the phoenix in medieval bestiaries. Like the phoenix myth, the bestiary images were shaped and reshaped throughout the Middle Ages in order to convey different philosophical understandings of the doctrine of the resurrection.

Philosophers of Hellenistic Greece were familiar with the idea of a disembodied, immortal soul after death. Inherited from Plato were views on the physical body which influenced later Christian beliefs. According to Platonic theory, the body is a tomb, incarcerating the divine and immortal element of the soul.[2] It is thus base or evil matter, a fetter from which man should escape. This was the general view shared by later Stoic philosophers. Cicero, for example, referred to the body as "a vase and a kind of container for the soul."[3] Early Christians in the East tended to retain the beliefs associated with the Stoics and the Hellenistic mystery cults, believing in the immortality of the soul, and its separation from the body at death. The possibility of a bodily resurrection was both denied and unwanted by some early Christians in favor of a spiritual rebirth.[4]

The apostle Paul, himself a convert from Hellenistic Judaism, set the tone for a longstanding dispute among Christians. In his sermons to converts in Corinth composed during the middle of the first century, Paul attempted to dissuade the general disbelief in any sort of resurrection by adopting a philosophical explanation of the transformation of the body at death. His view echoes the beliefs of Plato and the Stoics. In I Corinthians, he presents physical parallels from nature to demonstrate the possibility of a resurrection of the body, yet he refers to the new body as a spiritual one. He emphasizes the idea of a radiant spiritual body as a replacement for the natural one: "Therefore as we have borne the image of the earthly, let us bear also the image of the heavenly" (I Cor. 15:49). He compares the dead body to a seed which, when buried, yields a new, transformed body. Likewise, at death, a human being is given a new body, spiritual and imperishable, rather than a natural, perishable one. Distinguishing between the two types of bodies, Paul says: "So also is the resurrection of the dead. It is sown in corruption, it shall rise in incorruption. It is sown in dishonor, it shall rise in glory. It is sown in weakness, it shall rise in power. It is sown a natural body, it shall rise a spiritual body" (I Cor. 15:42-44). The use of an example from nature, the seed, to prove the physical reality of a resurrection is incongruous with Paul's spiritualized conception of the resurrected body: the resurrected will be of flesh but of a transformed, non-material flesh. In trying to convey the reality of a physical resurrection of the flesh, later theologians would use Paul's example of the seed for a new purpose: as natural proof of corporeal revival.[5]

Contrasting with Paul's view of the resurrection is the one presented by the Evangelists. In the Gospels of Luke and John, the flesh of the resurrected Christ is strongly emphasized. In Luke 24:39, Christ says, "See my hands and my feet, that it is I myself, handle, and see: for a spirit hath not flesh and bones, as you see me have." The bodily resurrection of Christ, so important in these texts, was the one generally accepted by the Church, because it distinguished Christian belief from

Hellenistic religious thought. On this point, Robert Grant succinctly observed,

> If Christians were to proclaim the historical reality of the rising of their Lord, they had to insist on a somewhat crude understanding of it in order to reach the masses. If they were to defend their faith from critical opponents, they had to insist on the novelty of the resurrection. Other gods died and rose; only Jesus rose in the flesh.[6]

In other words, the belief in a physical resurrection reinforced the historical reality of Christ's resurrection and thus made the doctrine of the resurrection of humankind more tangible to the unlettered masses.

During the second century, theologians struggled to reconcile the antithetical views concerning the nature of the resurrection. However, by this time, the Pauline conception of a spiritual resurrection was considered heretical, and the idea of a bodily resurrection became the canonical view, doubtless owing to its successful grasp by new converts. Subsequently, Church leaders such as Tertullian and Ignatius did not question the possibility of a physical resurrection. Rather than attempt to prove it outright, they proclaimed its truth based on beliefs surrounding the nature of Christ's resurrection. In his epistle to the Smyrnaeans, Ignatius wrote, "For myself, I know and believe that He was in the flesh even after the Resurrection."[7] However, although they did accept the idea of a bodily resurrection, other writers could not rely on faith alone. They could not accept the doctrine as absolute truth without seeking to prove its viability by using examples from the natural world. Athenagoras took this "scientific" approach to extremes. In his desire to understand and explain every contingency of a physical resurrection, he questions what happens to people who are drowned, eaten by animals, or even consumed by other people. He concludes that the misfortunate consumed or dismembered deceased will rise completely intact:

> Men say . . . that many human bodies become, through drowning by shipwreck or in rivers, food for fishes; many of those who die in war or by some other hard fate or whim of circumstance lie unburied, are food for the first animals that approach. Bodies then, they say, are thus done away and their proper portions and particles pass after decay into a multitude of animals and are by digestion united to the bodies that thus feed upon them, so that the separating of these

becomes impossible. Then there is a further and more awkward predicament. The animals that feed upon these human bodies such at least that are fit for human consumption pass through the stomachs of man and are incorporated into the bodies of men who eat them. . . . And from all this they prove—as they think—that resurrection is impossible for the reason that the same parts cannot rise again in two or more bodies. . . . Such men seem to me not to realize the power and wisdom of Him who made and governs this universe.[8]

In their various attempts to demonstrate the plausibility of a physical resurrection, many theologians sought parallels from the natural world, following Paul, who used the analogy of the seed and its new body after germination. However, unlike Paul, who sought an analogy for spiritual transformation, later writers were trying to prove the physical nature of the resurrection. Among the natural examples proffered were the monthly resurrection of the moon, the daily rising and setting of the sun, and the resurrection of the phoenix from death. It is this last example that figured prominently in the bestiaries and became such an important vehicle for communicating the nature of the doctrine of the resurrection throughout the later Middle Ages.

In medieval interpretation, the Classical phoenix myth was often cited in conjunction with other natural regenerative phenomena. It would appear, therefore, that the phoenix story was considered factual and thus used as "evidence" to prove wrong those who maintained beliefs in a solely spiritual resurrection. In his *De resurrectione carnis*, for example, Tertullian writes:

> Consider a very complete and reliable example of this hope. . . . What proof could be found more clearly and strikingly intended for this case? For what other matter is there such a proof? For in his scriptures God says: "And he will flourish like a phoenix," that is, from death. . . . The Lord declared that we are of more value than many sparrows; this would mean little if it did not also apply to phoenixes. And will men die, once and for all, when Arabian birds are sure of resurrection?[9]

St. Ambrose also offers the phoenix myth as evidence for human resurrection. In a funeral oration delivered for his brother in the year 375, St. Ambrose consoled his own fears about what lay in store for his deceased brother: "There is a bird in Arabia called the phoenix. After it dies, it comes back to life, restored by the renovating fluid in its own flesh. Shall we believe that men alone are not restored to life again?"[10]

In Christian literature, two versions of the phoenix myth were developed.[11] In one version, the phoenix dies after a long life and its flesh putrefies. A worm rises from the decayed flesh, and it is transformed into a new phoenix. This version was adopted by Clement, who was the first to use the phoenix myth in order to illustrate points of Catholic doctrine.[12] In his epistle to the Corinthians, written around 100, Clement likened the death of the phoenix to human death, thus comparing the phoenix's resurrection from decayed flesh to human resurrection:

> Let us consider the strange and striking phenomenon which takes place in the East, that is, in the regions of Arabia. There is a bird which is called the phoenix. It is the only individual of its kind, and it lives five hundred years; and when it approaches dissolution and its death is imminent, it makes itself a nest out of frankincense and myrrh and the other spices; this it enters when the time is fulfilled, and dies. But out of the decaying flesh a sort of worm is born, which feeds on the juices of the dead animal until it grows wings. . . . "[13]

Clement's version of the phoenix story was not entirely satisfactory from a christological point of view. For one thing, because it involves the concept of physical decay, it is not easily read as an analogy for the death of Christ. Furthermore, since the bird simply dies from old age, the story lacks the important element of self-sacrifice which is crucial to the success of the phoenix as a Christ analogy.

The second version of the myth was the more popular of the two, as it provided a clearer analogy for the resurrection of both Christ and humanity. According to this version, the phoenix builds for itself a funeral pyre into which it climbs and then sets itself on fire. In some versions, this self-incineration occurs every thousand years, perhaps alluding to the millennium before Christ's return.[14] A worm forms from the ashes, which then transforms into an egg from which a new phoenix emerges. This version was the one favored by the author of the second-century *Physiologus* included in the medieval bestiaries:

> There is a species of bird in the land of India which is called the phoenix, which enters the wood of Lebanon after five hundred years and bathes his two wings in the fragrance. . . . Then the bird enters

Heliopolis laden with fragrance and mounts the altar, where he
ignites the fire and burns himself up. The next day then the priest
examines the altar and finds a worm in the ashes. On the second day,
however, he finds a tiny birdling. On the third day he finds a huge
eagle . . . . [15]

The motif of bodily decay is eliminated through the return to the
Classical theme of self-incineration and death through cremation.
However, the extraneous detail of the worm often persists in the stories,
probably in order to retain the relation to human death and to
emphasize the possibility of a resurrection of the body intact even after
earthly decay. An invention of the author of the *Physiologus* is the
three-day waiting period between the phoenix's death and its
resurrection, further likening the bird to Christ.

Once the connection between the phoenix and Christ's resurrection
had been made, this important theme was elaborated in a variety of
literary contexts. The most important of these is the fourth-century
Latin poem, *De Ave Phoenice*. In this work, Lactantius emphasizes the
spiritual, transcendent nature of the resurrection. His phoenix is clearly
a Christ figure, returning to earth after a "thousand years of life . . . in
order to repair the age lapsed by declining periods."[16] The paradisiacal
quality of the phoenix's dwelling place is vividly described: "Here is
the grove of the sun, and a wood planted with many a tree, verdant with
the splendor of perpetual leafage."[17] In relating the events of the bird's
self-incineration and resurrection, the poet retains the motif of the
worm. However, he likens the worm's transformation to that of the
butterfly which emerges from the body of a caterpillar. He introduces
yet another significant element to the phoenix myth in his
characterization of the bird's gender or lack of it: "Happy indeed is that
bird, whether male or female or neither . . . . "[18] He further alludes to
the spiritual nature of the bird's resurrected body when he speaks of its
sustenance: "There is no food in our world granted to her. . . . She sips
the fine ambrosial dews from heavenly nectar which has fallen from the
starbearing pole."[19] Following the Pauline tradition, Lactantius
emphasizes the radiant beauty of the phoenix's new body:

Her color is like that of the tender pomegranate seeds. . . . Her
shoulders and beautiful breast shine with this covering; with this garb
her head, with this her neck and the ridge of her back gleam. Her tail
is drawn out, marked by metallic yellow, on the spots of which a

scarlet mixture blushes. From above this marks the feathers of her wings just as she is accustomed to paint her colors upon a cloud from her place in the sky. The bird gleams, marked with a shining mixture of emerald, and her gemmed beak glitters open with its clear horn.[20]

This poem was clearly not intended to quell the fear of death by assuring that the physical body will rise intact but rather to convey the splendor of Heaven and the spiritual beauty of Christ and the blessed at the Last Judgment.

The distinction between a physical conception of the resurrection as opposed to a spiritual one is marked in early Christian literature. The same conflicting ideas observable in literature—a Pauline belief in a spiritual body versus the renewal of the physical body set forth by Luke and John—are also prominent in bestiary images of the phoenix. In some cases, this dialectic is clearly conveyed. In an image from Royal 12.C.XIX, the story of the phoenix, first building the funeral pyre and then going up in flames, is depicted in a continuous narrative (figure 1). On the left, the phoenix is shown gathering twigs in its beak and claws and is next depicted on the right, burning atop a decorative pyre. Visual emphasis is on the dead, limp body of the burning phoenix. No attempt has been made to glorify the bird's body, nor to depict its resurrection. The phoenix is represented as a real bird, with a curved raptor's beak, like a hawk. It is part of the terrestrial world, existing amid naturalistic landscape elements, including leafy plants. At the same time, however, its transcendence is suggested by the solid gold ground.

The phoenix image in the Morgan Bestiary is rather different (figure G, p. xxviii). The bird's preparation of the funeral pyre and its self-incineration are depicted as two isolated events, each a frozen moment within a circular frame. The static, heraldic position of the bird glorifies the phoenix's self-sacrifice and renewal, emphasizing its symbolic significance. In the second frame, the bird rises from brilliant flames, its wings spread in a gesture of triumph. Unlike the Royal 12.C.XIX image, the bird's resurrection is depicted and presented as a glorious, timeless emblem. By means of independent framing devices, the bird's spiritual nature is separated from its physical nature, with frames enclosing the earthly and heavenly realms, respectively. The bird's mystical, ethereal nature is emphasized through the use of a gold ground on the left and gold flames against a red ground on the right.

In a later, thirteenth-century image from Bodley 764, a phoenix rising from its burning nest visually accords with the Pauline conception of the spiritual body after death (figure H, p. xxix). The accompanying text reads:

> The phoenix produces all the signs of the Resurrection; for the birds are there to teach man, not to teach the birds. It is therefore an example to us that the Author and Creator of birds does not suffer His saints to die eternally, but wishes to restore them by using His own life-force. Who then has announced to this bird the day of its death, so that it makes its chrysalis and fills it with sweet scents and goes into it and dies, so that the scents can overcome the stench of death? O man, make your chrysalis, and putting off the old man, and all his deeds, clothe yourself in the new man.[21]

This text shows clearly the influence of Pauline philosophy: "The first man was of the earth, earthly: the second man, from heaven, heavenly . . . Therefore as we have borne the image of the earthly, let us bear also the image of the heavenly" (I Cor. 15:47-49).[22] When the image is read in conjunction with the accompanying text, the phoenix positioned against an abstract, gold ground and rising from the flaming nest with outstretched wings is a striking verbal and visual pronouncement of the glory of spiritual renewal.

In a late thirteenth-century North French copy of Guillaume le Clerc's metrical *Bestiaire,* a markedly different view of the resurrection is suggested (figure 2). In this image, the phoenix's death and resurrection are placed in a liturgical context. The nest has become a bowl positioned atop a column, suggestive of a tall chalice, from which the bird's renewed body emerges. The mythical priests of Heliopolis described in the *Physiologus* (on which Guillaume's bestiary is heavily dependent) have been transformed into contemporary ecclesiastics. The message conveyed in this image accords with one set forth in the Gospel of John, in which the spirit of Christ is conceived as a material entity.[23] In particular, John connects Christ's resurrection to the Eucharist. In John 6:54-59, eating the flesh and drinking the blood of Christ is characterized as a means of attaining eternal life. In the fr. 24428 bestiary image, the iconography of the phoenix has been manipulated to accord with John's idea of direct participation in the resurrection of Christ through the sacrament. On the right side of the image, celebration of the Eucharist is suggested by situating the reincarnated phoenix in its chalice form next to a priest standing before an altar, thereby simultaneously evoking the idea of the resurrection of the body and the concept of Christ's physical presence.

The self-sacrifice and resurrection of the phoenix take place in eucharistic contexts elsewhere in Christian art. For example, in a sixth-century floor mosaic in the Church of Umm Jerar near Gaza, a phoenix with a rayed nimbus rises from a chalice-shaped altar.[24] The theme receives variant treatment in the bestiaries as well. For example, in the Ludwig XV/3 bestiary, a phoenix sacrifices itself upon a draped altar, as a clear reference to Christ's sacrifice and to the Eucharist (figure 3). In addition, the prominent architectonic trefoil framing device reinforces the allegorical nature of the image by evoking the number of the Trinity.

As images of the death and resurrection of the phoenix are transformed into visual references to the Eucharist, they are also related to the sacrament of Baptism. In the Gospels of Luke and John, baptism is a symbol of rebirth, a rebirth achieved through a death of the flesh. In baptism, one dies and rises with Christ, experiencing the transition, "from being 'in sin' to being 'in Christ', from death to life . . . The one rite is used to interpret the other: the rite that marked Christ's passage from death to his life 'to God' that lay beyond the grave is used as a metaphor of the passage in baptism from 'death' through death with Christ and burial with Christ to life with him 'to God'."[25] Thus, baptism is intimately linked with the resurrection of Christ: it is a way for Christians to symbolically participate in the resurrection of Christ, while insuring their own bodily resurrection. This concept found its way into the bestiaries. In some images, the phoenix is portrayed as emerging from what may be read simultaneously as a nest and as a baptismal font, for example, in the Cambridge Bestiary (f. 36v),[26] rather than from a more naturalistic nest constructed from twigs and branches.

Finally, some bestiary phoenix images attempt to synthesize the spiritual and physical views of the resurrection while at the same time exposing its dialectical nature. The two conflicting views of the resurrection are perfectly united in two images representing the death and the rebirth of the phoenix in the Ashmole Bestiary (figures 4, 5). In the first image, the body of the phoenix assumes a cruciform shape, its wings outspread and its tail stretched towards the ground, creating a strong vertical axis (figure 4). Its body is raised above the ground, supported by two flanking trees. Above the bird's head, the sun functions as a halo.[27] The outstretched body of the phoenix refers to the crucified body of Christ, and yet the body is emblematic and radiant as if already risen from the mundane world of flesh. In the pendant image, the transformed, renewed phoenix rises from its nest, which, like the Cambridge Bestiary image, may be read as a baptismal font (figure 5). Although the visual reference to baptism suggests the fleshly resurrection of Christ, the emphasis is on the bird's radiant, transcendent body rather than on its physical presence in the natural world. It is also significant that the device of the baptismal font occurs again in the Ashmole Bestiary image of the eagle (f. 74).[28] The eagle plunges three times into a basin of water, shaped much like the one in the phoenix image, in an act symbolic of baptism.

As a symbol of the resurrection of Christ and of the concomitant resurrection of humanity at the end of time, the phoenix myth must be evaluated in light of evolving Church doctrine. When examined in this context, the phoenix in Christian literature and its illustration in medieval bestiaries together provide insight into the beliefs and perceptions of the various patrons, churches, artists, and authors responsible for these works, as well as the views dominant at the time of their production. The bestiaries in particular helped shape prevalent beliefs concerning the resurrection of Christ and of humankind in beautifully economic and succinct images that both convey the essential tenets of the dogma but that still preserve its inherent mystery.

NOTES

1. Robert M. Grant, "The Resurrection of the Body," *The Journal of Religion* 28 (1948), 120-30; 188-208. The latest study on differing medieval views of the resurrection is Carolyn Walker Bynum, *The Resurrection of the Body in Western Christianity, 200-1336* (New York, 1995).

2. Plato, *Phaedo* 67C-D (*Plato*, trans. Harold North Fowler [London, 1933], I, 232-35).

3. Cicero, *Tusculane Disputationes* I.22.52 (Cicero, *Tusculan Disputations*, trans. J. E. King [Cambridge, MA, 1971], 62-63).

4. On Early Christian views of the resurrection, see Bynum 1995, 21-114.

5. Grant 1948, 193-94.

6. *Ibid.*, 127.

7. St. Ignatius, "Epistle to the Smyrnaeans," in *The Epistle of St. Clement of Rome and St. Ignatius of Antioch*, trans. James A. Kleist (New York, 1946), 91.

8. Athenagoras, *Embassy for the Christians, The Resurrection of the Dead*, trans. Joseph Hugh Crehan (New York, 1955), 84-85.

9. Tertullian, *Liber de resurrectione carnis* 2.13 (*PL* 2:857B-858A); trans. Grant 1948, 195. See also Bynum 1995, 34-38, 40-43.

10. St. Ambrose, "On His Brother, Satyrus: II," in *Funeral Orations by St. Gregory Nazianzen and St. Ambrose*, trans. Leo P. McCauley et al. (New York, 1953), 221.

11. A detailed discussion of both versions as well as other sources for the phoenix myth may be found in R. Van Den Broek, *The Myth of the Phoenix According to Classical and Early Christian Traditions* (Leiden, 1972), 146-232, from which the following description is summarized.

12. Bynum 1995, 23-26.

13. St. Clement, "Epistle to the Corinthians," *The Epistles of St. Clement of Rome and St. Ignatius of Antioch*, trans. James A. Kleist (New York, 1946), 25.

14. For example, see Gregory of Tours, *De cursu stellarum ratio qualiter ad officium implendum debeat observari* 12, ed. B. Krusch, in *Monumenta Germanicae Historica, Scriptores rerum Merovingicarum* 1.2 (Hannover, 1885).

15. Curley 1979, 13.

16. Lactantius, *The Minor Works*, trans. Mary Francis McDonald (Washington, D.C., 1965), 215.

17. *Ibid.*, 213.

18. *Ibid.*

19. *Ibid.*, 217.

20. *Ibid.*, 218.

21. Barber 1993, 143; with the exception of the last line of the passage, in which Barber has translated "hominem veterem" as "old Adam." In fact, Adam is not mentioned at all in this entry. "Ipsa sibi insignia resurrectionis instaurat, et utique aues propter homines sunt, non homo propter auem. Sit igitur exemplum nobis que auctor et creator auium sanctos suos in perpetuum perire non passus, resurgentem eam sui semine uoluit reparari. Quis igitur huic annuntiat diem mortis, ut faciat sibi thecam et impleat eam bonis odoribus atque ingediatur in eam et moriatur, illic ut odoribus gratis fetor funeris possit aboleri? Fac et tu, homo, tibi thecam, et, expolians te ueterem hominem cum actibus suis, nouum indue" (Bodley 764, f. 70).

22. That the bestiarist had Paul in mind is evidenced later on in the Bodley 764 entry, when Paul is identified as the author of the famous passage, "I have fought a good fight, I have finished my course, I have kept the faith . . . there is laid up for me a crown of justice"(2 Tim. 4:7-8): "Et Paulus qui ait,'Bonum

certamen certaui, cursum consummaui, fidem seruaui. Reposita est michi corona justicie" (Bodley 764, f. 71).

23. A.J.M. Wedderburn, *Baptism and Resurrection* (Tübingen, 1987), 246.
24. Reproduced in Van Den Broek 1972, pl. XXXII.
25. *Ibid.*, 61.
26. Reproduced in White 1954, 126.
27. Hassig 1995, 74-75.
28. Reproduced in Rowland 1978, 53; and Graz 1982 (color).

filij auem in uetati tc.g-claū ate. uus. ecaum.
Vocaui ū plebem meam ſi plebē meā.t ū dilectā
dilectā meā. Hictionax ipā eſt cg-noctua. et ē
auis lucrfuga.cg-folem uidere ū patriur

st aluud uolacile qd dr fenjr arrhie ut ata
bis aur. eo qd coloze fenicei habear uel

Figure 1. Phoenix. London, British Library, MS Royal 12.C.XIX,
f. 49v. Photo: by permission of the British Library.

leil canl elungu   & nlesgardeu se renouele\
tenroit chter   a utreli com fait li oisele\
avoit vigour   & us en vrai soleil q cel fit\
ntre lauoz   & tout les elemens attist\
le guerpront\
n entremetroit.\
si se renouele\
l'ample bonez bele\
xuroit ouret\
vient renoucler\
sit ancien\
u sort crestien\
de sonturer seroient

la nature dou fenis\
Vn oisel qui a non fenis\
en vne isle maint tout dis

Figure 2. Phoenix. Guillaume le Clerc, *Bestiaire*. Paris, Bibliothèque Nationale, MS fr. 24428, f. 58v. Photo: Bibliothèque Nationale, Paris.

Est ҂ aliud uolatile
qd dr beniɔ. Hoc
figura gerit dni nri
ihu xpi. q dicit in
euuangelio. porestate
heo ponendi anima
mea ҂ irerū sumdi
eam. ibr̄ heo uerba
irati lunt iudei· et

uolebat eu lapidare.
Est q̄ auis ꞇ yndie
ptib; q̄ dr pheniɔ.
de hac phylolophuɛ
dicit. qa ɔpleɑ̄ ɛn
orenttʃ annuʃ uice
sue. urait ꞇ lignuʃ
lybani· ҂ replet uɩ̄
q₃ alaʃ suaʃ dulſis

Figure 3. Phoenix. Los Angeles, J. Paul Getty Museum, MS Ludwig XV/3,
f. 74v. Photo: The J. Paul Getty Museum, Los Angeles, California.

in ercsia chartholica. ii domini babri
vomo ibioz; habeat cocidianum uici
mortalitcacipotum ii pciosum sangu
mel i fauum suauissimis eloquis

Figure 4. Phoenix. Oxford, Bodleian Library, MS Ashmole 1511, f. 67v.
Photo: The Bodleian Library.

Figure 5. Phoenix. Oxford, Bodleian Library, MS Ashmole 1511, f. 68.
Photo: Bodleian Library.

PART 3

Classical Inheritances

Did Imaginary Animals Exist?

Pamela Gravestock

The bestiary pages are filled with imaginary animals, including the basilisk, bonnacon, caladrius, centaur, dragon, griffin, manticore, parandrus, phoenix, serra, siren, unicorn, and yale, to name some of the most familiar. Less often, some bestiaries include other creatures drawn directly from Classical mythology and tradition such as the Minotaur, chimera, and Cereberus as well as the Monstrous or Fabulous Races.[1] This essay will explore the following question, often posed: to what extent did medieval people believe these creatures actually existed?[2] As modern viewers, we tend to separate the real from the imaginary animals in the bestiaries and assume that medieval readers recognized these same categories.[3] But is this really a safe assumption? When medievals viewed the imaginary animals alongside known animals in the bestiaries, did they make such a clear distinction?

One artistic measure of an animal's perceived existence might be the degree of naturalism observable in its rendering. However, this is not a useful gauge, as there are countless examples in the bestiary of known animals that are not rendered naturalistically. Among others, images of elephants, beavers and panthers are more often than not depicted in a nonnaturalistic way or given physical features that they do not have. For example, the elephant is frequently shown with "flowery" ears, feet that resemble paws, and a trumpet-like trunk (figure I, p. xxx). A similar situation occurs with images of the beaver, in which the animal tends to look more like a wolf, fox, or dog, with a bushy tail rather than a flat one covered with epidermal scales (figure F, p. xxvii). Far from a sign of artistic ability or lack thereof, the degree of naturalism observable in a given bestiary image was clearly a matter of choice and was often related to the accompanying moralization.[4]

It is also true that for the most part, artists were not working from direct observation of nature, especially in the cases of animals which were in distant places, much less when the animals were imaginary! Even in those rare instances of animal images supposedly drawn from life, such as Villard de Honnecourt's famous lion, the final product may still be decidedly non-naturalistic.[5] In the bestiaries, it is assumed that the artists worked from written descriptions and from pictorial models and in this were in keeping with illuminators of other types of manuscripts during this same period.[6] The same method was used whether the artist was depicting real or imaginary animals, which more than anything must account for their stylistic similarity and uniformity of treatment.

Although the twelfth century was a period of scientific discovery and direct observation from nature, this did not inform traditional bestiary iconography until much later.[7] Necessarily, most medieval writers on science and nature relied heavily on the works of Classical authors for much of their information, especially for those animals located at a geographical distance.[8] It should also be remembered that the *Physiologus*, which provided the core roster of bestiary creatures, is believed to have been compiled in second-century Alexandria and describes animals, such as the crocodile and the elephant, that would have been virtually unknown to the English bestiarists,[9] aside from those few who might have had access to a monastic zoo or menagerie of exotics. In a sense, then, to the bestiary readers, many of the animals that actually existed may have seemed as imaginary as the unicorn or the dragon.

It is therefore impossible to look at the manner in which the bestiary animals were rendered or described as a way to distinguish those that were considered real from those that were not. In general, the imaginary animals are not treated in a more fantastic manner or given any special attributes or qualities that would serve to separate them from living animals, except of course for those features that identify them as a particular imaginary "species" (such as the unicorn's horn or the griffin's beak, wings, and paws). Nor are they given more negative or positive moralizations than the other animals. In fact, in the bestiaries, the imaginary animals are given the same treatment—both pictorially and textually—as those animals that were known to exist.

Pictorial renderings of imaginary animals do sometimes inject a certain element of ambiguity, however. For example, the bestiaries indicate that the manticore is a beast found in India, with a triple row of teeth, the face of a man, and grey eyes. It is blood-red and has a lion's body and a pointed tail; it stings like a scorpion and has a hissing voice. It is a powerful jumper, and it delights in eating human flesh. According to the moralization, the manticore is a figure of the devil.[10] The creature is frequently depicted in the bestiaries as disturbingly humanoid, with a maned body and the head of a man.

The composite nature of the manticore described in the text is also expressed visually, but in different ways that suggest opposing perceptions of this creature. In the Rochester Bestiary, the manticore is positioned in a landscape surrounded by other animals and plants (figure 1), while the manticore image in Bodley 764 underscores the creature's humanoid qualities by the attribute of a Phrygian cap (f. 25).[11] Taken together, the different types of representation—in a landscape as if "real" or more emblematic and isolated—communicate the ambiguity of the creature itself and the unanswerable question of its actual existence.

One way of solving the imaginary/real dilemma posed by the bestiary creatures is to assume that all of the animals were real but just severely misinterpreted to be ultimately unrecognizable. This school of thought seeks to match each of the imaginary creatures to animals that have actually been known to exist or that still exist today.[12] Such an approach is based on the assumption that the animals were misunderstood or their written descriptions mistranslated during antiquity, resulting in severe verbal and visual confusion.

This is actually a very old method of analysis, known as rationalism, familiar from the Classical period. Rationalism's most masterful proponent was Palaephatus, who in the fourth century B.C. made one of the earliest attempts to debunk the existence of various mythological creatures in his treatise, *On Unbelievable Tales*.[13] In this work, Palaephatus rationalizes such creatures as the centaurs, the Amazons, Pegasus, and Scylla, by attributing their "existence" to a pun, a misunderstanding of a name, or a misreading of a physical form.[14] Believers in the subsequently discredited creatures are inevitably characterized as feeble-minded.

In modern times, numerous bestiary creatures have been subjects of rationalist scrutiny. In these studies, the physical descriptions of the animals and their geographical origins are used to narrow down the possible identifications until a real-life counterpart for the imaginary beast is selected and defended. For example, using this method, modern rationalists have identified the manticore described above as a cheetah or some other type of large cat.[15]

Another imaginary animal subjected to rationalist treatment is the yale (figure 2). The yale is described in Pliny's *Natural History* as well as by Solinus.[16] The creature was not discussed in the *Physiologus*, but by the twelfth century it was regularly included in the bestiaries.[17] The yale is described as a beast the size of a horse with the tail of an elephant, and outlandishly long, adjustable horns that can be moved about at will.[18]

Most scholars have chalked up the yale to Pliny's imagination.[19] Others, however, have identified the beast as a gnu, a mountain goat, or some type of exotic cow.[20] Alternatively, it has been suggested that the yale actually represents an Indian water buffalo. This hypothesis emerged after comparing a number of bestiary illustrations of yales and *mappa mundi* images as well as written physical descriptions and accounts of its geographical origins. Finally, after other possible prototypes were eliminated, the Indian water buffalo emerged as the yale's "true" identity.[21]

The rationalists offer an interesting explanation for the siren, the half-woman, half-fish or half-bird sea creature known from antiquity, and a very popular figure in the bestiaries as well as in other artistic contexts (figure B, p. xxiii). It has been suggested that the siren was a misunderstanding of the Mediterranean monk seal, which superficially fits the siren description. That is, because this type of seal has a round head and large eyes, it is said to have a somewhat human look, and the fact that it coos purportedly inspired the ancient tale of the sweet music of the sirens: "Imagine the treacherous reef where the monk seals with fishes in their mouths splash in and out of the crashing waves and the diving sea-birds wheel and screech against the sky—what sailor struggling at the helm to avoid the rocks would not think the coast bewitched by the carnivorous sirens?"[22] Whether or not there is any merit to this theory, the traditional description of the siren does not suggest anything specific to a monk seal, in that any round-headed, big-eyed sea creature might just as well suffice as the siren "mistake." It is quite reasonable, however, to speculate that ancient sailors may have interpreted the cries of various sea creatures as sirens singing *after* the fact, that is, once they were familiar with the legend and expected to find sirens lurking in the sea.

The main problem with taking a rationalist approach to the imaginary bestiary animals is that it concentrates on just one aspect of a very complex problem. That is, to categorically assume that imaginary animals are the result of "mistakes" or sloppy thinking on the part of Classical and medieval writers is to denigrate the human imagination, and represents a misguided attempt to force "reality" into the same mode of thought as the imaginative.[23] Another difficulty is that real-life counterparts for imaginary animals are sought from where the animals are said to originate in the writings of Pliny, Aristotle, and on the world maps. In these sources, many animals are located in India or Ethiopia, but these two place names were almost used generically to refer to anywhere far away or exotic. That is, "India" and "Ethiopia" were more ideas than actual places, making attempts to locate imaginary animals in their modern-day equivalents anachronistic.[24] Interestingly, rationalism was not without its critics even in Ancient times; Plato himself condemned this "dismal business," aptly remarking, "Anyone who does not believe in [mythical creatures], who wants to explain them away and make them plausible by some sort of rough ingenuity, will need a great deal of time."[25]

The same rationalist method has been applied to the imaginary Monstrous Races, cycles of which are sometimes included in the bestiaries as noted above. Like the yale or the siren or even the ant-lion (identified as a ratel),[26] the Monstrous Races have been "explained" as misunderstandings of living groups or tribes. Accordingly, Giants have been identified as Watusi; Pygmies as the modern-day tribe known by the same name; one-legged Sciopods are yogis, and Amyctyrae, with their giant lower lips, are Ubangi.[27] But again, this approach proves ultimately unsatisfactory, because it is unsustainable, arbitrary, and most importantly, it diminishes the role of these creatures as carriers of moralized meanings. To put it another way, it is apparent that the viability of the rationalist theory hinges on the assumption that medievals were extremely literal-minded in their descriptions of the natural world. However, Christian religious commentaries—in particular the "nature" genre that includes the bestiaries and aviaries— as well as a consistently demonstrated love of the symbolic and multivalent clearly shows they were not.

Another way of approaching the problem of imaginary animals is to hypothesize that most medievals really believed in their existence. We can point to their inclusion in the bestiary alongside other known animals as indirect evidence. That is, in a type of manuscript that by the thirteenth-century ordinarily presented the various creatures in consistently recognizable categories—exotics, domestics, birds, reptiles, and fishes—there was no separate category that grouped together the unicorn, griffin, siren, and yale. Rather, these creatures were placed in various bestiary locations based on the defining characteristic(s) for each group. For example, the unicorn and griffin normally appear with the exotics, the caladrius is presented alongside other birds, and owing to her complicated iconographical history, the siren was sometimes categorized as a fish and at other times a bird.[28] The only prominent example of a bestiary that includes what appears to be a separate "fabulous" section is the Westminster Abbey Bestiary, but even so, only certain mythological monsters are included, while the phoenix, dragon, unicorn, griffin, and yale may be found integrated with the "real" animals and birds.

Much stronger evidence that medievals believed in the existence of certain imaginary animals is suggested from their inclusion in contemporary treatises on natural history. The thirteenth century, in particular, saw the emergence of a number of treatises devoted to the natural sciences, most notably Albert the Great's *On Animals*, written between 1258 and 1262.[29] This comprehensive look at some four hundred and seventy-seven species in over twenty-six books includes a number of imaginary animals, such as the phoenix, griffin, unicorn, and Unisexual Bird. Albert began this work as an attempt to paraphrase Aristotle's *History of Animals* but went significantly further in his analysis and included many of his own observations.[30]

Much later, Edward Topsell continued discussion of some of the same imaginary animals described by Albert the Great and the bestiarists in *The Historie of Foure-footed Beastes* (1607) and *The Historie of Serpents* (1608).[31] However, neither Albert nor Topsell merely repeated the earlier animal stories. Unlike the bestiarists, both Albert and Topsell tried to discern the living animals among the fictive ones.[32] Nevertheless, Albert, as a man of the church, had as his ultimate agenda the support of Scriptures rather than strict empiricism,[33] which meant that debunking imaginary animals might at times conflict with that creature's importance as a religious symbol or the mere fact that it is mentioned in the Bible. In such cases, the animals in question are never entirely discredited as noted below.

This highlights an interesting problem and offers another possible explanation for the continued acceptance and inclusion of imaginary animals: many were referred to in the Bible and were perhaps therefore hard to explain away without going up against divine authority. This is, in fact, precisely the way Edward Topsell justifies his continued defense of the unicorn: "The main question to be resolved is whether there be a unicorn. . . . Do we think that David [in Ps. 92] would compare the virtue of his kingdom and the powerful redemption of the world unto a thing that is not or is uncertain and fantastical?"[34]

This was not a new sentiment. Earlier, the inclusion of imaginary animals in the Scriptures had motivated their treatment in the *Physiologus*, the writings of the Fathers, and the thirteenth-century encyclopedias, all of whose contents either informed or overlapped with the bestiaries. For example, Peter Cornwall in his *Pantheologus* aims to present an alphabetical list and brief interpretation of all animals mentioned in the Bible, including the fantastic ones, such as the basilisk and unicorn.[35] The great spiritual encyclopedias of the thirteenth century, including the *Speculum naturale* compiled by Vincent of Beauvais, and Batholomew the Englishman's *De proprietatibus rerum*, also include information about imaginary animals. In this practice, later medieval writers, including the bestiarists, were simply continuing a tradition of exegesis on animals from Scriptures—whether observable in the countryside or not—begun much earlier;[36] and the combined authoritative weight of antiquity and Scriptures ensured the continued acknowledgment of certain mythological creatures. Later, from Edward Topsell's point of view, as a compilation of both biblical and Classical learning, it is likely that the bestiary itself also enjoyed a certain authoritative status.

Even those writers who sought to get at the "truth" of the fantastic animal stories by relying on the authority of antiquity were faced with the realization that much of this information was based on fable, making it even more difficult to distinguish "fact" from "fiction."[37] That this was still a recognized problem by the seventeenth century is apparent in Topsell's introduction to *The History of Four-Footed Beasts*:

> The second thing which I have promised to affirm in this discourse is the truth of the history of the creatures, for the mark of a good writer is to follow truth and not deceivable fables. I would not have the reader of these histories imagine that I have inserted or related all that is ever said of these beasts but only so much as is said by many. And if at anytime, I have set down only a single testimony, it was because the matter was clear and needed no further proof. . . . [38]

Topsell, like Albert the Great, bases much of his information on
Pliny, Aelian, Solinus, and Aristotle, and in this way his approach is a
continuation of the medieval tradition. In fact, there are some important
parallels in Albert's and Topsell's respective investigative methods,
which can be observed by a close look at their treatment of a few
selected imaginary creatures.

One of the fantastic creatures of great interest to both men is the
dragon. The Bodley 764 entry on the dragon is representative of the
prevailing wisdom at the time of Albert's compilation:

> [the dragon is] larger than all the rest of the serpents and than all
> other animals in the world. . . . It has a crest, a small mouth and
> narrow nostrils, through which it breathes, and it puts out its tongue.
> Its strength is not in its teeth, but its tail, and it harms more by blows
> than by force of impact. It has no harmful poison. But it is said that it
> does not need poison in order to kill, because it slays anything which
> it embraces. . . . Its homes are Ethiopia and India, where there is
> always heat.[39]

According to the bestiary moralization, the dragon symbolizes the
devil, who deceives "fools with hopes of vainglory and human
pleasures." The dragon is also identified as the devil in Scriptures:
"And the great dragon was cast out, that old serpent, called the Devil,
and Satan, which deceiveth the whole world . . . " (Apoc. 12:9). In the
Bible, dragons are so consistently identified with evil that the term,
"dragon" was used during the Middle Ages to denote sin in general.[40]

The dragon is also a major player in the stories of other bestiary
animals, most notably in those about the panther and the elephant, in
which it functions as a figure of the devil in opposition to the other
beasts, who symbolize Christ.[41] There is some variety in the bestiary
dragon images, but in general they represent a serpentine, four-legged,
winged beast with a bestial head, not unlike depictions of dragons in
other medieval contexts.

Albert and Topsell both testify to the existence of dragons.
Interestingly, Albert dismisses the findings of some earlier writers on
the creature but accepts the word of others such as Semerion and
Avicenna, the latter whom Albert records as having actually
encountered a dragon. He indicates that the term "dragon" refers to
numerous species that range widely in size and type. He asserts that
"investigation has shown that immense dragons exist not only in India

but also in other regions," mentioning the Middle East as one such additional location.[42] Some of the bestiary claims he dismisses or questions include the belief that dragons can fly and that they can crush elephants with their tails as depicted in many bestiary illustrations. (figure I, p. xxx).[43]

Following the bestiary tradition, Topsell categorizes dragons under the heading of "serpents" but says that they are distinguishable from other serpents by the comb on their heads and by their beards.[44] His account also includes physical descriptions of the various types, their preferred foods, where they can be found—including Ethiopia and India—as well as how to kill them. He also discusses evidence for the existence of some tame dragons as well as some interesting miscellaneous facts such as that dragons will become fat if they eat eggs.[45] The "truth value" of this information is enhanced by the very factual and straightforward manner in which it is presented, a common rhetorical persuasive strategy applied to the description of fantastic things since the Classical period.[46]

The modern rationalists, on the other hand, have postulated that the term "dragon" (*draco*) has been widely misinterpreted. According to this theory, the bestiary dragon is simply a type of serpent, probably a python or other constrictor snake based on the description of the method it uses to kill its prey and supported by certain of the bestiary images that depict the dragon crushing an elephant in constrictor fashion (figure I, p. xxx).[47] While this particular type of image indeed depicts a decidedly serpentine "dragon," if imagery is to be used as evidence of a particular identification, then the constrictor hypothesis certainly does not fit the other more bestial, flying and fire-breathing dragons illustrated in the bestiaries, such as Harley 3244 (figure 3), or for that matter, dragons depicted in other artistic contexts.

Both Albert the Great and Topsell are especially interested in the unicorn, a fantastic animal that played an important religious role in the bestiaries. The Bodley 764 entry for the unicorn reads as follows;

> The unicorn . . . is a little beast, not unlike a young goat, and extraordinarily swift. It has a horn in the middle of its brow, and no hunter can catch it. But it can be caught in the following fashion: a girl who is a virgin is led to the place where it dwells, and is left there alone in the forest. As soon as the unicorn sees her, it leaps into her lap and embraces her, and goes to sleep there; then the hunters capture it and display it in the king's palace.[48]

The bestiarist states that the unicorn is a figure of Christ and quotes a number of Bible passages that refer to the unicorn, such as Psalm 92:10: "My horn shalt thou exalt like the horn of an unicorn." The horn is said to represent Christ's unity with his father and its small size to signify Christ's humility in assuming humanity.[49]

Albert treats the unicorn in a brief entry in which he presents a general description of the animal and repeats the bestiary story of the virgin entrapment, introducing an element of doubt as to the veracity of the latter with the comment, "It is alleged. . . ." On the other hand, he cites the example of a unicorn once exhibited by Pompey in Rome and notes that young unicorns can be caught and tamed.[50] Thus he treats this creature with some degree of ambivalence, probably because as a churchman, he is unwilling to deny the existence of an animal mentioned in Scriptures.

Topsell makes very clear in his excerpt on the unicorn in the *History of Four-Footed Beasts* that he is referring to the "true" unicorn and not some other one-horned creature.[51] Although it is not entirely certain what other one-horned creature he might have had in mind, he seems to be acknowledging the fact that there are conflicting reports on this animal. One clue may be the double entry the unicorn often receives in the bestiaries, albeit under three different names: *rhinoceros, monoceros,* and *unicornis.* In general, the story of the unicorn and the virgin, the religious moralization, and narrative illustration is reserved for *unicornis* (figure E, p. xxvi), while the *monoceros* or *rhinoceros* entries simply describe a ferocious, one-horned animal accompanied by a simple portrait of a single-horned creature.[52] In spite of the confusion surrounding the unicorn, Topsell indicates that to doubt the beast's existence would involve a lack of faith in the power and glory of God, as noted above.[53] He also includes a rather lengthy discussion dismissing the claims that the unicorn had been mistakenly identified and was actually an animal such as the Indian ass.[54] In this he seems to be anticipating the arguments made by the modern rationalists.

That is, like the dragon and the siren, the rationalists have sought to find a real-life counterpart for the unicorn in order to suggest another case of mistaken identity. One investigation points to the oryx as the animal erroneously identified by the ancients as the unicorn. Physical resemblance (!) is the main thrust of the argument. The oryx has the body of a horse with the cloven hooves of an antelope and is known to live in both Africa and the Near East. The horns of an oryx are very soft and thus often become deformed as the animal grows and can result in one horn being reduced to a curly stump. Therefore, it has been asserted that the unicorn could represent either the one-horned Indian rhinoceros or the two-horned black rhinoceros.[55]

The caladrius is another famous bestiary creature popular in both ancient and medieval sources.[56] For example, it is described by both Aristotle and Albert the Great, both of whom seem to accept its existence.[57] Numerous rationalist suggestions have been made as to its "prototype," and thus it has been identified as various birds from parrots to seagulls.[58] Again, the argument is unresolvable and does not take into account the function of the caladrius in the bestiaries as a prognosticating figure of Christ.

The caladrius is most notable for its ability to predict the future, especially in matters of health. It was believed to be able to give signs to indicate whether or not a person would recover from an illness. If the bird turned and faced the ailing person, that person would recover and live as illustrated in Harley 4751 (figure J, p. xxxi). The caladrius first leeches the illness from the sick one and then "it flies up to the sun, burns off the sickness, scatters it in the air, and cures the sick man."[59] If, on the other hand, the caladrius turns away from the person, then he would surely die, as depicted in Harley 3244 (f. 52).[60]

In the bestiaries, the caladrius is an entirely white bird. Like the unicorn, the caladrius is likened Christ, who is "wholly white, without a speck of black" and who turned away from the Jews because of their lack of faith in him.[61] Albert's comments on the caladrius are based on its prognosticating power as discussed in the bestiaries, and, while he does not dispute the story outright, he hedges somewhat by noting "augury by the use of these birds does not fall within the scope of our present inquiry."[62]

In antiquity, it was believed that the caladrius could cure jaundice and that its dung was useful in curing eye ailments, especially failing sight.[63] Like the unicorn, the griffin, and the dragon, the caladrius was of interest for its medicinal value. Various ancient and medieval medicinal remedies required the use of animal body parts, both real and imaginary.[64] For example, the bestiarists note that the beaver is hunted for his testicles, which have special medicinal value.[65] In the realm of the imaginary, dragon fat is useful in treating ulcers and scaring away demons, and their tongues when boiled with wine can ward off nightmares.[66] The unicorn's horn is of special interest for its ability to detect and act as an antidote for poisons.[67] In addition, if the horn is ground down and boiled in wine it may be used as a whitener for the teeth.[68] The continuing trade in narwhale horns, which passed for unicorn horns, bears witness to a thriving belief in the unicorn's magical and medicinal powers.[69]

Medicinal uses of animals were by no means restricted to the imaginary type, but the fact that certain ailments required body parts from the latter raises an interesting question. Did the dissemination of remedies involving the use of imaginary animals constitute indirect evidence of belief in their existence? It is difficult to speculate on this, but in a world where people died from common ailments such as the flu, it has been suggested that remedies involving *exotica* gave people hope who were otherwise well aware of the limitations of local treatments.[70] Viewed negatively, that cures for various afflictions involved fantastic animals may have underscored the fact that chances of recovery were rather slim.

Perhaps the most useful way to approach the problem of imaginary animals is to hypothesize that medievals knew quite well that these animals did not exist and to view the question as to whether or not they actually existed as irrelevant. That is, what was important was that imaginary creatures serve a didactic purpose. As mentioned earlier, real animals were frequently represented in very non-naturalistic ways which strongly suggests that the bestiary images did not function as field guides or direct representations of the natural world. Especially in the bestiaries, animals—both real and fantastic—had a different role to fill, which was to provide metaphors or symbols for a variety of Christian mandates and beliefs. Perhaps, then, the imaginary animals in the bestiaries were used to fill certain "spiritual gaps" for which the real animals were not as readily adaptable.

Not all of the imaginary creatures were moralized, however, and these may have had other types of functions. One example is the bonnacon, a composite creature with the body and mane of a horse and the head of a bull. The bonnacon was described by Pliny and Solinus, the bestiarists, and Albert the Great and is still of interest centuries later in Topsell's treatise. Interestingly, Topsell attempts to correct the earlier accounts of this animal, in that he notes that bonnacons can be found in Paonia and "not in Lydia and Phrygia, as Solinus and Albertus have delivered."[71]

The bonnacon's horns curled in on themselves and were therefore useless as a defense mechanism. The bestiarists describe the creature's alternative means of defense: "When it flees, the excrement from the stomach of the beast produces such a stench over an area of two acres that its heat singes everything it touches. By this poisonous dung it keeps all pursuers at bay."[72] It is this intriguing characteristic of the bonnacon that is usually chosen for bestiary illustration. For example, both the Ashmole Bestiary and Harley 4751 show a group of hunters spearing the bonnacon who looks back at them to assess the effectiveness of the attack (figure 4).

Modern rationalists have suggested that the bonnacon is actually a European bison, pointing to its physical characteristics which position it in the family of cloven-hoofed animals.[73] It has also been pointed out that the bonnacon's defense strategy is similar to what actually happens when some animals are frightened,[74] albeit greatly exaggerated in the bestiary texts and images. It is again impossible to say whether this animal may have been based on a bison, but as bison do not launch anal attacks, the creature—if indeed based on something "real"—is at best a composite invention. Lacking a moralization and given the apparently comical nature of the images, it has been suggested that the bonnacon may have functioned as a humorous figure in the bestiaries.[75]

Whether people believed in imaginary animals whole-heartedly, half-heartedly, or not at all, studies that seek a one-to-one matchup between imaginary and actual living beasts serve only to deny medievals a richly faceted imagination that allowed for inventive use of animals in symbolic ways and as carriers of theological meaning. In pragmatic terms, today as in ancient times, the rationalist approach brings us no clearer understanding of contemporary views of imaginary animals, nor does it afford any insights into the function of animal symbolism in medieval Christianity. It is therefore more useful to hypothesize that medievals knowingly and effectively used fantastic creatures in art, literature, and theology, and that they had discernible reasons for doing so. Ultimately, focusing on these reasons rather than on problems of animal identification will provide a better understanding of how animal symbolism functioned in the bestiaries and within the broader context of medieval popular religion.

NOTES

1. See, for example, the Monstrous Races and mythological creatures depicted in the University Library Bestiary, Fitzwilliam 254, the Westminster Abbey Bestiary, and Douce 88.

2. A study that explores the question of fabulous beings in a more general context is Gerhardt Von Christoph, "Gab es im Mittelalter Fabelwesen?" *Wirkendes Wort* 38 (1988), 156-71. Apropos the bestiary creatures, Von Christoph stresses their symbolic rather than "empirical" significance (p. 164).

3. Modern catalogs of imaginary animals include John Vinycomb, *Fictitious and Symbolic Creatures in Art* (London, 1906); Richard Barber and Anne Riches, *A Dictionary of Fabulous Beasts* (Woodbridge, 1971); Malcolm South, *Mythical and Fabulous Creatures* (New York, 1987); and *Mythical Beasts*, ed. John Cherry (London, 1995). Like the bestiaries, Rowland 1973 and Rowland 1978 treat both real and imaginary creatures.

4. On naturalism in the bestiaries, see Hassig 1995, 91-92, 141-43.

5. On Villard's lion, see Hans R. Hahnloser, *Villard de Honnecourt* (Graz, 1972), 143-50.

6. Jonathan Alexander, *Medieval Illuminators and Their Methods of Work* (New Haven, 1992), 95-120.

7. See Lynn White, Jr., "Natural Science and Naturalistic Art in the Middle Ages," *American Historical Review* 52 (1947), 421-35; and Brunsdon Yapp, "Birds in Bestiaries: Medieval Knowledge of Nature," *The Cambridge Review* 105 (1984), 183-90.

8. Klingender 1971, 340.

9. The crocodile is mentioned and depicted in entries devoted to the hydrus. See White 1954, 178-80; Barber 1993, 190-91.

10. White 1954, 51-52; Barber 1993, 63-64.

11. Reproduced in Barber 1993, 63.

12. Proponents of this view include T.H. White (1954) and Wilma George (see below). The identification of bestiary animals with "real" ones is an organizing principle in Wilma George and Brunsdon Yapp, *The Naming of the Beasts: Natural History in the Medieval Bestiary* (London, 1991).

13. Palaephatus, *On Unbelievable Tales*, trans. Jacob Stern (Wauconda [IL], 1996).

14. See Paul Veyne, *Did the Greeks Believe in Their Myths?: An Essay on the Constitutive Imagination* (Chicago, 1988). In this study, Veyne seeks to invalidate the question posed by the title by collapsing the distinction between "myth" and "truth."

15. George and Yapp 1991, 52-53.

16. Pliny, *Naturalis historia* 8.30.73-4 (Rackham 1940, 54-5); Solinus, *Collectanea rerum memorabilium* 52.35 (ed. Mommsen 1958, 189; trans. Arthur Golding, *The Excellent and Pleasant Worke of . . . Caius Julius Solinus* [London, 1587] [1955 reprint], cap. lxiiii, f. Dd4v).

17. Wilma George, "The Yale," *Journal of the Warburg and Courtauld Institutes* 31 (1968), 423.

18. For the Cambridge Bestiary yale entry, see White 1954, 54.

19. G.C. Druce, "Notes on the History of the Heraldic Jall or Yale," *Archaeological Journal* 68 (1911), 181.

20. George 1968, 423; Payne 1990, 47.

21. George 1968, 428.

22. George and Yapp 1991, 100.

23. Stern 1996, 7.

24. See J.M. Courtès, "The Theme of 'Ethiopia' and 'Ethiopians' in Patristic Literature," in J. Devisse, *The Image of the Black in Western Art II: From the Early Christian Era to the "Age of Discovery,"* Part 1: *From the Demonic Threat to the Incarnation of Sainthood*, trans. W.G. Ryan (New York, 1979), 9-32.

25. Stern 1996, 8; Plato, *Phaedrus* 229 C-D (trans. Alexander Nehamas and Paul Woodruff [Indianapolis, 1995], 5).

26. Wilma George, "The Bestiary: A Handbook of the Local Fauna," *Archives of Natural History* 10/2 (1981), 191.

27. See Friedman 1981, 24-25. A rationalist view of the Monstrous Races is also taken in Robert Garland, *The Eye of the Beholder: Deformity and Disability in the Graeco-Roman World* (Ithaca, 1995), 160-61.

28. On siren classification, see Hassig 1995, 108.

29. Scanlan 1987 is an English translation of Books 22-26 of the *De animalibus*, which include a number of imaginary animals.

30. Scanlan 1987, 12-14. On Albert's borrowings, errors, and "barbarous Latin," see Pauline Aiken, "The Animal History of Albertus Magnus and Thomas of Cantimpré," *Speculum* 22 (1947), 205-25.

31. Edward Topsell, *The History of Four-Footed Beasts and Serpents and Insects*, 3 vols. (New York, 1967) is an unabridged republication of the 1658 edition. Excerpts from both *The Historie of Foure-footed Beastes* and *The Historie of Serpents* have been edited by Malcolm South in *Topsell's Histories of Beasts* (Chicago, 1981).

32. Scanlan 1987, 17; South 1981, xi.

33. Alberto M. Simonetta, "La conoscenza del mondo animale dalla romanità al medioevo," in *L'Uomo di fronte al mondo animale nell'alto medioevo*, 2 vols. (Spoleto, 1985), I, 122.

34. South 1981, 169.

35. London, British Library, MS Royal 7.C.XIV.

36. One notable ninth-century example is Rabanus Maurus, *Allegoriam in universam sacram scripturae* (*PL* 112:849-1088).

37. South 1981, xi.

38. *Ibid.*, 4.

39. Trans. Barber 1993, 183. "Draco maior cunctorum serpentium siue omnium animantium super terram. . . . Est autem cristatus, ore paruo, et artis fistulis per quas trahit spiritum, et linguam exerit. Uim autem non in dentibus sed in cauda habet, et uerbere potius quam rictu nocet. Innoxius tamen est a venenis. Sed ideo huic ad mortem faciendam uenena non esse necessaria dicunt, quod si quem ligauerit, occidit. . . . Gignitur autem in Ethiopia et in India ubi in ipso incendio est iugis estus" (Bodley 764, f. 93).

40. Vinycomb 1906, 70.

41. See White 1954, 14-15 (panther) and 25-26 (elephant). In the elephant entries, depiction of the elephant giving birth while being menaced by the dragon was less common than that of the battle elephant, even though the dragon story is emphasized in the *Physiologus*. An especially dramatic image of the elephant-dragon episode is in Laud Misc. 247 (f. 163v).

42. *De animalibus* 25.25 (trans. Scanlan 1987, 402).

43. *De animalibus* 25.27 (trans. Scanlan 1987, 403-404). See also the color reproduction of the dragon crushing the elephant in Royal 12.C.XIX (f. 62) in Payne 1990, 82.

44. South 1981, 75. The bestiaries often describe the dragon as largest or king of serpents.

45. South 1981, 76.

46. François Hartog, *The Mirror of Herodotus: The Representation of the Other in the Writing of History*, trans. Janet Lloyd (Berkeley, 1988), 256-58.

47. George and Yapp 1991, 200.

48. Trans. Barber 1993, 36. "Unicornis, qui et rinoceros a grecis dicitur, hanc habet naturam: pusillum animal est, simile hedo, acerrimum nimis. Unum cornu habens in medio capite, et nullus uenator eum capet potest. Sed hoc argumento capitur: puella uirgo ducitur ubi moratur, et ibi dimittitur in silua sola. At ille mox ut uiderit eam, insilit in sinu eius et complectitur eam, et sic in gremio eius dormiens; ab exploratoribus comprehenditur et exhibetur in palacio regis" (Bodley 764, f. 10v).

49. McCulloch 1962, 179-80. For a comprehensive study of the unicorn, see J.W. Einhorn, *Spiritalis Unicornis* (Munich, 1976).

50. *De animalibus* 22.144 (trans. Scanlan 1987, 180-81).

51. South 1981, 169.

52. See for example the *monoceros* entry in Bodley 764, f. 22 (trans. Barber 1993, 57). On double entries in the bestiaries, see Hassig 1995, 94-96.

53. South 1981, 169.

54. *Ibid.*, 170.

55. George and Yapp 1991, 87.

56. See George C. Druce, "The Caladrius and Its Legend, Sculptured upon the Twelfth-Century Doorway of Alne Church, Yorkshire," *Archaeological Journal* 69 (1912), 381-416.

57. Aristotle, *Historia animalium* 8.3 (615a 1) (Aristotle, *History of Animals*, trans. D. M. Balme [Cambridge, MA, 1991], 269); Albert the Great, *De animalibus* 23.31 (trans. Scanlan 1987, 210-11).

58. White 1954, 115, n. 1.; Rowland, 1978, 17.

59. Trans. Barber 1993, 130.

60. Reproduced in Payne 1990, 66.

61. White 1954, 115-16; Barber 1993, 130-31.

62. *De animalibus* 23.31 (trans. Scanlan 1987, 211).

63. Aelian, *De natura animalium* 17.13 (Aelian, *On the Characteristics of Animals*, trans. A. F. Scholfield [London, 1959], III, 339); Peter Murray Jones, *Medieval Medical Miniatures*, London, 1984, 75.

64. The bestiaries make occasional references to an animal's medicinal value. Besides Albert the Great's *De animalibus*, another prominent treatise on the medicinal use of animals is Hildegard of Bingen's *Physica* (*PL* 197:1117-1352).

65. White 1954, 28-29; Barber 1993, 43-44.

66. South 1981, 83.

67. South 1981, 172; Einhorn 1976, 241-44.

68. South 1981, 173. On other uses of the unicorn's horn, see Einhorn 1976, 244-47.

69. Margaret B. Freeman, *The Unicorn Tapestries* (New York, 1976), 29.

70. Nancy G. Sirasi, *Medieval and Early Renaissance Medicine* (Chicago, 1990), 147.

71. Topsell 1967, I, 53.

72. Trans. Barber 1993, 48.

73. George and Yapp 1991, 75.

74. White 1954, 33, n. 1.

75. Hassig 1990/1991, 159.

Figure 1. Manticore. London, British Library, MS Royal 12.F.XIII, f. 24v.
Photo: by permission of the British Library.

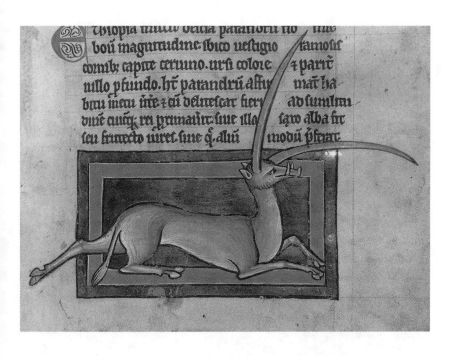

Figure 2. Yale. London, British Library, MS Royal 12.C.XIX, f. 30.
Photo: by permission of the British Library.

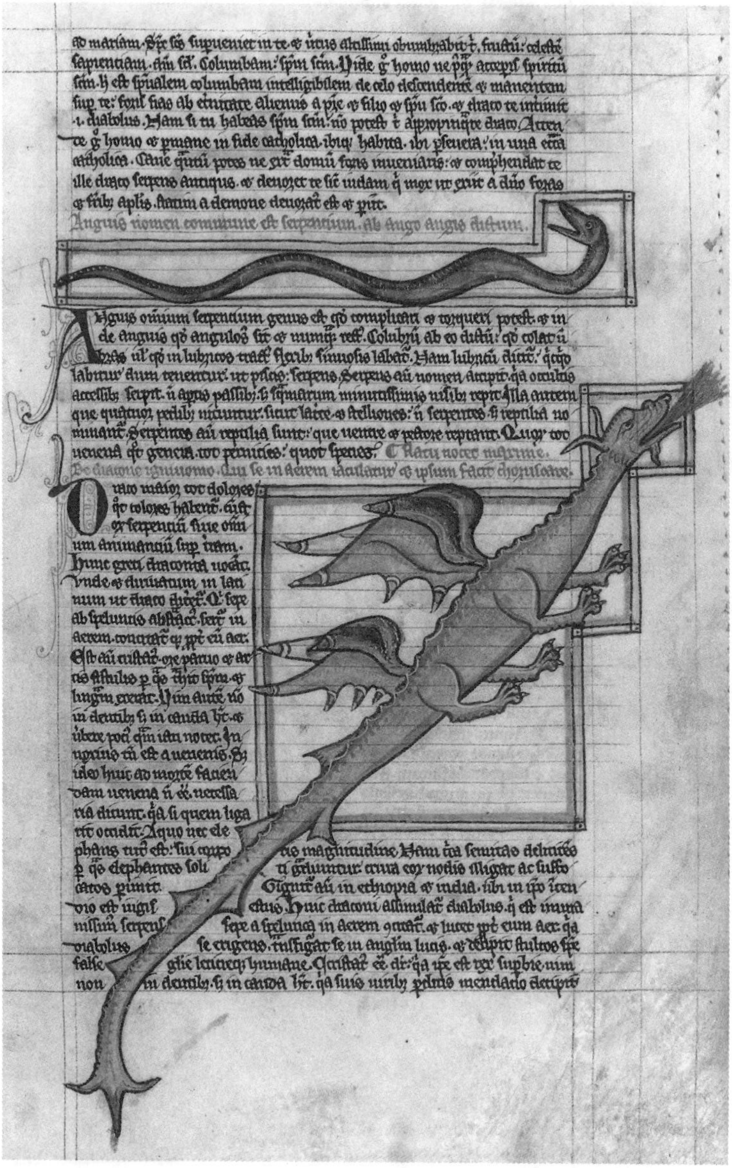

Figure 3. Dragon. London, British Library, MS Harley 3244, f. 59.
Photo: by permission of the British Library.

Figure 4. Bonnacon. London, British Library, MS Harley 4751, f. 11.
Photo: by permission of the British Library.

Classical Ideology in the Medieval Bestiary

J. Holli Wheatcroft

The links between the medieval bestiaries and Classical art and culture are multiple and pervasive. The significant degree to which the bestiaries appropriate and reshape ancient traditions and iconography is often acknowledged but rarely addressed in detail. In fact, ancient sources were incorporated into the later medieval bestiaries both directly and indirectly, by way of the animal imagery established in the early *Physiologus* manuscripts as well as in Classical imagery in different media. This essay will focus on relationships between the bestiary snake and phoenix and the art and culture of the Romans, predominantly from the first to fourth centuries A.D. Roman art of this period exerted the greatest influence on bestiary iconography doubtless owing to its strong impact on the development of medieval art in general as well as to the fact that the core *Physiologus* text was compiled in Alexandria while it was under Roman rule.[1]

The difficulty of identifying a specific source for any given bestiary animal legend has been duly noted, as these often represent the culmination of several strands of tradition.[2] Scholars have incorporated this idea into their analysis of literary sources, but in the case of iconographical study of the bestiaries, the imagery's formal indebtedness to Classical animal illustration is usually acknowledged without extensive elaboration.[3] Most of these discussions of the bestiary's reliance upon Classical art focus either on the assimilation of Classical literary sources into the bestiary texts or on the iconographical and stylistic similarities between the bestiaries and early medieval manuscripts, such as the Vatican Vergil, Cotton Genesis, and the Utrecht Psalter. Although both types of studies demonstrate the undeniable impact of earlier traditions on the bestiaries, they only partially address specific issues relevant to a highly complex problem.[4] This essay will attempt to take a close look at how the medieval bestiarists appropriated and reworked not only Classical iconographical motifs but also pagan religious beliefs in their descriptions and images of selected animals. Focus will be on the snake and the phoenix because both of these creatures enjoyed a long tradition from ancient times, were essential to the early *Physiologus* roster, and continued as ubiquitous inclusions in the later medieval bestiaries.

It has been well established that at the time of the *Physiologus'* compilation during the second century A.D., Early Christian art was a compelling synthesis of Roman pagan art invested with Christian meanings and iconographical invention which drew heavily upon Roman imperial models.[5] Such syncretic art helped facilitate the necessary ideological shift from the earlier religious system to the new one. In order to establish its status as a superior and powerful institution as well as to clearly communicate the new ideology, the Church's visual dialog had to be in the "vernacular," and hence the familiar subjects, compositions, and iconographical formulae of the Roman emperors were appropriated for use in the new context. Owing to the high recognition factor, pagan motifs thus allowed the Church to communicate ideas which conscripted the support of well-established and powerful symbols in order to shift public allegiance from the Roman emperors to Christ.[6]

The *Physiologus* tradition was an integral part of this syncretic process, relying as it does in numerous ways on Classical Roman texts and imagery but recasting and reshaping these in order to communicate new Christian moralizations. However, art historical study of these manuscripts thus far has been limited to a search for stylistic and iconographical forerunners for the animal imagery. In this regard, the ninth-century Bern Physiologus, as the earliest extant illustrated copy of the *Physiologus*, is frequently cited as heavily indebted to Alexandrian painting, therefore providing a distant window on Classical style and iconography.[7]

This can be readily demonstrated with a few brief examples. In the Bern Physiologus, the depiction of the lion huddling in a cave shows a dependence on Classical compositions (f. 8). In particular, the presentation of the cave interior as a cross-sectional view can be traced to Classical representations of caves, such as that observable in the image of the lioness and her cubs on one of the so-called Grimani reliefs.[8] The antique garb worn by the hunter spearing the snake in the Bern manuscript (f. 12v) is another obvious and frequently-cited vestige of Classical illustration, and also similar to figure types depicted in Classical zoological manuscripts.[9] The anthropomorphized image of the sun as a symbol of Christ in the image of the sun-lizard (f. 8v) is an appropriation of the Classical Helios image, observable in various media in Early Christian art, such as the famous third-century mosaic in the Tomb of the Julii in the Vatican.[10] Aerial views of small bestiary creatures such as moles and frogs have been compared to zoological drawings in Early Christian copies of Dioscorides' *De materia medica.*[11] Other bestiary animal images based directly on Classical models include those of two snakes horizontally intertwined in the manner of the Classical *caduceus*[12] and the popular bestiary image of the caladrius, which retains the essentially Classical pose of a figure reclining in bed (figure J, p. xxxi).[13]

The survival of Classical culture in the bestiaries, however, was not limited to style and iconography. Despite the fact that Christians necessarily modified pagan legends for their own purposes, they incorporated recognizable portions of texts from Classical literature in both the *Physiologus* and the later bestiaries. Michael Curley clearly demonstrates this sometimes "radical metamorphosis" in his discussion of the transformation of Classical animal legends into stories which were reshaped in order to communicate important tenets of Christian belief.[14] The legend of the snake is a premier example, which Curley analyzes in relation to the text tradition,[15] and that I will reexamine in order to highlight specific relationships between Classical depictions of the snake, its illustration in the Bern Physiologus, and ancient ideological beliefs and practices concerning snakes.

According to the *Physiologus* and the later bestiaries, the snake has three natures. First, when the snake grows old, its eyes become dim. In order to rejuvenate itself, it fasts for forty days and forty nights, after which its skin cracks. It then crawls through a narrow crevice in a rock in order to slough off its old skin. The moralization indicates that the old skin signifies past sins, and by sloughing off the skin, the snake physically and spiritually renews itself. Second, when the snake is thirsty, it leaves its poisonous venom in the pit where it lives, so that the water from which it will drink is not contaminated. This behavior compares to the faithful, who must not bring their unworthy desires to church. Third, when the snake is attacked, it will expose its body and protect its head, "For the head of every man is Christ" (1 Cor. 11:3).

It is easy to detect the Christian additions to the pagan accounts of the snake, such as fasting for forty days and forty nights, and the moralized interpretation of the snake's other "natural" habits. As Curley has shown, it was Classical lore that informed the *Physiologus* stories, providing the core around which the Christian author(s) worked their moralizations. In fact, it has been suggested that the Christian elements of the *Physiologus* may well have been grafted upon a pre-existing collection of animal lore, which has led to a two-author theory vis-à-vis its composition: the first author compiled the tales, and a subsequent author provided the religious moralizations.[16]

Pagan imagery, like the appropriated texts, was either modified or left largely intact, albeit in the new Christian context. In the first representation of the snake in the Bern Physiologus (figure 1), we have an example of a modified version of ancient iconography.[17] The Bern image depicts the first of the snake natures described in the text and thus shows the animal sloughing off its old skin. In the later bestiaries, such as the Cambridge Bestiary, the snake typically crawls through a small gate rather than the rock described in the text (figure 2), thus providing an allegorical visual reference to the famous biblical passage to which the snake's behavior refers: "The gate is narrow and there is tribulation on the way which leads toward life, and few are those who enter through it" (Matt. 7:14). At first glance, it appears that the Bern image illustrates the snake in precisely this way, showing a large blue snake slithering through an architectural form. However, I would suggest that the snake is crawling not through a gate but through an altar.[18] Owing to its poor state of preservation, the imminent appropriateness of the gate motif in light of the biblical verse just cited and the fact that the later bestiaries normally depict a gate, a strong argument could be made in favor of a gate identification. But if Classical iconography and religious beliefs are taken into account, its identification as an altar is perhaps more convincing. In particular, the image possesses strong visual affinities with Roman funerary monuments featuring snakes and altars, and may therefore constitute an appropriation and subsequent Christianization of pagan views of death and the afterlife.

In the ancient Roman world, snakes had a predominantly positive reputation. Snakes were kept as pets, were associated with fertility and healing, were believed to have prophetic powers, and were regarded as the beneficent spirits of the dead.[19] It is this last association that wrought a key influence on the snake image in the Bern Physiologus. In Classical art, the snake as the spirit of the dead is either depicted among other figures of the deceased or of favored deities, or else it lies beside an altar which bears one or more eggs. In both types of imagery, the snake represents the family's founding ancestor or ancestress. Therefore, a *lararium* (shrine) wall painting from Pompeii depicts snakes approaching an egg-bearing altar in order to devour the eggs, ancient symbols of life (figure 3).[20]

Incorporating Classical snake funerary iconography into the Christian *Physiologus* helped fulfill the political and religious objectives of the early Church, by transforming a familiar symbol from a pagan to a Christian context after investing it with new meaning. That is, just as the text concerning the snake was modified to serve the new religion, so the imagery accompanying it harnessed the power of pre-existent symbology. In this new context, the snake has transformed from the dead founder of the family to the Christian sinner seeking spiritual renewal.[21] The altar retains its significance as bearer of life, but the motif of the eggs is absent. This is likely the case because to have included them would have been to render an unequivocal representation of a pagan, rather than Christian, altar. Another possible explanation for their exclusion is that the eggs play no discernible role in the *Physiologus* version of the snake story, and therefore do not appear in the image, while the altar arguably functions as an allegorical interpretation of the rock through which the snake must crawl to slough off its skin. That the later bestiary images depict gates rather than altars (or do they?) may be the consequence of greater distance from Classical artistic tradition, plus the fact that a syncretic function for images was no longer a crucial one in a world where, by now, Christianity was the undisputed dominant religion. That is, in the later bestiaries, the snake's altar may have transformed into a gate, much as Helios disappeared from the lizard iconography, and most human figures stopped wearing togas.

Another way of explaining the change from an altar to a gate may be to hypothesize a shift in interpretive emphasis of the snake story. The gate may signify the actual moment of the soul's salvation as it departs from one world and enters another, as the bestiaries sometimes indicate, "And we may seek the spiritual rock, Jesus, and the narrow crack, that is, the narrow gate."[22] The earlier image of the altar, on the other hand, may be the signifier of the actual process of salvation, whereby the sinner receives redemption by passing through the life-giving altar of Christ.

In sharp contrast to their dedicated entries, snakes in the *Physiologus* and bestiaries assume an extremely negative role in stories of other animals that identify snakes as symbols of evil and of the devil himself. One such story is that of the peridexion tree, also illustrated in the Bern Physiologus (figure 4). According to the text, the peridexion tree is a haven for doves seeking escape from the dragon, a term interchangeable both textually and pictorially with that of "snake" in the bestiaries.[23] The peridexion tree text indicates that the fruit of the tree is very sweet, and doves delight in eating it. The dragon is the enemy of doves, but it is afraid of the tree and especially of the tree's shadow. So the dragon waits outside of the shadow for a dove to stray, and if one does, the dragon slays it. The dove signifies the Holy Spirit; the tree, God the Father; and the shadow, the Son. The fruit is the wisdom of the Lord, and the serpent is the devil. This story teaches Christians the importance of maintaining their faith and of living in the protective arms of the Church: should the Christian stray outside the doors of the Church, he will be prey to the devil and perish just as Judas did when he left the Lord.[24]

Some of the later bestiary depictions of the peridexion tree show the snake squeezing through the trunk (figure 5). Still others show a pair of dragons, symmetrically positioned underneath a tree full of symmetrically-arranged doves.[25] However, the Bern image does not show the snake squeezing through the tree, nor does it depict a pair of dragons posed below it, but rather shows a single snake slithering below and hissing at the doves roosting in the tree's protective branches.

It is not immediately clear what all of this has to do with Classical snake iconography and religious meaning, but the iconography of the peridexion tree in fact relates to the idea of salvation expressed in the Bern image of the snake crawling through the altar (figure 1). The additional iconographical element of meaning is the tree. The tree has many functions in Christian iconography, one of which is as a symbol of knowledge. Such a symbol can be intricately linked to the snake-and-altar motif, as it is only through a knowledge of God that salvation is attained, and it is salvation, or ever-lasting life, that is offered through the altar. Whether the snake is crawling through an altar or through the trunk of a tree, the image may be said to draw upon the earlier idea of the snake as sinner, combined with the newer motif of the tree as knowledge. Therefore, such images may on at least one level represent the sinner seeking knowledge of God.

Other prominent medieval trees as signifiers of knowledge include the Tree of Knowledge in images of the Transgression and depictions of Christ's cross as the Tree of Life. The former is especially relevant to the present analysis, combining as it does the motif of a tree with that of a snake symbolizing the devil, just as the snake represents the devil in the bestiary peridexion tree images. Both the Tree of Knowledge and the Tree of Life have sacrificial connotations as articulated in a prayer recited before the canon of the Mass: "Death came from a tree, life was to spring from a tree; he who conquered on wood was also to be conquered on the wood."[26] Christ himself as well as Christ in the form of the Eucharist were both offered at the altar, the former metaphorically and the latter literally. In this sense, the motif of the snake crawling through a tree may also denote Christ's sacrifice that was necessary to redeem humanity.

The example of the peridexion tree points up the fact that allegorical representations of the snake, like many other bestiary motifs, are often contradictory. When the snake is featured alone, it is associated with goodness, but when the snake is depicted with other animals, such as in the entries for the peridexion tree, the ibis, the elephant, and the stag, it consistently symbolizes evil or the devil.

For example, the ibis is an unclean bird who feeds snake eggs to its young and thus represents the sinner who eschews spiritual matters in favor of evil and the mundane matters of this world (figure K, p. xxxii).[27] It is interesting to note the presence of eggs as a central motif in this story, perhaps a distant vestige of the Classical snake-altar imagery. In the entry for the dragon/snake, Bodley 764 indicates that the elephant fears suffocation by the coils of this creature which "lurks on the paths which elephants use because the devil lays the coils of sin in the path of all those who make their way to heaven and kills them when they are suffocated by sin."[28] The bestiaries also describe how the stag tramples the snake to death as figures of Christ and the devil, respectively.[29] This shifting significance of the snake would seem to undermine theories that assert an essentially mnemonic role for the bestiary imagery, of which it is claimed that the portrayal of an animal was "a kind of pictorial shorthand"[30] as "an alternative or a substitute for reading in an age of secular illiteracy."[31] In fact, such antithetical meanings fit well into the concept of duality that is an inherent part of Christian ideology and hence of the bestiaries. As expressed in the

Physiologus, many creatures have a dual nature, both laudable and blameworthy.[32]

This concept of duality is also present in Classical ideology, in which the snake also represented both good and evil. Favorable qualities include those of prophecy and fertility as outlined in the accounts of Propertius and Aelian.[33] But in other contexts, the snake symbolized an indulgence in sinful or earthly pleasures or else was a figure of evil. An example of the latter is the battle between the snake and the eagle in the myth of Ganymede, where the eagle carries the snake into the sky in its talons and functions as an allegory for the triumph of the heavenly realm over the dark chthonic forces.[34] The bestiaries express the same idea, as in the stag entry mentioned above, in which the stag's triumph over the snake is an allegory for Christ's triumph over the devil.[35]

The phoenix is another bestiary creature with a distinguished and ancient pedigree that in the bestiaries retained links with its past associations. The relationships between Classical traditions and the bestiary treatment of this bird are complex, because the exceptionally long history of the phoenix, traceable to ancient Egypt, ensured multiple meanings over time and in different cultural milieux. The phoenix has been portrayed in a variety of ways, but its identifying feature in both Classical and medieval art is the attribute of its funeral pyre (figure H, p. xxix).

According to ancient writers, after a very long time, the phoenix realizes it must die. It proceeds to construct a nest of spices and either lies in it and waits to die or else beats its wings to ignite the pyre in order to sacrifice itself.[36] Apropos this part of the phoenix story, the bestiaries put much emphasis on the spices, by identifying them allegorically as the "good works and virtues of the soul, and the sweet odors of good deeds."[37] However, the use of spices in burial practices is not a medieval invention but rather an ancient tradition. Spices were instrumental in the preparation of the deathbed, the grave, the bier, or the pyre, and their quantities indicated both the deceased's importance and the family's wealth.[38] In ancient rites, the pleasing fragrance of the spices symbolized the triumph of life over death. Much like the first nature of the snake in the Bern Physiologus, ancient funerary imagery is preserved in the later medieval bestiaries. This is again a case of ideological appropriation from pagan lore to facilitate Christian belief, demonstrated in both the *Physiologus* account of the phoenix and in Lactantius's famous poem, in which an association is made between the use of spices in the death of the phoenix and the acquisition of one hundred pounds of myrrh and aloe for the burial of Christ.[39] Of course, the most important aspect of the phoenix story from the Christian point of view is the bird's physically intact return from its own ashes, a powerful symbol of the resurrection of Christ as well as the general resurrection at the end of time.[40]

In the bestiaries, the phoenix not only sits in or beside its pyre but sometimes also perches in a tree or rests in a nest of branches.[41] The phoenix perched in a tree is a popular Early Christian symbol of Paradise, observable on death monuments. For example, on an Early Christian sarcophagus depicting the *traditio legis*, a phoenix is positioned above and to the right of the standing figure of Christ, who seemingly gestures to it with his raised hand.[42] This simple gesture communicates the idea that it is only through Christ that the true path to Paradise may be found. In some of the bestiaries, the phoenix is represented in two separate images, intended to signify the two important stages in the phoenix story. For example, in the Morgan Bestiary, the first illumination depicts the phoenix perched in the top of a tree gathering branches, and in its pendant image, the phoenix rises from the flames with outstretched wings (figure G, p. xxviii). In a Christian context, it has been suggested that the phoenix gathering branches to bring about its self-sacrifice is analogous to the story of Christ's Passion.[43]

A certain ideological overlap existed between the phoenix and the eagle in both Classical thought and in the medieval bestiaries. Close relationships between the phoenix and other "birds of the sun" such as the eagle, griffin, *benu*, *ziz*, *parodars*, and others resulted in the transference of characteristics from bird to bird.[44] For example, in Hebrew legend, the eagle performs the act of self-renewal by consuming itself in the fire of its own funeral pyre.[45] The related characteristic of the eagle illustrated and discussed in the bestiaries is that the eagle must renew its eyesight by flying into the sun's heat. To cool itself, the eagle then plunges three times into the water below, thus linking its behavior to the Christian concept of spiritual renewal via baptism.[46]

The phoenix and eagle were also closely associated in the ancient world. For example, flying into the sun's heat was an aspect of both eagle and phoenix behavior according to both Claudian and Dionysius.[47] In Roman art, both the phoenix and the eagle were symbols of the Empire, with the eagle representing primarily the

Empire's power and victory in battle[48] and the phoenix functioning as a symbol for the immortality of Rome.[49] Evidence of the latter symbolic value of the phoenix includes its frequent appearance on the reverse of Roman coins depicting the emperor on the obverse.[50]

It is interesting to note that the physical form of the phoenix rarely follows the description set forth in the bestiary texts, that is, as purple with multi-colored feathers. Instead, the bestiary phoenix often resembles an eagle[51] and although this is apparently not the case in Roman art, the conflation does apply to Roman thinking about phoenixes and eagles as outlined above.[52] For example, the eagle on a Greco-Roman tombstone functioned as a symbol of immortality, just as the phoenix functioned during the Middle Ages as a sign of the resurrection.[53] Also, just as the phoenix image was used in conjunction with that of the emperor, so was the eagle, as observable on a leaf from a Roman diptych depicting the apotheosis of Antoninus Pius or Julian.[54] Thus, in Classical art, both the phoenix and the eagle could symbolize immortality and the divinity of Emperors, just as the phoenix symbolized resurrection and the divinity of Christ in the medieval bestiaries.

The examples of the phoenix and snake demonstrate very well how the ideological and iconographical elements employed to communicate the Christian morals of the medieval bestiary owe much to earlier Classical traditions. While the focus of the present essay has been on Classical Roman art, it is certainly true that the iconographical and ideological history of many of the bestiary animals also carries influences from other ancient cultures not discussed such as those of Egypt, Greece, and India.[55] However, we can perhaps observe more clearly and easily links between the bestiaries and the art and thought of the Romans, since the Romans assimilated many earlier and neighboring cultures into their own, and it was Roman art that was most prevalent in Alexandria at the time of the compilation of the *Physiologus*. It is also true that medieval art in general owes its greatest debt to Classical Roman forms. Building upon the foundations first established by the *Physiologus* compilers, the bestiarists inherited from Classical antiquity a rich cultural interest in the natural habits and religious significance of animals. The ideological and iconographical traditions that arose from this interest formed an important legacy that was left to the medieval bestiarists, who skillfully manipulated Classical imagery and beliefs to serve Christian moral purposes as part of the larger syncretic process so crucial to the acceptance, development, and dissemination of early medieval Christianity.

NOTES

1. The *Physiologus* is generally dated to the second century A.D. (Curley 1979, xxx). It is in any case securely datable before 494 A.D., when it was cited by Gelasius I as a heretical book (Muratova 1984, 14).
2. Curley 1979, xxx.
3. See for example Muratova 1984, 41; and Carola Hicks, *Animals in Early Medieval Art* (Edinburgh, 1993), 106. Xenia Muratova ("Problemes de l'origine et des sources des cycles d'illustration des manuscrits des bestiaires," in *Épopée animale, fable, fabliau* [Paris, 1984], 390) states that the problem of determining whether there were antique prototypes for the bestiary images is unsolvable.
4. Earlier studies have focused on Classical influence on the earliest *Physiologus* manuscripts. See Helen Woodruff, "The Physiologus of Bern: A Survival of Alexandrian Style in a Ninth Century Manuscript," *Art Bulletin* 12 (1930), 226-53; Kurt Weitzmann, *Ancient Book Illumination* (Cambridge, 1959), 16-17; and Dimitri Tselos, "A Greco-Italian School of Illuminators and Fresco Painters," *Art Bulletin* 42 (1956), 1-30.
5. "The subtle reinterpretation of pre-Christian motifs, enabling them to survive as biblical and bestiary illustrations, encouraged continuity of belief in an age of massive spiritual transition, and was positively supported by the main patron, the church" (Hicks 1993, 272).
6. On the relationship between Early Christian and Roman imperial models, see the important revisionist study by Thomas Mathews *(The Clash of Gods: A Reinterpretation of Early Christian Art* [Princeton, 1993]).
7. See especially Woodruff 1930.
8. On the Grimani relief, see J.M.C. Toynbee, *Animals in Roman Life and Art* (London, 1973), 67 and pl. 21. On the stylistic similarity between the cave motif in the *Physiologus* and representations of caves in Hellenistic reliefs, see Woodruff 1930, 237.
9. Zoltan Kadar, *Survivals of Greek Zoological Illuminations in Byzantine Manuscripts* (Budapest, 1978), 48.
10. See Michael Gough, *The Origins of Christian Art* (London, 1973), fig. 10; and John Beckwith, *Early Christian and Byzantine Art*, 2d ed. (New Haven, 1979).
11. Kadar 1978, 21. See for example the St. Petersburg Bestiary, f. 46 (Muratova 1984).

12. See for example the intertwined snakes in the St. Petersburg Bestiary (f. 80v; Muratova 1984).

13. See George C. Druce, "The Caladrius and Its Legend, Sculptured Upon the Twelfth-Century Doorway of Alne Church, Yorkshire," *Archaeological Journal* 69 (1912), 381-416.

14. Curley 1979, xxiii-xxv; "'Physiologus,' . . . and the Rise of Christian Nature Symbolism," *Viator* 11 (1980), 1-10.

15. Curley 1980, 8-9.

16. Curley 1979, xxi.

17. The Bern Physiologus entry for the snake includes two subsequent snake images on f. 12 (depicting two snakes drinking and leaving poison in the pool) and f. 12v (showing a man spearing a snake, who exposes his body to the blow but protects his head). For these and subsequently cited images, see *Physiologus Bernensis*, ed. Christoph von Steiger and Otto Homburger (Basel, 1964) (facsimile).

18. Woodruff (1930, 248) identifies the object as an altar, and von Steiger and Homburger (1964, 36) describe the snake as crawling through a stone hewn as an altar, but neither offers any further discussion of the altar's significance.

19. Toynbee 1973, 223.

20. *Ibid.*

21. Curley 1979, 16.

22. "Et queramus spiritualem petram, Christum, et angustam fissuram, id est, angustam portam" (Ashmole Bestiary, f. 84).

23. Technically, "dragon" is designated in the *Physiologus* and bestiaries by the Latin *draco*, while "snake" is designated *serpens*. However, bestiary stories that refer to *draco* often depict a slithering snake as in numerous images of the dragon battling the elephant. For example, the St. Petersburg Bestiary shows what appears to be a large boa constricting the elephant, even though the text refers to *draco*, not *serpens* (f. 79). In fact, the bestiary entry for *draco* defines this creature as the "largest of serpents" (*draco maior cunctorum serpentium*); see White 1954, 165-67. Conversely, a reference to *serpens* might be accompanied by an image of a winged, bestial dragon. An example is the *jaculis*, described as a type of "flying snake" (*jaculis serpens volans*) and often depicted as a winged dragon with a dog's face as in the St. Petersburg Bestiary (f. 87). On the interesting relationship between dogs and bestiary serpents, see James I. McNelis, "A Greyhound Should Have 'Eres in the Manere of a Serpent,'": Bestiary Material in the Hunting Manuals *Livre de chasse* and *The Master of Game*," in Houwen 1997, 67-76.

24. White 1954, 160-61.

25. See, for example, Bodley 764 (f. 91v; Barber 1993, 180).

26. Gertrude Schiller, *Iconography of Christian Art*, trans. Janet Seligman (London, 1971), II, 134.

27. White 1954, 119-20.

28. Trans. Barber 1993, 183-84. "Circa semitas per quas elephantes gradiuntur delitescit, quia iter eorum ad celum nodis peccorum illigat, ac suffocatos perimit" (Bodley 764, ff. 93-93v). See also note 23, above.

29. White 1954, 37-40.

30. Klingender 1971, 383.

31. Hicks 1993, 278. See also Mary J. Carruthers, *The Book of Memory: A Study of Memory in Medieval Culture* (Cambridge, 1990), 126-27.

32. Muratova 1984, 23. "Duplicia autem sunt creatura, laudabilia et uituperabilia" (*Physiologus latinus versio Y*, ed. Francis J. Carmody [Berkeley, 1944], 106).

33. Toynbee 1973, 235. See Propertius, *Elegies*, 4.8.3-14 (Propertius, *Elegies*, trans. G.P. Goold [Cambridge, MA, 1990], 418-19); and Aelian, *De natura animalium* 11.16 (Aelian, *On the Characteristics of Animals*, 3 vols., trans. A.F. Scholfield [London, 1959], II, 380-83).

34. Rudolf Wittkower, *Allegory and the Migration of Symbols* (London, 1977), 29.

35. See Michael Bath, *The Image of the Stag: Iconographic Themes in Western Art* (Baden-Baden, 1992), 237-74; and Hassig 1995, 40-51.

36. See, for example, Pliny, *Naturalis historia* 10.2 (Rackham 1940, 292-95); Solinus, *Rerum memorabilium collectaneae* 33.12 (ed. Th. Mommsen [Berlin, 1958], 149-51), and Ovid, *Metamorphoses* 15.391-407 (Ovid, *Metamorphoses*, 2 vols., trans. F.J. Miller [London, 1933], II, 392-93). See also R. van den Broek, *The Myth of the Phoenix According to Classical and Early Christian Traditions* (Leiden, 1972), 67-69.

37. White 1954, 125-28.

38. van den Broek 1972, 169-71.

39. *Ibid.*, 170, n. 5.

40. On the phoenix and resurrection, see Jones in this volume.

41. See, for example, Bodley 764, f. 70 (Barber 1993, 141).

42. S. Giovanni in Valle, Verona, c. 400; see van den Broek 1972, pl. XXV,1.

43. van den Broek 1972, 76. Hassig (1995, 74-75) interprets the first of two phoenix images in the Ashmole Bestiary as parallel to crucifixion iconography.

44. van den Broek 1972, 398. For a functional comparison of the phoenix with the pelican, see Rundle Clark, "The Origin of the Phoenix, Part II," *University of Birmingham Journal* 2/2 (1950), 131.

45. Clark 1950, 135.

46. White 1954, 105-107.

47. Claudian, *Phoenix,* 30-35 (ed. and French trans. in Jean Hubaux and Maxime Leroy, *Le mythe du phénix dans les littératures grecque et latine* [Liège, 1939], XXI-XXVI); Dionysius, *De aucupio* 1.32 (van den Broek 1972, 161).

48. Wittkower 1977, 29.

49. Mary C. Fitzpatrick, *Lactanti De Ave Phoenice* (Philadelphia, 1933), 28; Hubaux and Leroy 1939.

50. For examples of such coins dated to the second century, see van den Broek 1972, pl. VI.

51. Hassig 1995, 225, n. 25.

52. Wittkower 1977, 37.

53. *Ibid.,* 31.

54. See Toynbee 1973, fig. 11.

55. On these and other cultural influences on Western medieval animal art, see Klingender 1971, 28-141.

Figure 1. Snake. *Physiologus*. Burgerbibliothek Bern, cod. 318, f. 11v.
Photo: Burgerbibliothek Bern.

Figure 2. Snake. Cambridge, University Library, MS Ii.4.26, f. 52.
Photo: by permission of the Syndics of Cambridge University Library.

Figure 3. Snakes at altar. *Lararium* wall painting. Naples, Museo Archeologico Nazionale. Photo: Museo Archeologico Nazionale.

Figure 4. Peridexion tree. *Physiologus.* Burgerbibliothek Bern, cod. 318, f. 17v.
Photo: Burgerbibliothek Bern.

erudenf eft arbo2 in india. fructuf autem huiuf arbo2if dul
cif eft totuf. et ualde fuauif. Columbe aū delectantū in fructi
buf hui' arbo2if. habitantez in ea pafcentef fructuf ef. Draco aū
inimicuf eft columbif. timetz arbo2em z umbm ef ubi colū
be mo2antur. et no poteft appinā́re arbo2i neqz umbze ef. Si enim vmbra
arbo2if uenit ad occidente. fugit ad o2iente. et fi uerit umbra ef ad o2ien
tem. fugit d2aco ad occidente. Si aū eueńte ut columba in emafḗ erit.
vmbram eiuf aut arbo2em. occidit eam d2aco.

A2bo2em. deum p2em intellige. vmbram. filium. Sicut gab2iel dicit
ad mariam. Spc sanctuf fupueniet in te. z vnt' altiffimi obub'.t.
fructum celeftem p2iam sapiencia. Deum. 'filiz columbam fpm scm. ideft
fpūalem columbam intelligibilē de celo defcendentē z manentē fup2e ne fo
rif fiat ab ec̄nitate amen. a p̄e z fp̄u sc̄o ū d2aco te no inclinat. ideft d2abol'.
Nam fi habeaf fpiritum sanctum. no poteft tibi appinquiare d2aco.
Attende homo et permane in fide catholica. ibiz habita. ibiz perseuera.
tum ea catholica. Caue quantum potef ne ex2a domū tuū inueni
arif et comprehendat te ille d2aco serpenf antiquuf forif et deuo2et te.
Sicut iudam qui mox ut ex2it a domino fo2al et fratribuf apoftol'
ftatim a demo ne deuo2atuf eft. et per iit.

Figure 5. Peridexion tree. Oxford, Bodleian Library, MS Douce 88 (I), f. 22.
Photo: The Bodleian Library.

Reading Beasts

Taboos and the Holy in Bodley 764
Alison Syme

Psychoanalytical approaches to the bestiaries reveal levels of meaning present in both texts and images that often harmonize with medieval notions of good and evil, sin and salvation, but that nevertheless are covertly presented under the guise of spiritual guidance. This dovetailing of medieval and modern perspectives helps bring to the fore the presence of certain themes central to the didactic function of the bestiaries, as well as the power of imagery that directly communicates fundamental ideas and fears that both underlie and transcend their accompanying texts.

The human horror of foul odors, those of feces or decay, is not natural. Animals do not share it. Bataille writes, "our horror of the life of the flesh, of life naked, undisguised, [is] a horror without which we would resemble the animals . . . bespeaks a negation of nature."[1] Humans distance themselves from nature and animality by washing and dressing and, most significantly for this analysis, by the establishment of certain taboos pertaining to sex, nakedness, feces, corpses and decay, as described in Leviticus 15 and 18. It has been suggested that such taboos are grounded in religious beliefs—such as the notion that the sacred must be protected from defilement—and that they also function as an important means of social control.[2]

"The loathing of nothingness [is] at the origin of the loathing of decay."[3] Decay is a taboo subject because it ultimately leads to the nothingness that marks the end of mortal existence, in other words, death. Excrement and waste are also taboo, because they run counter to man's ideal or dream of himself, which is atemporal and which seeks order, reason, and clarity; that is, the eternal Godhead. In the bestiaries, both the dream and its disruptions are presented by way of a series of metaphors based on the fear of animality (or mortality) and on the desire to preserve the holy. These metaphors operate consistently in Bodley 764, one of the most celebrated of the English medieval bestiaries. The texts and images in this bestiary communicate taboos fundamental to human existence, but they always do so under the cloak of spiritual guidance.

According to Saint Augustine, "we are born between feces and urine."[4] A similar description of mankind reduced to excrement, worms, and waste was graphically put forward centuries later by Pope Innocent III in *On the Misery of the Human Condition*.[5] This is our underside, a dark and temporal site of loss, waste, death. Our countering dream is immortality and spirit, literally the breath that animates life, one of the fundamental Scriptural metaphors.

Breath has symbolic importance in the bestiaries, in that various stories and images address aspects of spirituality and immortality by metaphorically casting these in the form of voice and odor. One prominent example is the panther, who "lets forth a great roar; and out of his mouth comes a very sweet smell that seems to contain every kind of scent" (figure 1).[6] He is a figure of the resurrection of Christ when he rises from his sleep on the third day, emerges from his cave, and "sends out a great cry and pours out sweetness."[7] Similarly, the phoenix's immortality is expressed as scent, in this case, of sweet spices. According to the text, "the scents [of the spices] can overcome the stench of death."[8] The accompanying image shows the phoenix rising intact from its nest, which is, unlike other bird nests pictured in this manuscript, constructed of crosses emblematic of the instrument of Christ's death (figure H, p. xxix). The reader is advised to fill Christ, his chrysalis, with "the sweet soul of [his] virtues . . . [and] the odor of [his] good deeds."[9]

Breath takes the metaphorical form of voice to signify life-giving power in the description of the nightingale, who "gets its name because its song signals the end of night and the rising of the sun" and "comforts itself in its sleepless toil by singing sweetly." Voice has the power to quicken, as the nightingale brings her chicks to life "no less with sweet melodies than with the warmth of its body."[10] In these traits, the nightingale is compared to the virtuous woman who shows her maternal devotion by singing soothing songs to her children at night.

Life-giving power is also ascribed to the lion's breath. The lion father approaches his still-born cubs and "blows in their faces, and awakens them to life."[11] Similarly, the bear licks her formless cubs into shape and gives them life, an act that forms the central focus of both the text and accompanying image.[12] The motif of the parent reviving the cub is similar in both the lion and bear stories, and the images communicate an additional level of meaning not mandated by the text. That is, in both of the images in Bodley 764, one of the cubs is red, connoting the real blood of childbirth.[13]

Breath—of God, life, and of spirit—is contrasted to negative animal functions of the mouth or of the other more sinister orifice. The opposite of life-giving breath is suffocation, which is the demonic dragon's *modus operandi*. The dragon's strength "is not in its teeth, but its tail."[14] It slays anything it embraces, implying an unnatural sexuality decidedly taboo. Most importantly, it kills elephants—bestiary figures of Christ[15]—by suffocating them to death, in other words, by choking out the breath, the life, the God. Suffocation as demonic is also expressed in the hoopoe entry, which typically reads, "if you smear yourself with [the hoopoe's] blood before you go to sleep, you will see demons that will threaten to suffocate you."[16]

Breathing problems in the bestiaries, then, are related to a lack of faith. The raven "gets its name from the sound of its voice, because it rasps."[17] This entry follows that of the nightingale, notable for its sweet singing. The respective images do not illustrate different degrees of spirituality in terms of "breath" but rather in terms of carnality, expressed allegorically in the relative height of their nests. The nightingale, a sign of maternal devotion, calmly rests in a nest raised above the ground into the sky, nourishing its young with its voice, its singing. By contrast, the raven's nest is dug out of the ground like a pit, in which it rests while depositing a worm into the open mouth of its young. The lower, earthly positioning of the raven is in keeping with the textual allegory, which compares the blackness of the raven to the blackness of sin or unfaithfulness.[18]

The image of the violently animalistic manticore emphasizes the opposition between the breathing, life-giving, and divine function of the mouth and its devouring, demonic, or animal function. The text states that the manticore "delights in eating human flesh" (note the three rows of teeth).[19] Because he has the face of a man, the leg he chews in the accompanying image invokes not only the taboo of corpses but also the taboo of cannibalism. In addition, there exists a well-recognized and close relationship between cannibalism and incest: both confuse the structures that function to separate the identity of self and the identify of other. Cannibalism threatens a more frightening annihilation than death, because it involves a metamorphosis into the other. That is, the death and decay of an individual's body at least retains the integrity of self, but the absorption of one's body by another suggests a perverse continuation of self as part of another, resulting in a grotesque and confused existence.[20]

Spiritually speaking, the manticore is a wholly negative figure, not just because of his violation of various taboos but also owing to his rapacity or voraciousness. Voraciousness, like lust, is a serious sin because it expresses a fundamental carnality from which the faithful strive to escape. In other words, the spiritual sin of voraciousness in the bestiaries is yet another disguise for animality. In addition to the manticore, the wolf is a primary exemplar. According to the text, "wolves kill everything they find when they are ravenous . . . the wolf . . . thirsts for blood."[21] In Bodley 764, the image of the voracious, animalistic wolf may be considered an antithetical counterpart to that of the spiritual, life-giving panther discussed above (figures 1, 2). The wolf's teeth are bared, the panther's are concealed. The animals assembled before the voracious wolf are all prey, whereas the panther has drawn the animals to him in order to save them. Concomitantly, the heads of the animals gaze upward in the panther image toward salvation while those in the wolf image are lowered to signify their violent earthly end. Not surprisingly, the panther's animals look peaceful and alert, while the prey of the wolf look worried and anxious. The panther's eyes are rolled upward, toward heaven; they seem to be, like the eyes of the surrounding animals, in prayer, imploring. The wolf's eyes, by contrast, are frontal, focused on his prey. The blueness of the wolf distinguishes him from his prey of different colors, but the multiple colors of the panther repeat those of the surrounding animals, suggesting the spiritual communion possible among the faithful but denied to those divided by earthly desires. A further visualization of unity is conveyed in the panther image by a Scripturally-derived lion and lamb standing peacefully together in the background.

The animalistic act of voracious devouring signifies sexual taboo in the text and image devoted to the viper. The viper, the text informs us, "in her sexual ecstasy, bites the male's head off."[22] The focus of the image is on the act that precedes this moment, in which the male puts his head into the female's mouth in order to release the semen or perhaps this image conflates both the sexual act and the devouring that immediately follows. If so, this qualifies as another spiritual disguise—

the dangers of lust and its consequences—for taboo sexual practices. Vomit, feces, and the anus are all powerfully taboo as signifiers of waste, decay, and death. All three feature in various of the bestiary stories, again disguised as spiritual lessons. For example, vomit, to which the dog always returns, signifies sin and the double-sexed hyena imitates human vomiting in order to solicit assistance, at which point s/he kills those offering help. In this, the hyena's behavior is compared to the deceit of the devil.[23] Earthbound vanity is signified by feces in this description of the properties of crocodile dung: "From [crocodile] dung is made an ointment with which old women and faded whores anoint their faces, and appear beautiful until their sweat washes it off."[24] This statement appears to condemn the sin of vanity, but it also reveals the illusory nature of all earthly beauty, subject to decay and disappearance. Excrement also figures centrally in the story of the bonnacon, who defends himself by forcefully ejecting burning feces from his anus, whose behavior is not moralized in the bestiaries, but which represents literal antithesis of the panther, who emits sweet breath from his mouth.[25]

Castration and the fear of loss that underlies it is another taboo cloaked in spiritual terms in the bestiaries. According to medieval Christian belief, God demands a sacrificial castration or "feminization" from the faithful, interpreted as a surrender of earthly desires, pride, and defiance. This is in keeping with the suggestion that the Israelites were God's bride, and that their "spiritual castration"—or the relinquishing of earthly desires—was a prerequisite for the reception of God's Word.[26] In Bodley 764, certain images convey the castration theme quite literally, either through depictions of testicles or of their removal, but accompany them with spiritual moralizations. The most prominent presentation of this theme is the beaver's graphic sacrifice of his testicles (figure F, p. xxvii). The accompanying text proclaims that, like the beaver who castrates himself to escape the hunter, so anyone "who wants to live chastely in accordance with God's commandments should cut off all vices and shameless deeds and throw them in the devil's face."[27] In the bird section, the cock, who "gets its name because it is sometimes castrated", is depicted on a flaccid, brown branch. The text goes on to state that this is the only bird whose testicles are cut off, and that the ancients used to refer to eunuchs as cockerels.[28] Interestingly, the cock comforts and encourages, roles typically assigned to females in medieval thought and exegesis, perhaps as a sign of diminished masculinity as a result of this devastating loss.

The *onager*, or wild ass, would seem to exhibit castration anxiety. A jealous beast who bites off the testicles of his newborn young so that they cannot usurp his place, he is compared in the text to the devil.[29] Castration anxiety is also suggested in the image of the fox's deception of birds, in which one bird bites his testicles, perhaps to ensure that he is really dead, while another bird attacks the fox's anus. According to the text, the impious fox jumps up at this point and devours his would-be devourers.[30]

Besides literal castration, both Bible and bestiary abound with its symbolic forms, the most common being blindness.[31] This is another example of the cloaking of a taboo theme under a symbolic metaphor. According to psychoanalytical theory, the eyes, like the penis, express active, male, aggressive life-force. Therefore, the raven "pecks the eyes out of corpses before attacking the rest of the body" in order to confirm that the corpse is really dead.[32] According to medieval thought, the eyes, like the genitals, are a source of sin when the spectacle of reality becomes a distraction from spirituality.[33] This is probably why bestiary creatures use their appearance to deceive and lure their prey. For example, the scitalis, a type of lizard, "has such a brightly-colored back that all creatures that approach it slow down to admire its splendor" and thus they meet their demise.[34] Eyes, in addition to being vulnerable to temptation, can also transgress in their expression of defiance. Proverbs 21:4 warns that "haughtiness of the eyes is the enlarging of the heart: the lamp of the wicked is sin." Similarly, the bestiary raven entry warns against defying the Father: "the eye that mocketh at his father . . . the ravens of the brooks pick it out (Prov. 30:17)."[35]

The contrasting state of blindness is analyzed by Derrida: "faith, in the moment proper to it, is blind."[36] According to this view, physical blinding is a form of castration or submission to the law of God the Father which is necessary to allow inner light and vision to awake. "Inflicted violence is always at the origin of . . . revelation that opens one's eyes and makes one go from sensible light or the *lumen naturale* to the intelligible or supernatural light."[37] Faith "sacrifices sight, even if it does so with an eye to seeing at last."[38] The metaphor of faith as blindness also finds a place in Scriptures where it is stated that Jesus comes "that they who see not may see; and they who see, may become blind (John 9:39)."

Besides blindness, castration references may be found hidden in the bestiaries in imagery that emphasizes symbolic forms associated with genitalia. According to Freud, multiplication of genital symbols signifies castration.[39] Thus, the image of the panther may also be read as an image of symbolic castration, for the panther is "a beast marked with little circles of color, like eyes" (figure 1).[40] Moreover, the peacock, a symbol of Christ, has feathers marked with eyes, confirming the necessity of the faithful's castration (figure C, p. xxiv). Displaying itself, it "signifies the Gentiles, coming from the ends of the earth to Christ, who adorns them with the grace and splendor of many virtues."[41]

Bataille has explored the parallels between eggs, eyes, and testicles as symbols for castration.[42] In the bestiary, the ostrich "lays its eggs and covers them in sand . . . at once forgetting them and never returning to them," an act valorized in the bestiary because it is interpreted as a "laying aside of earthly things to follow the course of heaven."[43] Through the prominent rendering of and focus on eggs, the image depicts the necessity of symbolic castration for conversion (figure 3). This turning toward God is here represented through the literal turning of the ostrich toward the sun, as the image conflates the moments of before and after the conversion experience.

The reward of castration or blindness is inner vision, represented in the bestiary imagery as a normal, open eye. Thus, the lion who sleeps with his eyes open, represents Christ asleep on the cross "while his Godhead kept watch."[44] In a literal depiction of this idea, the lion in Bodley 764 sleeps with his eyes wide open.[45] Other bestiary entries present a central narrative of restoration of sight, such as the eagle and hoopoe. Like the ostrich, the eagle's sight is restored through the sun while the hoopoe's eye scales are pecked away by its nurturing offspring.[46]

True understanding, or inner vision, manifests itself pictorially in other ways, such as in the form of a horn. Horns are widely understood as a phallic substitute, even a supplement, communicating ideas of power and virility. From a spiritual point of view, though, horns spring from the head; their phallic nature is not sexual but rather legal in the Lacanian sense: they represent a creature thinking the Law of the Father. Not surprisingly, there are many examples of the connection between horns and the Law in the bestiary text. For example, the antelope's horns are compared to the two Testaments, and "rams are like the apostles because these animals have powerful foreheads and always overthrow whatever they strike."[47] Thus, the horn of the unicorn is "exalted" (Ps. 91:11) because it is a "horn of salvation" (Luke 1:69).[48] In the Bodley 764 image of the unicorn, the beast is sacrificed;

the hunters thrust their spears downward to the earth, while the unicorn raises his gaze along his horn up to heaven. Good, spiritual horns are always on a vertical axis, traveling upward, channeling the spirit toward heaven. Non-spiritual horns also travel upward—as erections. The bestiary also tells us that the ibex's two horns are so strong that if it falls from a high mountain, its horns bear the weight of its body and it escapes without injury. "This beast represents those learned men who understand the harmony of the Old and New Testaments, and if anything untoward happens to them, they are supported as if on two horns by all the good that they have derived from reading the witness of the Old Testament and the Gospels."[49] In Bodley 764, the ibex seems to exist in a different space than that of the hunters (figure 4). This is emphasized by the way the animal's horns fall in front of the frame: the hunters, as signs of carnality, are completely excluded from the ibex's space or the realm of its spiritual "being." Other "good horns" belong to the elephant, whose tusks are described as "a rampart of ivory,"[50] thus providing a metaphor for their protective power but also suggesting their masculine potential. In general, horns may be interpreted as spiritual substitutes for not only the penis—and in this regard, it may be significant that the Bodley 764 ibex entry follows on immediately after the story of the beaver's castration—but also for the eyes. Horns function like a blind man's cane in guiding the animal spiritually as a kind of optico-genital prosthesis.

As for "bad" horns, the premier example are the horns of the bonnacon, that "wind back on themselves in such a way that anyone who falls on them is not wounded. The protection which is denied to this monster through its horns is provided by its belly."[51] Good horns grow up from the head, while beards and hair (both sexual attributes) grow down. An excess of hair—and even of feathers, as in the entry for the owl (*bubo*)—is considered analogous to an excess of flesh.[52]

Horns, hairiness, and the sin of seeing are combined in the bestiary description of the goat to communicate the dual messages of animality and the sin of lust. Sin is the result of a physical eye "too natural, too carnal, too external."[53] For example, the he-goat is "a stubborn, lascivious animal, always eager to mate, whose eyes are so full of lust that they look sideways, from which they get their Latin name 'hircus', for Suetonius calls the corner of the eye the 'hircus'."[54] Such goats are compared to sinners. Good goats are good because they are far-sighted, and the goats and kids which directly precede the he-goat in Bodley 764 are literally upright creatures. The he-goat, though, has horizontal emphasis and is almost too large for his frame (he can barely contain himself), and his horns point downward, rather diabolically (figure D, p. xxv). The text asserts that the Latin "hircus" also means "hirsute" or "hairy," another sign of virility and lust. The he-goat is a figure of stubbornness, a blindness not of the eye but of the heart, because it is willed. In theological terms, such blindness is exhibited by sinners who do not wish to see the light, the "foolish people, and without understanding, who have eyes, and see not: and ears, and hear not" (Jer. 5:21).

Certain bestiary creatures, rather than providing secondary or indirect references to human sexual anatomy, represent it directly. The Bodley 764 scorpion might be served by Derrida's apt description: "[it] is stretched towards the . . . place of [its] desire in an energetic, determined, but uncontrollable movement, being sheer potential, potentially violent . . . all the more carnal . . . animal, in that sight does not protect [it] . . . more naked than others, [it] virtually becomes [its] own sex, [it] becomes indistinguishable from it because he does not see it."[55] The image of the scorpion accords with another description by Derrida of a "phalloid image, an unveiled sex from head to toe, vaguely obscene and disturbing" (figure 5).[56] The scorpion is shown in plan as a sign of inferiority, with all of its members stretched out, which increases its phallic connotations by making the beast appear rigid and enlarged. According to Charbonneau-Lassay in accordance with medieval astrological belief, the scorpion is the ruler of human genitalia.[57] The bestiary describes it as a "land worm," a type of parasite, which, according to Scriptures, "consumeth the heart" (Prov. 25:20). The text also asserts that the stinging scorpion "signifies the devil or those who serve him" and that it is also a sign of despair, the opposite of the joy of the faithful.[58] To emphasize this association, the scorpion in Bodley 764 is depicted stinging the palm of a human hand, inflicting a wound identical to the stigmata of Christ (figure 5). It is thus a murderer of love, the light, and the spirit. However, it is at the same time a phallus and all of its potentially uncontrollable power.

The scorpion is not the only "naked phallus" image in the bestiary. Like the scorpion, the bat, in reality, lacks hair or feathers. However, the bat in Bodley 764 sports feathers, even though the text states that it does not fly with the help of feathers but rather uses the folds of its skin.[59] Charbonneau-Lassay notes that bats' wings are not formed of feathers but of a naked membrane, whose appearance makes their evil character more evident. In Christian symbolism, wings of skin are connected with the idea of the perversion of the intellectual faculties.[60] In medieval art and thought, feathers are connected to flight and celestial existence, to the upward climb towards heaven, and to a liberation of the mind from carnal concerns. In Bodley 764, feathers notwithstanding, the bat is the only bestiary "bird" shown in plan, used as in the scorpion image to indicate its lowliness. Moreover, it is shown upside-down, another indicator of its infernal character, while at the same time a naturalistic feature of bats.

Derrida speaks of "the obscenity of a scar, the impossible suture of a slit, frontal genitality."[61] The Bodley 764 image of the boar shows two sequential bloody penetrations that entangle the hunters and the hunted. The open, bleeding wound of the boar suggests the female genital opening penetrated by the hunter's spear or by the other hunter's knife, especially since the latter hunter is lying directly underneath the boar while thrusting his knife into the belly. This, then, is another example of foregrounded "genitality." Interestingly, the accompanying text states that the boar signifies the fierceness of the rulers of this world, including Vespasian, persecutor of the Jews. In this light, the text then refers to a particularly significant taboo, mainly the Jewish prohibition against the eating of pork, in its statement that the Jews believe the boar is an unclean animal.[62]

Taboos associated with excrement are also conveyed through the nature of animal dwellings, which function consistently in the bestiaries as symbols either of temporal and earthbound or celestial and eternal existence. The dwellings of the evil and despised creatures are inevitably characterized by the presence of excrement, or, from the theological point of view, the disorder and defilement that symbolizes the unholy.[63] For example, the owl is "a loathsome bird because its nest is filthy from its droppings."[64] Similarly, the hoopoe lives among human dung and feeds on filth and excrement.[65] From the spiritual point of view, filth is equated with sorrow. Thus, the filthy owl is a "truly unhappy creature through its habits."[66] As well, "the hoopoe is said to love sorrow, because the sorrow of the world brings about the death of the spirit; and for this reason all those who love God must always rejoice and pray without ceasing, give thanks in all things because joy is the fount of the spirit."[67] As noted above, Proverbs 25:20 identifies sorrow as a parasite, suggesting that what is ultimately expressed in the owl and hoopoe entries is the human fear of susceptibility to bodily decay.

Creatures that function as signs of spiritual goodness, such as the dove, inhabit dwellings that are positive symbols. The bestiaries state that the dove nests in holes in the rock. In its hardness, the rock is a metaphor for eternity or resistance to decay and death, and as the text indicates, "the rock moreover was Jesus."[68] Etymologically and symbolically, the rock is also a metaphor for Peter (*petrus*) and for the church he founded. The eternal dwelling of the dove, free from filth and excrement, is hence not subject to death or decay.

In the Bodley 764 image of the dove, this idea is visually expressed by the pediment windows of the dovecote, which suggest the form of a church. Interestingly, enduring material, fine craftsmanship (evident here in the dressed stone of the masonry), and uprightness constitute the goodness of a dwelling in accordance with medieval aesthetic principles that define a good work of art,[69] and good is equated with the holy.

The nests of the swallows are "more precious than gold, because they are wisely built."[70] The text goes on to explain how the swallow builds its nest so that its young can move around safely inside of it and are protected from the cold.[71] The swallow's nest has the additional virtues of being raised above the earth and of adjoining human dwellings: by shunning the perils of the wilderness, the swallow demonstrates its desire for spirituality over its own animal nature. Like swallows, bees also live in skillfully built homes, pictured in Bodley 764 as tall and upright, in keeping with bees' exceedingly virtuous nature achieved through hard work and avoidance of sex.[72]

The taboo of corpses is violated repeatedly in the bestiaries but always under the guise of spiritual decay. One of the primary corpse-violators is the hyena, who "lives in the graves of dead men and feeds on their bodies."[73] Owing to its possession of both male and female genitalia, the hyena also violates a fundamental sexual taboo, but this is given a spiritual interpretation in the text which identifies the hyena as the duplicitous Jew.[74] In Bodley 764, the hyena is thus shown outside of the church, excluded from it. In this image, the corpse covering his genitals displays a greater sense of decorum than the hyena, whose double sex is left exposed for all to see.[75] Interestingly, the state of hermaphroditism also may have had a positive significance, in that it has been interpreted as a transcendence of all opposition into unity, and thus an image of the divine.[76]

Another bestiary taboo-breaker is the ibis, who uses serpents' eggs and animal corpses "to make a very welcome meal for its young."[77]

The real taboo is graphically illustrated in Bodley 764, which depicts not only a human rather than animal corpse but specifically a head, the locus of reason, reduced to a raw, animal state with bared teeth (figure K, p. xxxii). Owing to its proximity, the nest may be read as the gaping hole of the man's stomach, reprising the theme of rapacity and voraciousness attributed to some of the more demonic bestiary creatures, such as the manticore and wolf discussed above. Moreover, the nest is rendered as a pit, a visual metaphor for hell, and the pictorial opposite of good, upright dwellings such as that of the bee.

In Bodley 764, fundamental human taboos related to sex, death, decay, and excrement are expressed visually yet are hidden in the text inside spiritual messages. An ideological opposition between animality and humanity clearly emerges, but this is also cloaked in metaphorical and spiritual terms. That is, the theme of animality/humanity is analogous to the unholy/holy antithesis consistently posed by the bestiary texts by way of animal metaphors. Subsequent investigation may reveal to what extent the analysis of Bodley 764 is applicable to other bestiaries produced during the same period. In any case, it is clear that the bestiaries address both the holy and the unholy with equal fervor, and it is a testimony to the power of the genre that this one type of book functioned simultaneously as a collection of animal lore, a guide to spirituality, and a handbook of primal fears.

NOTES

1. Georges Bataille, *The Accursed Share Volume II: Consumption*, trans. Robert Hurley (New York, 1991), 63.

2. The classic study of filth taboos and their religious and social significance is Mary Douglas, *Purity and Danger: An Analysis of the Concepts of Pollution and Taboo* (London, 1966).

3. Bataille 1991, 79.

4. "Inter faeces et urinam nascimur" (Bataille 1991, 62)

5. Lothario Dei Segni (Pope Innocent III), *De miseria condicionis humanae*, ed. Robert E. Lewis (Athens [GA], 1978); *On the Misery of the Human Condition*, trans. Donald R. Howard (Indianapolis, 1969).

6. Trans. Barber 1993, 30. "Post triduum ut exurgit a sompno et statim emittit magnum rugitum, et ab ore eius odor suauissimus exit atque si omnia aromata intra se haberet" (Bodley 764, f. 7v).

7. Trans. Barber 1993, 31. "Die autem tertio surgit a sompno et emittit magnum clamorem fragrans suauitatem" (Bodley 764, f. 8).

8. Trans. Barber 1993, 143. "Quis igitur huic annuntiat diem mortis, ut faciat sibi thecam et impleat eam bonis odoribus atque ingrediatur in eam et moriatur, illic ubi odoribus fetor funeris possit aboleri?" (Bodley 764, f. 71).

9. Trans. Barber 1993, 143. "Theca ergo tua est fides; imple eam bonis uirtutum odoribus tuarum, hoc est castitatis, misericordie, atque iustiae, et in ipsa penetralia fidei suauis factorum prestantium odore redolentia tutus ingredere" (Bodley 764, f. 71).

10. Trans. Barber 1993, 158. "Lucinia auis inde nomen sumpsit quia cantu suo significare solet surgentis exortum diei . . . Est enim per uigil custos cum oua quodam sinu corporis et gremio, fouet in sompnem longe noctis laborem cantilene suauitate solatur . . . Ut enim uidetur hec summa eis est intentio, quo possit non minus dulcioribus modulis quam fotu corporis animare fetus ouaque fouere" (Bodley 764, f. 78v).

11. Trans. Barber 1993, 24-25. "Custodit eos tribus diebus, donec ueniens pater eorum tertia die, insufflat in faciem eorum, et uiuificat eos" (Bodley 764, f. 4).

12. Barber 1993, 58-60; Bodley 764, ff. 22v-23v.

13. Barber 1993, 22 (lion image), 58 (bear image). According to Oppian (*Cynegetica* 3.139-169; trans. A. Mair [London, 1928], 125-27), bear cubs are born formless owing to the female bear's lechery during her pregnancy.

14. Trans. Barber 1993, 183. "Uim autem non in dentibus sed in cauda habet . . . Sed ideo huic ad mortem faciendam uenena non esse necessaria dicunt, quod si quem ligauerit, occidit" (Bodley 764, f. 93).

15. Hassig 1995, 134-35.

16. Trans. Barber 1993, 171. "Cuius sanguine si quis se inunxerit dormitum, purgens demones suffocantes se uidebit" (Bodley 764, f. 85).

17. Trans. Barber 1993, 159. "Coruus siue corax nomen a sono gutturis habet, quod uoce crociter" (Bodley 764, f. 79).

18. "Coruus nigredo peccati uel infidelitatis" (Bodley 764, f. 79; trans. Barber 1993, 159).

19. Trans. Barber 1993, 63. "Humanas carnes auidissime affectat" (Bodley 764, f. 25). On the manticore, see also Gravestock in this volume.

20. David Williams, *Deformed Discourse: The Function of the Monster in Mediaeval Thought and Literature* (Montreal, 1996), 145-46.

21. Trans. Barber 1993, 69. " . . . 'licos' autem a morsibus appellatur, quod rabie rapacitatis queque inuenerint trucidant" (Bodley 764, f. 28).

22. Trans. Barber 1993, 186. " . . . illa, autem ex uoluptate in rabiem, uersa caput maris ore receptus percidit" (Bodley 764, f. 94v).

23. Bodley 764, ff. 30-32 (dog), f. 15 (hyena); Barber 1993, 76 (dog), 46 (hyena).

24. Trans. Barber 1993, 62. "Stercus eius fit unguentum unde uetule et rugose meretrices facies suas per ungunt, fiunt que pulchre donec sudor defluens lauet" (Bodley 764, f. 24v).

25. Hassig 1995, 165. See Barber 1993, 47-48 (bonnacon). On the bonnacon, see also Gravestock in this volume.

26. Howard Eilberg-Schwartz, *God's Phallus and Other Problems for Men and Monotheism* (Boston, 1994), 18, 36. "Feminization" accomplished through castration is discussed by Freud in several contexts, including "A Child Is Being Beaten: A Contribution to the Study of Sexual Perversions," in *Standard Edition of the Complete Works of Sigmund Freud*, trans. James Strachey, 24 vols. (London, 1953-74) (hereafter *SE*), XVII, 1919, 198; *Group Psychology and the Analysis of the Ego*, in *SE* XVIII, 1921, 105-6; and "The Ego and the Id," in *SE* XIX, 1923, 33.

27. Trans. Barber 1993, 44. "Sic omnis qui iuxta mandatum Dei uersatur et caste uult uiuere secat a se omnia uicia et omnis impudicitie actus et proiecit eos a se in faciem diaboli" (Bodley 764, f. 14v). On the beaver, see also Hassig in this volume.

28. Trans. Barber 1993, 172. "Gallus a castratione uocatus inter ceteras. Enim aues huic soli testiculi adhimuntur; veteres enim abscisos gallos uocabant" (Bodley 764, f. 85v).

29. Barber 1993, 99-100; Bodley 764, ff. 45-45v.

30. Barber 1993, 65-66; Bodley 764, ff. 26-26v.

31. Sigmund Freud, "The Uncanny," in *SE* XXIII, 1964.

32. Trans. Barber 1993, 159. "Hic prior in cadaueribus oculum petit" (Bodley 764, f. 79).

33. On the medieval sin of seeing, see Michael Camille, *The Gothic Idol* (Cambridge, 1989), 302-306.

34. Trans. Barber 1993, 189. "Scitalis serpens est uocata quod tanta profulget tergi uarietate ut notarum genera aspicientes se retardet"(Bodley 764, f. 97).

35. Barber 1993, 159; Bodley 764, f. 79.

36. Jacques Derrida, *Memoirs of the Blind: The Self-Portrait and Other Ruins*, trans. Pascale-Anne Brault and Michael Naas (Chicago 1993), 30.

37. *Ibid.*, 92.

38. *Ibid.*, 30.

39. Sigmund Freud, "Medusa's Head," in *SE* XVIII, 1955, 273.

40. Trans. Barber 1993, 32. "Pantera est bestia inimitis orbiculis superpicta ita ut oculatis ex fuluo id est circuli nigra uel alba distinguatur varietate" (Bodley 764, f. 8v).

41. Trans. Barber 1993, 170. "Significat populum Gentilem de longinquis partibus terre ad Christum uenientem, qui etiam eius gracia multarum uirtutum ornatu resplendet" (Bodley 764, f. 84v). On the peacock, see also Brown in this volume.

42. Georges Bataille, *The Story of the Eye*, trans. Joachin Neugroschel (New York, 1977), 105.

43. Trans. Barber 1993, 137, 138. ". . . fodit in terram, ubi ponat oua sua . . . ascendit de loco illo, statim obliuiscitur eorum et nunquam reddit ad oua sua. . . . Si ergo assida cognoscit tempus suum et obliuiscitur posteritatis sue, ac terrena proponens sequitur celestia . . . " (Bodley 764, ff. 67, 67v).

44. Trans. Barber 1993, 24. "Secunda natura eius est quia cum dormit oculos apertos habere uidetur. Sic et Dominus noster, corporaliter obdormiens in cruce, sepultus est et Deitas eius uigilabat" (Bodley 764, f. 3v).

45. Bodley 764, f. 2v; Barber 1993, 22.

46. Barber 1993, 118-19 (eagle) and 145-47 (hoopoe); Bodley 764, ff. 57v-58 (eagle) and ff. 72v-73 (hoopoe). On the hoopoe, see also Hassig 1995, 93-103.

47. Trans. Barber 1993, 80. "Arietes autem bene sunt apostolis comparati quam ut diximus animalia ipsa plurimum fronte ualent et obiecta semper inpingendo deiciunt" (Bodley 764, f. 35). On the antelope, see Barber 1993, 34; Bodley 764, ff. 9-9v.

48. Barber 1993, 37; Bodley 764, f. 11.

49. Trans. Barber 1993, 45. "Significat autem eruditos homines qui duorum testamentorum consonancia, quicquid eis aduersi acciderit, qui quodam salubri temperamento temporare solent et uelud duobus cornibus fulti bona que perpetrant ueteris testamenti ac euangelice lectionis attestatione sustentant" (Bodley 764, f. 15).

50. Trans. Barber 1993, 40. "Rostrum autem promuscida dicitur quam illo pabula ori admouet, et est angui similis uallo munitur eburneo" (Bodley 764, f. 12v).

51. Trans. Barber 1993, 48. "Cornua autem ita multiplici flexu in se recurrentia ut si quis in eo offendat non uulneretur. Sed quicquid praesidii monstro illi frons negat, aluus sufficit" (Bodley 764, f. 16v).

52. Bodley 764, f. 74. See Barber 1993, 149, where the *bubo* is identified as a screech owl. The entry for the screech owl (*ulula*) is found in Bodley 764, ff. 84v-85 (trans. Barber 1993, 170-71). On the various bestiary owls, see Miyazaki in this volume.

53. Derrida 1993, 18.

54. Trans. Barber 1993, 83. "Hircus lasciuium animal et petulcum, et feruens semper ad coitum, cuius oculi ob libidinem in transuersum aspiciunt,

unde et nomen traxit, nam 'hirci' sunt oculorum anguli secundum Suetonium" (Bodley 764, f. 37).

55. Derrida 1993, 106.

56. *Ibid.*

57. Louis Charbonneau-Lassay, *The Bestiary of Christ*, trans. D. M. Dooling (New York, 1992), 342-43. Medieval astrological images that position the scorpion over the male genital region include that of the anatomical man (f. 14v) in the fifteenth-century Très Riches Heures (Chantilly, Musée Condé). See Millard Meiss, *The Très Riches Heures of Jean, Duke of Berry*, New York, 1969 (facsimile).

58. Trans. Barber 1993, 197-98. "Scorpio uermis terrenus . . . Scorpio diabolum significat uel ministros eius" (Bodley 764, f. 102).

59. Barber 1993, 158; Bodley 764, ff. 78-78v.

60. Charbonneau-Lassay 1992, 289.

61. Derrida 1993, 92.

62. Barber 1993, 86; Bodley 764, f. 38v.

63. Douglas 1966, 29-40.

64. Trans. Barber 1993, 149. "Auis fetida esse dicitur quia fimo locus eius in quo habitat commaculatur" (Bodley 764, f. 74).

65. Barber 1993, 171; Bodley 764, f. 85.

66. Trans. Barber 1993, 149. "Infelix ergo bubo est qui ea que praediximus operatur" (Bodley 764, f. 74).

67. Trans. Barber 1993, 171. "Hupupa etiam luctum amare dicitur, quod seculi tristicia mortem spiritus operatur; propter quod oportet eum qui Deum diligit semper gaudere sine intermissione orare, in omnibus gratias agere, quod gaudium fructus est spiritus" (Bodley 764, f. 85).

68. Trans. Barber 1993, 162. "Petra autem erat Christus" (Bodley 764, f. 80v).

69. See C. Barret, "Medieval Art Criticism," *Journal of British Aesthetics* 5 (1965), 25-36.

70. Trans. Barber 1993, 165. " . . . preciosiores auro nidos instruit quia sapientur nidificat" (Bodley 764, f. 82).

71. Cold in the form of the winter frost is identified in the text as "spiritual numbness"(*refrigerate mentis*) as opposed to the "warmth of love" (*ardor caritatis*) symbolized by the heat of summer (Bodley 764, f. 83; trans. Barber 1993, 167).

72. Barber 1993, 177-79; Bodley 764, ff. 89-91. On sex and the bee, see Hassig in this volume.

73. Trans. Barber 1993, 45. "Est animal quod dicitur yena in sepulcris mortuorum habitans eorum que corpora uescens" (Bodley 764, f. 15).

74. On the hyena as a figure of the Jew, see Hassig 1995, 145-55.

75. On sex and the hyena, see Hassig in this volume.

76. Williams 1996, 168-75.

77. Trans. Barber 1993, 136. "Hec serpentium ouis utitur et morticinis et ex eis gratissimus cybus pullis suis" (Bodley 764, f. 66).

Figure 1. Panther. Oxford, Bodleian Library, MS Bodley 764, f. 7v.
Photo: The Bodleian Library.

Figure 2. Wolf. Oxford, Bodleian Library, MS Bodley 764, f. 28.
Photo: The Bodleian Library.

Figure 3. Ostrich. Oxford, Bodleian Library, MS Bodley 764, f. 67.
Photo: The Bodleian Library.

Figure 4. Ibex. Oxford, Bodleian Library, MS Bodley 764, f. 14v.
Photo: The Bodleian Library.

Figure 5. Scorpion. Oxford, Bodleian Library, MS Bodley 764, f. 102.
Photo: The Bodleian Library.

Silence's Beasts
Michelle Bolduc

The associations between bestiary and romance abound despite their disparate traditions.[1] Perhaps the best studied in terms of its bestiary/romance hybridism, Richard of Fournival's *Bestiaire d'amour* shows itself to be a meeting of the two genres: a catalog of animals within the frame of courtly love, a clerical and scientific work infused with eroticism.[2] Less well studied, however, are references to the bestiary tradition within particular romances. In her study of the figure of the lion in two thirteenth-century works, the *Chevalerie de Judas Macabé* and the *Roman de Kanor*, Meradith McMunn explores both the use of "direct visual and verbal quotation" and the "allusion or echo" of bestiary material in these two works.[3] Although McMunn does not focus solely on romance, her analysis suggests that both the text and the images of works not explicitly concerned with natural history may reveal significant relationships to the bestiary genre. Using McMunn's article as a point of departure, I will examine the influence of bestiaries on a thirteenth-century French romance, *Le Roman de Silence*.[4] I intend to show how both direct references to and indirect invocations of the bestiary tradition further multiply the levels of meaning of this text.

While *Le Roman de Silence* follows the narrative structure of many romances (and indeed traces the adventures of a solitary heroine), this thirteenth-century romance is remarkable because of its seemingly postmodern focus on the intersections between gender and language.[5] This 6706-line romance about a cross-dressed chivalric heroine pushes at the textual and sexual limits of the genre of romance. Extant in a single manuscript (Nottingham University Library, MS Middleton Mi.LM.6), *Silence* is accompanied by fourteen miniatures, eleven of which are narrative in form and content. *Le Roman de Silence*'s general interest in language is recorded in these narrative images which depict the interaction and dialogues of the characters rather than the transgendered heroine's musical and military exploits. Since these narrative images accompany for the most part speeches or monologues, they are in direct rapport with the focus of the written text.

According to Lewis Thorpe, the first modern editor of the romance, these eleven miniatures were probably all by the same artist; indeed, the stylistic details—such as the heavy drapery, the simple drawing of facial features and the stylized hair of the figures—as well as the repetition of clothing color and pose (in order to aid in identification of the characters), suggest a single artist.[6]

Thorpe proposes that the remaining three miniatures were probably executed by a second artist and characterizes these miniatures as "stock decorations which bear no relationship to the story at all." These three miniatures, which are portraits of hybrid creatures, certainly seem out of place in comparison with the more numerous narrative images; unlike the narrative images, the relationship of these creature portraits to the text is neither explicit nor direct. Indeed, Peter Allen describes the creatures as mythical and suggests that they might be in the text "only to remind us that the texts belong to the domain of fantasy."[7] Although Allen and Thorpe discount the possibility that these creature portraits may generate meaning through their relationship with the text, it seems unlikely that they represent only an illustrator's flights of fancy. The creature portraits are not hastily drawn nor are they marginal doodles; instead, the artist treats them in much the same way as the narrative images: they are enframed and carefully executed. The size of the creature portraits duplicates that of the narrative images, and further, their similar *mise-en-page* also indicates their parallel iconographic importance. If we are meant to recognize a clear link between the text and the narrative images (and the sheer number of narrative images suggests this), certainly the creature portraits play some role in this visual *significatio*.

More importantly, creature portraits of this type were not unfamiliar to a medieval audience. These images of animals, isolated from their narrative contexts and presented as portraits, would have been immediately recognizable as images drawn from the bestiary tradition. This tradition, first begun in a monastic, Latin context, was also popular among the laity in a vernacular—albeit less luxurious—form beginning in the thirteenth century and thus was part and parcel of a medieval reader's cultural knowledge.[8] In a text such as *Le Roman de Silence*, the juxtaposition of common narrative images and the surprising creature portraits recalls the interpolation of different textual sources common to the bestiary tradition.[9] Because the relationship between the text and these particular creatures is not explicit, I would propose that a Bakhtinian "open endedness" between text and image results: as McMunn has suggested, these predetermined associations with the bestiary serve to enrich the polysemy of the narrative.[10]

The images of these creatures appear rather late in the romance; the first only after 4780 lines. In addition, the three creatures are depicted in relative proximity (on folios 213, 217, and 218v). An abridged version of the catalog of the miniatures provided by Thorpe reveals (in terms of the ordering of the folios themselves) a desire to depict the creatures as a unified group.[11]

Folio 188	Author portrait of Heldris de Cornüälle
Folio 195v	Count of Chester talks to Euphemie
Folio 199	The nurse and Euphemie holding the baby Silence
Folio 201	The seneschal and Cador
Folio 203	Silence with the two jongleurs
Folio 206v	Old man talks to Cador
Folio 209	Silence and Queen and Eufeme
Folio 211	Silence presents the letter to the king of France
Folio 213	dog
Folio 214v	Ebain's chancellor explains how the letter was changed
Folio 217	bird with griffin's head
Folio 218v	bird with serpentine head
Folio 221	Merlin sitting on a rock
Folio 222v	Silence naked, with Ebain

Although the miniature on folio 214v—Ebain's chancellor explaining how the letter was changed—interrupts the catalog of animals, the creature miniatures are distributed across only four folios. Their proximity links the creatures together, but more importantly, it visually recalls the form of the bestiary catalog.

The first animal portrait, identified as a dog by Thorpe, appears at line 4781 (figure 1). At this point in the romance, the king of France has just welcomed the male-attired heroine, Silence, to his court. However, Silence's letter of introduction, purportedly from King Ebain, orders the king of France to kill the bearer (lines 4380-97). The letter states that Silence committed deeds too horrible to name and that Ebain dared not kill Silence because he was of high lineage (lines 4434-53). The king of France is quite naturally upset, not understanding why his most faithful ally would ask that he be avenged so secretly and so calls for counsel (lines 4459-4530). The lengthy passage that follows resembles a judgment poem: the members of the French court engage in debate, offering various arguments as to how the king should react to this brutal letter.[12] During these deliberations, several counts suggest that the king wait for forty days to see if there will be a reprieve from Ebain (lines 4531-4770). The count of Clermont, on the other hand, insists that the request is not a sign of true friendship since it might harm the king of France's reputation. Clermont suggests that the king of France write a short letter to this effect and send it along with the longer letter to Ebain (lines 4771-4879). In terms of the narrative thread, then, the image of the first creature appears just as the count is beginning his speech on friendship between political allies.

Although Thorpe has identified this first creature as a dog, knowledge of the bestiary tradition suggests that it is instead a lion. It has the curly mane, tufted tail, and the paws of a lion, strongly resembling the bestiary lions, such as those depicted in the Ashmole bestiary (ff. 10, 10v),[13] although its complex, heraldic posture is quite different from the frozen posture of the Ashmole lions. Besides the obvious heraldic nature of the stance, the dynamic pose of *Silence*'s lion may also be compared to various bestiary lions with similarly open mouths and raised paws.[14]

The lion is most often characterized as a noble beast, and consequently became a symbol of royalty.[15] This notion of the lion as king has at its roots a confusion in linguistic transmission. Isidore in his *Etymologies* explains the "corrupted" translation from the Greek and how as a result, the Latin *leo* signifies both "lion" and "king." According to Isidore, this confusion led to the popular belief that the lion is the king of the beasts.[16] Lions in earlier romances also characterize the lion as royal. For example, the lion of the *Roman de Renart* is named *Noble* and delivers judgment before a court of animals (lines 1-1678), and Chrétien de Troyes' Yvain, in slaying the evil dragon, wins a lion as his noble companion (lines 3341-3484).[17] Some bestiaries depict the lion as crowned.[18] Ludwig XV/3 depicts the lion against a royal background, which combines the heraldic arms of St. Louis with those of his mother, Blanche of Castille.[19] Viewed in this light, then, the *Silence* lion may also function as a reference to the King of France. This notion of the lion as doubly significant fits well in this particular romance and may comment upon Silence's doubly significant gender as well as a play on her changeable name. In addition, that the lion appears at the point in the romance when the count of Clermont pleads for clemency for Silence relates to the traditional bestiary characterization of the lion as merciful, and links by analogy the king with this specific character trait. While both Pliny and Isidore note the lion's compassionate attitude toward humans, Pliny singles out the lion as unique among all the wild beasts for this trait.[20] The identification of this beast as a lion with its royal associations recalls the natural history tradition's focus on the lion's clemency, thereby accentuating the ideal role of the king as merciful, as indeed the French king's decision to follow Clermont's advice demonstrates his *clementia*.

In addition to its merciful attitude toward humans, the lion is also characterized by its vigilance, by its watchful and protective nature. In *De bestiis et aliis rebus*, a major bestiary text source, the lion appears not only as virtuous and steadfast but also as a symbol of God, the guardian of the tribe of Israel, and by extension, of our souls.[21] In the bestiaries, then, because of his vigilance at night, the lion protects us from sin and the temptations of the devil and consequently is interpreted as a figure of Christ. Similarly, in *Silence*, the king of France (again, following Clermont's advice) has decided to protect Silence from this unsavory business by treating Silence honorably and not informing him of the contents of "Ebain's" letter (lines 4868-73).

In addition, according to Pliny, lions indicate their state of mind by means of their tails. When the lion is calm, he does not move his tail; when angry, the lion will first strike the earth with his tail, and then as his anger grows, his own back, as if to incite further anger.[22] Perhaps recalling Pliny, the lion in *Silence* appears to be biting his own tail as if in anger. In the context of the romance, the lion may thus visually communicate the French king's angry response to Ebain's request. In fact, a certain amount of anger—as well as pain—is revealed in the king of France's reaction to "Ebain's" letter:

> The king said, "I am in a dreadful dilemma.
> I don't know what in the world I can do,
> For the man requesting my help in this message
> Is my most faithful ally.

It is contemptible of him; I don't understand
Why he is asking me secretly,
In the name of all the honors he has paid me,
To avenge him.[23]

The king of France emphasizes his feeling of betrayal first by alluding
to Ebain as the man who loves him most in the world and then indicates
their feudal bonds by repeating, *"me prie et me semont"* and later,
declares Ebain's stubbornness (*onerance*). However, the French king
undercuts the symbolic glory of this language by using it in the context
of a base, indeed cowardly, request for vengeance. Moreover, the
French king names Ebain as *forfait*, a very strong adjective in this
context: to call a lord *forfait* is to identify him as *recréant*, to accuse
him of treason. Thus, the image of the lion biting his tail over his back
may indeed function as a visual sign of the king's anger toward Ebain.

   Despite the rich significance of the lion identification and
subsequently with King Ebain, I think this image is designed to carry
multiple meanings. Indeed, the stance of the creature—with its head up
and chest forward—strongly resembles that of the bestiary *pardus*
instead of a lion. Although they may be faced in different directions,
with manes more or less curly, the *pardus* in the Ashmole (f. 12v),
Douce 88 (f. 6v), Bodley 764 (figure A, p. xxii), and St. Petersburg
bestiaries (f. 36v) all exhibit an extraordinary similar *passant* body
position.[24] The identification of the *Silence* creature as a *pardus* can
also be linked to the accompanying text. The author of *De bestiis*,
quoting Isidore directly, characterizes the *pardus* as a hybrid, *ferarum
genus varium*.[25] Moreover, the author reworks the Plinian notion that
the *pardus* is born of the coupling of a leopard and a lioness by passing
a moral judgment on the relationship as adulterous and noting that from
this unholy union is born a degenerate creature.[26] He denies Pliny's
assertion that a *pardus* can be born via the copulation of either a male
leopard/female lioness or female leopard/male lion, and opts instead to
pursue Pliny's idea that within the lion couple, it is the lioness who is
unfaithful.[27] By insisting that it is a male leopard and a female lioness
who give birth to this hybrid creature, the *De bestiis* author not only
defends the male lion's purity but also imposes an age-old misogynist
characterization—woman as lustful temptress—from the tradition of
patristic exegesis upon the animal world.[28] If we read the romance
creature, then, as a hybrid *pardus*, it may signify the double and thus
inverted nature of Silence. In addition, by recalling the adulterous

circumstances of the pardus' birth, the image may also point toward the attempts of the lustful Eufeme to seduce the innocent Silence.

Instead of offering a single identity—lion or pardus—for this creature, I would like to suggest that all of these interpretive threads are possible despite their seeming contradictions and indeed may exist simultaneously in keeping with much medieval imagery. In fact, how a medieval reader identified this creature would depend on his or her own knowledge of both the bestiary tradition and the text of *Silence* itself.

The next creature pictured in the romance has been characterized by Thorpe as a bird with a griffin's head (figure 2). However, it more closely resembles a bestiary dragon; such as that depicted in Ludwig XV/4 (figure 3). In both the *Silence* and bestiary imagery, the creature's tail is long and sinuous like that of a snake, and it lacks the beak and birdlike crest that defines a medieval griffin. In fact, this image is very similar to the many bestiary reptiles, such as the asp or siren serpent.[29]

In the romance, the scene preceding the dragon miniature is that of an epic battle: Silence has returned to England in order to help King Ebain in his war against the count of Chester. Although the reason for the war is not explicit in the text, it appears that the count has illegally usurped power from the king or defied him in some way. The passage that introduces this image thus describes the frenzy of battle: the fragments flying, the piercing of entrails, blood and brains splattering. More important, just before the dragon image, the text describes the king surrounded by enemy troops amid this fierce combat and Silence leading the charge into the fray to rescue him. The French troops are impressed by Silence's heroism and scream, *"Montjoie!"* in an obvious allusion to Silence's status as a brave, perhaps even epic, heroine (lines 5485-5556). It is at this point in the narrative that the miniature of the dragon appears.

Expanding on Isidore's comments on the dragon, the author of *De bestiis* associates the dragon with the serpent and, consequently, with the devil.[30] While Isidore notes the dragon's physical prowess,[31] the *De bestiis* author points to the dragon's tongue as its instrument or weapon of deceit, venom, and betrayal.[32] According to the author of *De bestiis*, then, the dragon is a powerful enemy, one whose bodily characteristics can not only physically overcome very large animals but also may deceive humans and lead them to spiritual damnation.

Many medieval literary works describe dragon battle scenes. In Geoffrey of Monmouth's *Historia Regum Britanniæ*, Merlin explains the clash between a red and a white dragon as the fight between the

British and the Saxons; Robert de Boron's Merlin interprets this same
scene as the battle between Vertigiers and Constant.[33] When Chrétien
de Troyes' Yvain happens upon a lion warring with a dragon, he helps
the lion and so gains a loyal companion.[34]

Relative to the narrative of *Silence*, the dragon may thus symbolize
on several levels the dangers that Silence will encounter: first, his hand-
to-hand combat with the count of Chester and, later, his more spiritual
battle against the seductress Eufeme. Like an ill-willed devil, the count
of Chester is described as filled with hatred, unable even to respect
Silence and the French for their military prowess:

> Now things were going badly for the count.
> He was filled with hatred for Silence.
> He simply couldn't manage to like him
> Or the French. He didn't know
> Who they were, but he certainly disliked them.[35]

The count's excessive hate signals his demonization; Silence's one-on-
one battle with Chester, which is described immediately following the
image, as a result becomes a battle of good versus evil. Silence, after
nearly being killed, manages to cut off the count's right arm, effectively
rendering him incapable of further fighting. In disabling the count,
Silence has thus single-handedly won the war for King Ebain, thereby
restoring power and glory to the monarchy. Once the count has been
dispatched and this physical danger has been overcome, the narrative
returns to the evil Eufeme who, having heard of Silence's spectacular
victory, again plots to seduce Silence.

> The queen was obsessed with thoughts of Silence:
> She could not wait to find out
> Whether he would agree to be her lover
> Or choose his own destruction.
> Her old mad passion was renewed.
> Damn her, body and soul![36]

Eufeme, whose belly is the euphemistic site of her excessive lust
("*Maldis soit li cuers de son ventre!*"), is determined either to have her
way with Silence or to destroy him. Eufeme's lust is a threat to Silence
on several levels: a relationship with Eufeme would involve not only
adultery (and thus peril for Silence's soul) but also the betrayal of

Silence's liege lord, King Ebain, indeed, unlawful usurpation of royal power. These spiritual/sexual threats culminate in the "impossible" task assigned to Silence—finding Merlin. The dragon image may thus represent and foreshadow these dangers, both physical (via the count of Chester) and spiritual (via Eufeme) that Silence will encounter. Merlin's engenderment by a demon may also signal an association between Merlin and the dragon.[37]

The last of the creature portraits depicts a long-necked bird that seems to be preening itself (figure 4). This image appears in the manuscript at the point when Silence is in the wilds of Britain looking for Merlin. In the passage that accompanies this image, an old man with flowing white hair approaches Silence and asks Silence why he is out in the wasteland, and then proceeds to instruct Silence on how to capture Merlin (lines 5873-5986).

With its characteristic long legs and neck, this bird may represent a crane, one of the popular bestiary birds. In the bestiaries, cranes are often depicted as white birds holding a rock in one claw, a reference to their sentry-like nature. While bestiary cranes tend to be light in color, *Silence*'s bird is dark with red wings. However, it does have the characteristic red marking on its head observable in bestiary depictions of cranes, such as that found in Bodley 764 (f. 62).[38] The blackness of the bird in the *Silence* image may be linked to the bestiary texts rather than the images. Both Isidore and Hugh of Fouilloy in his *De avibus*, excerpted in the bestiaries, refer to the tradition that cranes turn black as they age. For Hugh, this fact is significant: he repeats the phrase, "for they grow black with age" (*nam in senectute nigrescunt*), in both the opening and closing sections on the crane. Furthermore, this darkening of the crane is important in terms of lay piety and concerns especially those who, concerned about their salvation, might enter a monastery late in life. Hugh creates an analogy between the crane and humans based on a penitential theme: like cranes that turn black, old people become contrite for the sins they committed in their youth and thus—in an act of physical as well as spiritual penitence—enter into a religious community.[39] This change in color of the cranes, then, is a physical, literal sign of contrition in *De avibus*. Employing verbs such as *prodit*, *nigrescunt*, and the repetition of *mutat*, Hugh stresses the aspect of transformation by referring again and again to the process of change.

Within the narrative of *Silence*, this image of the crane—and its invocation of the theme of metamorphosis—invites comparison to the figure of Merlin. Although it is not stated in the text, it is possible that the old man who reveals to Silence how to entrap Merlin is Merlin himself. In the French tradition, Merlin appears quite often in an unrecognizable form (for example, as a peasant or an old man), and later appears in his more recognizable form of the wild man, the savage who lives in the woods and eats berries.[40] Reading the image as a crane, with its own tradition of metamorphosis, thus suggests a connection to Merlin. Furthermore, the identification of the bird as a crane provides a reference to other figures in the narrative who alter their appearance, including Silence and the "nun" in Queen Eufeme's retinue. The notion of transformation as signified by the crane may also foreshadow the imminent unveiling of these characters by Merlin.

That this bird may be an allusion to Merlin is also suggested by its gesture of placing its beak in its breast. Although the bird could simply be preening, this position quite obviously recalls that of the bestiary pelican, who is regularly shown piercing its own breast, sacrificing itself in a Christly gesture in order to resurrect its murdered brood (figure 5).[41] Merlin also has this trait of self-sacrifice. In Robert de Boron's *Merlin*, Merlin often transforms his appearance in order to show those people searching for him exactly how to find him.[42] As a figure of the quarry who leads the hunters to himself and willingly allows himself to be captured, Merlin may be seen as self-sacrificial and consequently may be invoked by this bird's pelican-like gesture.

In addition to their specific narrative references, the three *Silence* beasts may also be linked together through visual analogy.[43] That is, all three creatures symbolically invoke royalty: the lion, as the king of beasts, the dragon, as the king of reptiles,[44] and by analogy, perhaps the bird as an eagle, the king of the birds.[45] In addition, the bird's pelican gesture may also allude to royalty. In the Ludwig XV/3 bestiary (figure 5), pelicans are depicted upon the same royal patterned background of St. Louis and Blanche of Castille's heraldic symbols found on the earlier lion folio, thus linking the pelican—and perhaps its associated characteristic of piety—with the French monarchy.[46] As symbols of royalty, the three *Silence* creatures signal the conclusion to the narrative: the reestablishment of hierarchy, the restoration of a monarchical state in its most institutionalized and stable form. Indeed, all of the possible threats to the royal and patriarchal hegemony are neatly resolved by this conclusion.

> In accordance with royal decree,
> The nun was executed,

And the queen was drawn and quartered.
Thus was the king's justice accomplished.
[. . .] They dressed Silence as a woman.
Lords, what more can I say?
Once he was called Silentius:
They removed the -us, added an -a,
And so he was called Silentia.
After Nature
Had recovered her rights,
She spent the next three days refinishing
Silence's entire body, removing every trace
Of anything that being a man had left there.
She removed all traces of sunburn:
Rose and lily were once again
Joined in conjugal harmony on her face.
Then the king took her to wife—
That's what it said in the book where I found this story—
On the advice of his
Most loyal and trusted advisers.
And then the count her father
And her mother, Eufemie, came to court.
They were overjoyed, as was only fitting.[47]

With the execution of Eufeme and the "nun," and the unveiling of
Silence's true sex as female, the king reasserts not only his royal but his
masculine power as king and husband.[48] By ordering that Silence's sex
be openly revealed, Ebain effectively consolidates both royal and
patriarchal prerogative over her: Silence is literally stripped naked
before the court in this ritual show of power (lines 6569-75). Clearly
then, it is not only the royal throne whose legitimacy is reestablished
but also the institution of the patriarchal family and, by extension, the
subservient silent role of women in society. Even the colors on
Silence's face—rose and lily—are remarried in an evocation of the
heterosexual institution of marriage (lines 6669-76). Once she is
refashioned by Nature, Silence becomes the embodiment of her name;
her place in the world, as woman, queen, wife, is one that prescribes
silence and obedience.[49]

In addition to the three creature portraits, there is yet another
miniature in the *Silence* manuscript that does not quite fit with the main
body of narrative images. That image, which depicts Merlin reclining

on a rock, not only directly follows the series of creature portraits but also exhibits the same portrait-like traits: Merlin is not shown interacting with Silence or Ebain, nor is he depicted as a wild man in the woods, framed by trees. Instead, like the creatures, Merlin is static, isolated from his narrative or natural context (figure 6). As a result, this image of Merlin also visually invokes the bestiary tradition—albeit in a much more complicated and implicit way—and thus stands apart from the other narrative miniatures.[50] Merlin's general association with animals is very well documented by Geoffrey of Monmouth. Merlin is a wild man living among and like the animals.[51] In addition, Merlin's prophecies in both the *Historia Regum Britanniæ* and the *Vita Merlini* function on the level of animal symbolism; the numerous references to lions, dragons, deer, serpents, and eagles were likely informed by the bestiary tradition.[52] Furthermore, Geoffrey's *Vita Merlini* reads very much like an unmoralized bestiary. In part an encyclopedic catalogue, the *Vita Merlini* notes different kinds of birds and fish and their attributes or natural habits. For instance, Merlin notes the pelican's resuscitation of its young much as a bestiary would.[53] Merlin even lists springs, rivers, and islands with their magical traits, such as the Gorgades and their hairy women, much like some of the bestiaries, the *Travels* of John Mandeville, and other medieval literature devoted to marvels.[54] The *Vita Merlini*, then, clearly draws on the structure and content of the bestiaries for much of its material. The Merlin miniature in the *Silence* manuscript is thus clearly linked by means of an intertextual resonance to the bestiary tradition.

In conclusion, the three creature portraits as well as the image of Merlin in the *Silence* manuscript bear witness to the influence of the bestiary tradition in this romance; moreover, the bestiary subtext of these images may redirect our reading of the text itself. In other words, material from the bestiary does not simply stay enframed within the visual image but also interacts with the narrative. In a sense, one might read these creature portraits as emblematic, although the levels of possible meaning clearly exceed a fixed, single symbolic association. Furthermore, while McMunn suggests that several genres borrow from bestiary material, it is arguable that the link between bestiary and romance is a particularly strong one; critics such as Ker and Bakhtin note that romance, like the bestiary, is ultimately a flexible genre, characterized by its plasticity.[55] Among romances, *Le Roman de Silence* is a particularly polysemous example; the meaning of *Silence* seems to exist somewhere between the shifting verbal and visual signifiers. Just as Allen proposes that we "read and be read, see what we can experience of the mute -*e* in the gap between -*us* and -*a*, in the ambiguity of silence,"[56] the invocation of the bestiary tradition in this romance challenges us not only to break the frame between text and image but also to read as significant the ambiguity between them.

NOTES

1. The influence of the bestiary tradition on other genres and media has also been explored. See for example, Michael Curley, "Animal Symbolism in the Prophecies of Merlin," in Clark and McMunn 1989, 151-63; Sion Segre Amar, "Su un codice parigino del Tresor," *Studi Francesi* 24/2 (1980), 256-61; and G. C. Druce, "The Medieval Bestiaries and Their Influence on Ecclesiastical Decorative Art," *Journal of the British Archaeological Association* n.s. 25 (1919), 40-82; n.s. 26 (1920), 35-79.

2. In the introduction to his edition of the *Bestiaire d'amour*, Cesare Segre (1957, vii-xxviii) examines in detail this synthesis of the didactic and the lyrical. Moreover, Florence McCulloch (1962, 46) indicates that of vernacular bestiary texts, the *Bestiaire d'amour* was the most popular. See also Jeanette Beer, "Duel of Bestiaries," in Clark and McMunn 1989, 96-105; Helen Solterer, "The Master at Work: Richard de Fournival's Bestiaire d'amour," and "Contrary to What Is Said: The Response au Bestiaire d'amour and the Case for a Woman's Response" both in *The Master and Minerva: Disputing Women in French Medieval Culture* [Berkeley 1995], 79-94; 97-130; and Hassig in this volume.

3. Meradith McMunn, "Bestiary Influences in Two Romances," in Clark and McMunn 1989, 134-50.

4. *Le Roman de Silence: A Thirteenth-Century Arthurian Verse-Romance by Heldris de Cornuälle*, ed. Lewis Thorpe (Cambridge, 1972). For bibliography and an edition with facing English translation, see *Silence: A Thirteenth-Century French Romance*, ed. and trans. Sarah Roche-Mahdi (East Lansing, 1992). Quotations are taken from this last edition.

5. Recent articles focusing on language and gender include R. Howard Bloch, "Silence and Holes: The Roman de Silence and the Art of the Trouvère," *Yale French Studies* 70 (1986), 81-99; Kate Mason Cooper, "Elle and L: Sexualized Textuality in Le Roman de Silence," *Romance Notes*, 25/30 (1985), 341-60; Michèle Perret, "Travesties et Transexuelles: Yde, Silence, Grisandole, Blanchandine" *Romance Notes*, 25/3 (1985), 328-40; Simon Gaunt, "The Significance of Silence," *Paragraph: A Journal of Modern Critical Theory* 13/2 (1990), 202-16; and Peter L. Allen, "The Ambiguity of Silence:

Gender, Writing, and Le Roman de Silence," in *Sign, Sentence, Discourse: Language in Medieval Thought and Literature*, ed. Julian N. Wasserman and Lois Rooney (Syracuse, 1989), 98-112.

6. Thorpe 1972, 6.

7. Allen 1989, 102.

8. McCulloch 1962, 45-69.

9. McMunn (1989, 138) suggests that the association of the bestiary and romance may account for the interpolations of bestiary-influenced material into other romances, citing as an example the extended lion episode in Chrétien de Troyes' *Yvain*.

10. McMunn 1989, 138. Bakhtin specifically links this open-ended polyvocality with the genre of romance. See M.M. Bakhtin, "Epic and Novel: Toward a Methodology for the Study of the Novel," in *The Dialogic Imagination: Four Essays*, ed. Michael Holquist (Austin, 1981), esp. 11-12, 22-40.

11. Thorpe 1972, 6-8. I am also following Thorpe's identification of the miniatures in this table.

12. This narrative scene of the public debate of a contentious issue before a person of authority, generally a count or king, forms the basis for, and is reminiscent of, many debate and judgement poems. See for example the Anglo-Norman *jugement d'amour* poems *Blanchflor et Florence* and *Melior et Ydoine* and Guillaume de Machaut's *Le Jugement dou roy de Navarre* and *Le Jugement dou roy de Behaingne*, among others. See *Blanchflor et Florence* in Paul Meyer, "Notice du MS. 25970 de la Bibliothèque Phillips," and "*Melior et Ydoine*," *Romania* 37 (1908), 209-235, 236-244; *The Judgment of the King of Navarre*, ed. R. Barton Palmer (New York, 1988); and *The Judgment of the King of Bohemia/Le jugement dou roy de Behaingne,* ed. R. Barton Palmer (New York, 1984).

13. Color reproductions in Morgan 1982, fig. 63; and Graz 1982.

14. See for example Ludwig XV/3, f. 68; and Ludwig XV/4, f. 111; reproduced in Anton von Euw and Joachim M. Plotzek, *Die Handschriften der Sammlung Ludwig*, Band 4 (Cologne, 1985), figs. 81, 105.

15. On bestiary lions and medieval kingship, see Haist in this volume.

16. "*Leonis* vocabulum ex Græca origine inflexum est in Latinum. Græca enim 84 vocatur, et est nomen nothum, quia ex parte corruptum . . . Leo autem Græca, Latine *rex* interpretatur, eo quod princeps sit omnium bestiarum" (*PL* 82:434A).

17. *Le Roman de Renart*, ed. Mario Roques (Paris, 1982), 1-57; Chrétien de Troyes, *Le Chevalier au Lion (Yvain)*, ed. Mario Roques (Paris, 1967), 102-106.

18. See for example Paris, Bibliothèque Nationale, MS lat. 11207, f. 1.

19. Reproduced in von Euw and Plotzek 1985, fig. 77. A similar pattern forms the background of the pelican image (figure 5). These heraldic patterns may establish a link between this bestiary, which dates from c. 1277, and the Sainte Chapelle, begun c. 1240 and commissioned by Saint Louis, the walls and stained glass of which employ the symbols of Louis and his mother, in similar patterns. Sydney Cockerell interpreted the heraldic patterns in Ludwig XV/3 as evidence that Louis was the manuscript's patron (*Monumenta codicum manu scriptorum* [New York, 1974], 53), but later opinion recognizes only their decorative function (von Euw and Plotzek 1985, 186).

20. "Leoni tantum ex feris clementia in supplices; prostratis parcit, et, ubi saevit, in viros potius quam in feminas fremit, in infantes non nisi magna fame" (Pliny 8.19.48 [Rackham 1940, 36-37]). Isidore notes, "Circa hominem leonem natura est benigna, ut nisi lœsi nequeant irasci. Patet enim eorum misericordia exemplis assiduis. Prostratis enim parcunt; captivos obvios repatriare permittunt; hominem non nisi in magna fame interimunt. De quibus Lucretius: *Scymnique leonum*, etc." (*PL* 82:434B).

21. *PL* 177:57A-57C.

22. Pliny, *Naturalis historia* 8.19.49 (Rackham 1940, 38-39).

23. Cho dist li rois: J'ai grant anguisce.

Ne sai sos ciel que faire puissce,

Car li hom el mont ki plus m'ainme

De cest message a moi se clame,

Forfais li est, jo ne sai dont,

Por cho me prie et me semont

Sor quanque il m'a fait d'onerance

que jo en prenge la venjance (lines 4459-66).

24. Reproduced in Graz 1982 (Ashmole pardus); Muratova 1984 (St. Petersburg pardus). On the pardus, see also Haist in this volume.

25. *PL* 177:83D. Isidore calls the pardus a "genus varium" (*PL* 82:435B).

26. "Leopardus ex adulterio leœnœ et pardi nascitur, et tertiam originem efficit, sicut et Plinius in naturali historia dicit leonem cum parda, aut pardum cum leœnœ concumbere, et ex utroque coitu degeneres partus creari, quales sunt ex diversis speciebus progeniti mulus et burdo" (*PL* 177:83D).

27. "Odore pardi coitum sentit in adultera leo totaque vi consurgit in poenam" (Pliny, *Nat. hist.* 8.17.43; Rackham 1940, 32-33).

28. The Church Fathers, in turn, were informed by earlier Classical notions of the biological inferiority of women, as articulated by Aristotle in *De generatione animalium* 4.467b (Aristotle, *Generation of Animals*, trans. A.L. Peck [Cambridge, MA, 1990], 400-405).

29. For example, see the St. Petersburg Bestiary, ff. 79, 82v. 87 (reproduced in Muratova 1984).

30. "Huic draconi assimilatur diabolus, qui est immanissimus serpens" (*PL* 177:72A).

31. Although its venom is not poisonous, the dragon's huge size and strong tail can suffocate even elephants, according to Isidore (*PL* 82:442C-443A). Many bestiary dragons, such as the one depicted in the Morgan Bestiary (figure I, p. xxx), indeed appear well on their way to suffocating the enemy elephants. On dragons, see also Gravestock in this volume.

32. Moreover, the *De bestiis* author associates the dragon with the devil, who changes shapes in order to beguile human souls (*PL* 177:72A).

33. *The Historia Regum Britanniæ of Geoffrey of Monmouth*, trans. Acton Griscom and Robert Ellis Jones (London, 1929), 384-5; *Merlin: Roman du XIII° siècle*, ed. Alexandre Micha (Geneva, 1979), 29.43-51 (p.115); 30.4-10 (p.118).

34. *Yvain*, lines 3341-3415 (Roques 1967, 102-104).

35. Or vait al conte malement.

Enviers Silence a gros le cuer.

Il nel puet amer a nul fuer

Ne les Franchois, et si ne set

Quels gens il sunt, mais moult les het (lines 5566-70).

36. La roïne est de maint porpens:

Ne cuide ja veïr le tens,

S'il violt u por son cors deduire

U s'il ne violt por li destruire.

En le viés derverie rentre.

Maldis soit li cuers de son ventre! (lines 5657-62).

37. Griscom and Jones 1929, 381-82.

38. Color reproduction in Barber 1993.

39. "Ætatem in illis color prodit, nam in senectute nigrescunt. Hic enim color in senectute seni competit, cum pro peccatis plangendo gemit. Cum enim quœ male gessit, senex commemorat, in senectute colorem mutat. Mutat enim amorem pristinœ delectationis in dolorem contritionis. Ecce qualiter per naturam volucrum doceri potest via religiosorum" (Clark 1992, 204-205).

40. In Robert de Boron's *Merlin* (32, 1-8; 34, 5-31), Merlin appears first as a dirty butcher, then as an elegant *prudhomme*, to the men sent by king Pandragons to find him (Micha 1980, 125, 132-33). On the wild man, see Richard Bernheimer, *Wild Men in the Middle Ages: A Study in Art, Sentiment, and Demonology* (Cambridge [MA], 1952); and Roger Bartra, *Wild Men in the Looking Glass* (Ann Arbor, 1994).

41. Hugh explicitly links the pelican with Christ: "Mystice pelicanus significat Christum" (Clark 1992, 168).

42. Dressed as the butcher, Robert de Boron's Merlin instructs the king's messengers seeking him: "Veu l'ai ge et bien sai son repaire, et il set bien que vos le querez, mais vos n'en trouverez point, se il ne viaut. Mais tant me comenda il que jo vos deisse que por noiant vos travailliez de lui querre, quar se vos le trouvoiez, il n'en iroit mie avec vos. [. . .] Et sachiez de cels qui vos distrent que vos queïssiez Merlin n'avoit que .V. en l'ost, et quant vos vendrez, vos n'i troveroiz que les .III. et a ces .III. dites et a vostre seingnor que, se il venoient en ceste vile et il cherchoient cez forez, il trouveroient Merlin" (32:20-25, 30-34; Micha 1980, 125-26).

43. Merlin's prophecies in *Historia Regum Britanniæ* contain a passage in which the dragon, lion, and eagle are linked: "Succedent duo dracones. quorum alter invidie spiculo suffocabitur. alter vero sub umbra nominis redibit. Succedit leo iusticie. ad cuius rugitum gallicane turres & urtica extorquebitur & argentum ex ungulis megientium manabit . . . Catuli leonis in equoreos pisces transformabuntur. & aquila eius super montem aravium nidificabit" (Griscom and Jones 1929, 387).

44. The dragon may also be an indirect allusion to King Arthur as glorious emperor. Arthur's dream before his battle with the Romans is filled with animal symbolism; moreover, he interprets the figure of the dragon as symbolizing himself. See Geoffrey's remarks in *Historia Regum Britanniæ* (Griscom and Jones 1929, 468).

45. Hugh of Fouilloy links the eagle with nobility and royalty in the *De avibus* (Clark 1992, 250-52).

46. See note 19, above.

47. Si com li rois le conmanda
I fu la none donc deffaite,
Et la dame a chevals detraite.
Li rois en a fait grant justice.
[. . .] Silence atornent come feme.
Segnor, que vos diroie plus?
Ains ot a non Scilensiüs:
Ostés est -us, mis I est -a
Si est només Scilentiä.
D'illeuc al tierc jor que Nature
Ot recovree sa droiture
Si prist Nature a repolir
Par tolt le cors et a tolir
Tolt quanque ot sor le cors de malle.

202 Michelle Bolduc

Ainc n'i lassa nes point de halle:
Remariä lués en son vis
Assisement le roze al lis.
Li rois le prist a feme puis—
Cho dist l'estorie u jo le truis—
Par loëment de son princhiers,
Qu'il plus ama et plus tint ciers.
Et dont I vient li cuens ses pere,
Et Eufemie avoec, sa mere.
Grant joie en ont, cho est a droit. (lines 6654-57, 6664-83)

48. However, The king's feelings for Silence do not seem to go beyond gratitude for her loyalty and recognition of her virtue in contrast to his emotion for his counselors, whom he loves and holds most dear. Compare lines 6629-34 to lines 6679-80.

49. One could view Silence's marriage as akin to Eufeme's execution: in both cases the woman who exceeds her appropriate role in society is literally silenced (killed off) in the narrative. The expectation that a woman be silent is made problematic in a striking and painful example in Chrétien de Troyes' *Erec et Enide* (ed. Mario Roques [Paris, 1973]). See especially lines 2764-2852 (pp. 83-87); 2959-3009 (pp. 90-92); and 3093-3112 (pp. 94-95).

50. Images of Merlin in the various Robert de Boron manuscripts are consistently narrative in form; that is, Merlin is shown interacting with other characters, illustrating a scene or dialogue from the narrative. See, for example, Paris, Bibliothèque Nationale MSS fr. 96, fr. 105, fr. 110, fr. 344, fr. 9123, fr. 19162 and fr. 24394.

51. "... fit silvester homo quasi silvis deditus esset" line 80 (Geoffrey of Monmouth, *Vita Merlini*, ed. and trans. Basil Clarke [Cardiff, 1973], 56-57). In addition, in at least one manuscript of Robert de Boron's *Merlin*, Merlin appears as naked and white, with fur all over, except when he is disguised as a peasant. See Paris, Bibliothèque Nationale MS fr. 9123, ff. 96, 116, and 141.

52. See Griscom and Jones 1929, 384-97; and *Vita Merlini*, lines 580-689 (Clarke 1973, 82-89). Curley (1989) explicitly links Merlin's prophecies in *Historia Regum Britanniæ* with the bestiary tradition.

53. "Est pellicanus avis pullos consueta necare/ et confusa tribus lugere dolore diebus./ Denique supposito laniat sua corpora rostro/ et scindens venas educit sanguinis undas, et vite reduces reddit rorando volucres" (*Vita Merlini*, lines 1365-69; Clarke 1973, 126-27).

54. *Vita Merlini*, lines 792-940 (Clarke 1973, 94-103). John Block Friedman (1981, 141-49) explores the influence of travel guides on representations of creatures familiar from the bestiary tradition.

55. Whereas Ker (m)aligns romance with(as) mystery and fantasy, Bakhtin refers specifically to the novel's plasticity. W. P. Ker, *Epic and Romance: Essays on Medieval Literature* (New York, 1957), 4, 352-70; Bakhtin 1981, 27.

56. Allen (1989, 110).

Figure 1. Dog. *Silence*. Nottingham, University Library, MS Middleton
Mi.LM.6, f. 213. Photo: The University of Nottingham Library.

Figure 2. Bird with griffin's head. *Silence*. Nottingham, University Library, MS Middleton Mi.LM.6, f. 217. Photo: The University of Nottingham Library.

de captuutrate dyaboli
z fociatut nos bonitati
fue· z pietatis prine fili

os adoptauit z iplenit
illud q̃o apl̃ia ante pre
dixerat· De dracone:
pernoz
arcus fi
fultis·p
quas t̃
hic fpm̃
z lingua
ererit·
uenenũ
nõ in̄ẽ

Draco maior eſt ōi
um ſerpentiũ fu
per tram· hũc greci dra
cantẽ uocant· vñ z diri
uatũ eſt i latinũ ut dra
co diceret· Qui ſepe a ſpe
luncis abſtractus· z aere
gettat· z iuter propter eũ
aer· Eſt aũ criſtatus· ore

tib3 b3 i cauda hc̃ z uibcr
pcius quã morſu noctr·
Innorius eſt enĩ a tene
no· hinc ad mortẽ facie
dam nõ eſt uenenũ ne
ceſſariũ· quia ſi quẽ liga
uerit occidit· A quo nec e
lephans tutus eſt ſui cor
pcis magnitudine· Ñã

Figure 3. Dragon. Los Angeles, J. Paul Getty Museum, MS Ludwig XV/4, f. 94. Photo: The J. Paul Getty Museum, Los Angeles, California.

tolt droit aloniere dun v
Salue le mit gentceme
oz elcolrel confairemer
ul
lo
do
ne
71
li
e
de

Silencel lirelpont biall
vol dioel bien der leuol

Figure 4. Bird with serpentine head. *Silence*. Nottingham, University Library, MS Middleton Mi.LM.6, f. 218v. Photo: The University of Nottingham Library.

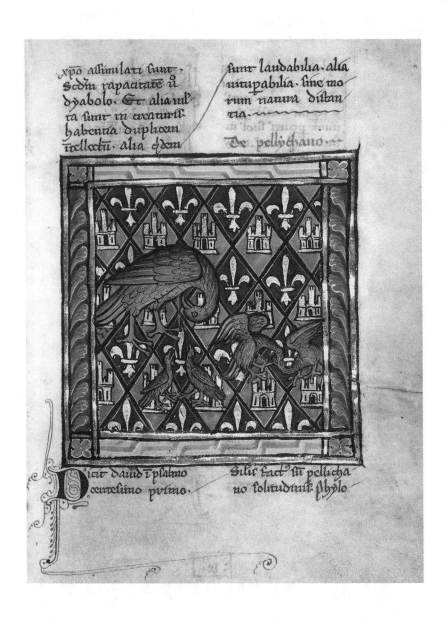

Figure 5. Pelicans. Los Angeles, J. Paul Getty Museum, MS Ludwig XV/3, f. 72. Photo: The J. Paul Getty Museum, Los Angeles, California.

Figure 6. Merlin. *Silence*. Nottingham, University Library, MS Middleton Mi.LM.6, f. 222. Photo: The University of Nottingham Library.

List of Bestiary and *Physiologus* Manuscripts

Add. 11283
London, British Library, Add. MS 11283
England, c. 1170

Ashmole Bestiary
Oxford, Bodleian Library, MS Ashmole 1511
England, c. 1200

Bern Physiologus (Bern 318)
Bern, Stadtsbibliothek, MS 318
Reims, 9th c.

Bodley 602
Oxford, Bodleian Library, MS Bodley 602
S. England, c. 1230

Bodley 764
Oxford, Bodleian Library, MS Bodley 764
Salisbury? c. 1240-50

Cambridge Bestiary
Cambridge, University Library, MS Ii.4.26
North Midlands? ca. 1200-10

Douce 88
Oxford, Bodleian Library, MS Douce 88
England, 13th c.

Douce 308
Richard of Fournival, *Bestiaire d'amour*
Oxford, Bodleian Library, MS Douce 308
Metz, early 14th c.

Fitzwilliam 254
Cambridge, Fitzwilliam Museum, MS 254
London region? c. 1220-30

Fitzwilliam 379
Cambridge, Fitzwilliam Museum, MS 379
England, c. 1300

fr. 14969
Paris, Bibliothèque Nationale, MS fr. 14969
Canterbury? or Oxford? c. 1265-70

fr. 24428
Paris, Bibliothèque Nationale, MS fr. 24428
N. France (Champagne), c. 1270

Harley 3244
London, British Library, MS Harley 3244
England, after 1255

Harley 4751
London, British Library, MS Harley 4751
Salisbury? c. 1230-40

Laud Misc. 247
Oxford, Bodleian Library, MS Laud Misc. 247
England, c. 1120

Ludwig XV/3
Los Angeles, J. Paul Getty Museum, MS Ludwig XV/3
N. France, c. 1270

Ludwig XV/4
Los Angeles, J. Paul Getty Museum, MS Ludwig XV/4
N. France, c. 1277

Morgan Bestiary
New York, Pierpont Morgan Library, MS M. 81
Lincoln? c. 1185

Rochester Bestiary
London, British Library, MS Royal 12.F.XIII
SE England, c. 1230

Royal 12.C.XIX
London, British Library, MS Royal 12.C.XIX
Durham? c. 1200-1210

St. John's 61
Oxford, St. John's College, MS 61
York? c. 1220

St. John's 178
Oxford, St. John's College, MS 178
London, Westminster Abbey, c. 1300

St. Petersburg Bestiary
St. Petersburg, State Public Library Saltykov-Shchedrin,
MS Lat. Q.v.V.I
North Midlands, ca. 1190-1200

University Library Bestiary
Cambridge, University Library, MS Kk.4.25
London, c. 1230

Westminster Abbey Bestiary
London, Westminster Abbey Library, MS 22
York? c. 1270-90

Contributors

Michelle Bolduc is a Fulbright Scholar who is completing her Ph.D. dissertation in Comparative Literature at the University of Oregon.

Carmen Brown is a graduate student in the Centre for Medieval Studies, University of Toronto.

Pamela Gravestock is a graduate student in the Fine Art Department, University of Toronto.

Margaret Haist holds the M.L.S. in Library Science and the M.A. in Art History from the University of Toronto and is Curator of Image Services for the Fine Art Department, University of Toronto.

Debra Hassig holds the Ph.D. in Art History from Columbia University and is a Research Fellow at the Institute for Advanced Studies in the Humanities, University of Edinburgh.

Valerie Jones is an artist and independent scholar working in Los Angeles.

Mariko Miyazaki is an independent scholar working in Toronto.

Alison Syme is a Ph.D. candidate in the Department of Fine Arts at Harvard University.

J. Holli Wheatcroft holds the M.A. in Art History from the University of Toronto and is Public Programs Assistant at the McCord Museum of Canadian History, Montreal.

Index of Creatures